"By linking developmental theory with p   ies, theology, and spiritual formation, Chris K   ir- ing picture of Christian discipleship acr   .ical ideas for pastors, parents, clinicians, and educators, *Discipleship for Every Stage of Life* offers clear pathways for helping people of all ages encounter Jesus in all of life. This is my new go-to resource for connecting contemporary human development with the timeless wisdom of the Christian faith."

—**David Setran**, Wheaton College

"Kiesling insightfully indicates how Christian formation can take place within stages of human development. The author has a deep understanding of both Christian ministry and the various psychological dimensions of human development. *Discipleship for Every Stage of Life* is well-documented and engaging as Kiesling provides personal examples and stories that illustrate how Christian formation can take place in different developmental stages. This book will be an invaluable resource for those working in or preparing for Christian ministry. We strongly recommend it to anyone who wants to know how churches can most effectively minister to the formational and developmental needs of their members."

—**Jack and Judith Balswick**, School of Psychology and Marriage and Family Therapy, Fuller Theological Seminary (retired)

"Kiesling provides a comprehensive look at faith formation across the human development life cycle, weaving together social science and the science of human development with biblical and theological understanding. The result is a well-informed, thoughtful, and practical resource. Whether read by a parent or a pastor, this work will help inform and inspire the intentional faith formation of infants through senior adults."

—**Colleen Derr**, Eastern Nazarene College

"In this thorough engagement with life span development studies, Kiesling advances the work of interpreting the social sciences as a tool for pursuing the way of Christ. To that end, his call for Christians to grow in 'moving from context to text' is apt, and his demonstration of doing so is deft. Here is the fruit of careful research and decades of faithful discipleship ministry. Readers seeking to be informed will benefit significantly. Readers willing to be spurred on will benefit abundantly."

—**John David Trentham**, The Southern Baptist Theological Seminary; editor in chief, *Christian Education Journal*

"*Discipleship for Every Stage of Life* could be written only by a senior scholar who has rich life experience as both a minister and a Christian educator. Kiesling has spent decades integrating insights from secular life span development theory with biblical and theological principles. He brings these fields together without simply tacking a truth from human development onto a biblical teaching or simply baptizing developmental insights. His careful work provides ministers and Christian educators with a nuanced, comprehensive book to aid us in our work."

—**Holly Allen**, Lipscomb University (retired); coauthor of *Intergenerational Christian Formation*; author of *Forming Resilient Children*

"Kudos to Chris Kiesling! *Discipleship for Every Stage of Life* is a treasure for academics and church leaders. He has filled an enormous gap in the literature for life span disciple making by combining insights from theology, theory, and practical ministry in a comprehensive and engaging text that will be helpful to present and future ministry leaders for years to come. Thank you, Dr. Kiesling, for recognizing that discipleship is a lifetime adventure!"

—**Chris Shirley**, School of Educational Ministries, Southwestern Baptist Theological Seminary

DISCIPLESHIP
for EVERY STAGE of LIFE

DISCIPLESHIP
for EVERY STAGE of LIFE

Understanding Christian Formation
in Light of Human Development

CHRIS A. KIESLING

Baker Academic

a division of Baker Publishing Group
Grand Rapids, Michigan

© 2024 by Chris A. Kiesling

Published by Baker Academic
a division of Baker Publishing Group
Grand Rapids, Michigan
BakerAcademic.com

Printed in the United States of America

Library of Congress Cataloging-in-Publication Data
Names: Kiesling, Chris A., 1963– author.
Title: Discipleship for every stage of life : understanding Christian formation in light of human
    development / Chris A. Kiesling.
Description: Grand Rapids, Michigan : Baker Academic, a division of Baker Publishing Group,
    [2024] | Includes bibliographical references and index.
Identifiers: LCCN 2023059658 | ISBN 9781540965943 (paperback) | ISBN 9781540966841
    (casebound) | ISBN 9781493442881 (ebook) | ISBN 9781493442898 (pdf)
Subjects: LCSH: Christian life. | Spiritual formation. | Faith development.
Classification: LCC BV4510.3 .K375 2024 | DDC 248.4—dc23/eng/20240129
LC record available at https://lccn.loc.gov/2023059658

Baker Publishing Group publications use paper produced from sustainable forestry practices and post-consumer waste whenever possible.

24 25 26 27 28 29 30   7 6 5 4 3 2 1

On a hill outside Bath, England, overlooking the River Avon in 1863, Folliott Pierpoint took in the beauty of God's magnanimous gifts of creation and of church. In gratitude, he wrote the text to a beloved hymn, "For the Beauty of the Earth."

After completing a text about the life span that in so many ways calls to mind in like gratitude the love that accompanies our journey and "over and around us lies," I found it only appropriate to borrow from the hymn writer's pen to dedicate this volume to all who have accompanied my life course, especially my wife, parents, siblings, children and extended family, friends, colleagues, and students. Though I could never name them all, I owe them a debt of gratitude for the life I have been fortunate to live. I hold you all near and dear to my heart, and to you I owe the living experience of this volume:

> For the beauty of the earth,
> For the glory of the skies,
> For the love which from our birth
> Over and around us lies,
>
> Lord of all, to thee we raise
> This our hymn of grateful praise.[1]

---

1. Pierpoint, "For the Beauty of the Earth."

Contents

Introduction

What institution in society is the most engaged in the wholistic flourishing of people through the entire span of a person's life? Hospitals focus on the physical health of people of all ages. Therapists address psychological needs and promote good mental health. Banks help people with their financial well-being across the life course. Social service centers, governmental agencies, and state universities support individuals and families with a broad scope of human flourishing, but they often do so void of any spiritual focus. The church has often been the originator of most if not all of these institutions, recognizing the breadth of its stake in how people apprehend and animate the course of their lives.

Salvation at its root is wholistic. The vision of the church is deep and wide, seeking nothing less than freedom from sin and abundant life in Jesus (John 10:10) that liberates people from misery, mortality, and meaninglessness.[1] As a result, the life of faith produces people interested in every sector that promotes betterment of self, society, relationships, and creation. Life reconstituted under a messianic King who rules with wisdom and justice calls followers to be involved in liberating actions that bring shalom to all people.

This text attempts to carry the wholistic, redemptive vision of salvation into an exploration of the human sciences, or rather, to bring the findings of human science into the service of that theological enterprise. It extends the impulse of "faith seeking understanding,"[2] whereby the church through the ages has brought faith into conversation with philosophy, science, the arts,

1. Peniel, "Salvation and Wholeness."
2. This phrase is attributed to the theological method of Augustine and Anselm. A person begins with faith and on the basis of that faith seeks further understanding.

1

and the cultural ideas of a particular time. This book seeks to help pastors, ministers, parents, and individuals to love God in deeper ways and to know people in the bio-psycho-social-spiritual ways that they grow and stay the same through the life course.[3] Loving God inevitably carries us into engagement with the disciplines of theology and biblical studies. Understanding people makes indispensable a deep probing of what social scientists have discovered in their research of how humans function.

Having served as a pastor in both a rural and a city church before assuming the role of a professor, I was always curious to discern the sources from which my congregational members were finding guidance and inspiration for their lives. I was trained and eager to offer them stories from Scripture, thoughts of great theologians through the ages, and hymns from the archives of church history that had become staples in my own formational journey. Though they engaged with what I shared on Sunday morning, I discovered that many in my flock were attuned to a myriad of voices during the week. Some found solace and direction from their therapists, who had an uncanny ability to understand their conundrums and speak truth into their lives. Coffee station talk was often about the latest pop psychology bestseller being touted on syndicated talk shows. Money and time were being spent to attend seminars on life-related topics or to read the latest self-help guidebook. I began to wonder why the Bible study I offered had a moderate attendance, while a licensed counselor in the congregation could regularly draw a crowd of thirty for a weekend seminar on relationship boundaries. I entered a doctoral program in Human Development and Family Studies eager to learn and to critique where these voices were coming from and why they were having such an influence.

My aim is to provide those who serve congregations a tool kit for thinking more comprehensively about discipleship at every stage of life, building on those before me who found meaningful correlation between faith formation and the study of human development. James E. Loder, for example, approached this task through theological formulation and the structure of human development,[4] and James W. Fowler gave conceptual description to the distinct form of faith through the stages of life.[5] I composed this text more akin to a practical theologian pondering how theological reflection may be operative in the everyday experience of passages through the life course. Hence, I foreground the stages of

---

3. At its simplest level, I can credit the origination of this book to a comment made by my college mentor, Steve Moore, when he shared that he sought two primary outcomes from his years as a seminary student. First, he wanted to know God better, and second, he wanted to know how people functioned. So began my attempt to integrate love for God with human development.

4. Loder, *Logic of the Spirit*.

5. J. Fowler, *Stages of Faith*.

the life course as the framework for my exploration.[6] This is not to dismiss the grand doctrines of the Christian faith (attentive readers will find these doctrines operative at an implicit level in every chapter of this text) but to discover how doctrinal implications might be revealed and give shape to thought forms that permeate the way social scientists organize human life. Taking this approach elevates questions that may not surface in a class on basic Christian doctrine or be addressed in a sermon that aims to interpret a text. It begins instead in a posture of listening to what people ponder and reach for in the lived situations of life and how those in the field of human development have informed those journeys. Some may find this overly accommodationist, a secularizing of theology. I would suggest instead that the dialogue is organic to the way people of faith naturally progress through and seek meaning from the stages of life. This approach locates theological reflection *within* social and cultural experience rather than *outside* it,[7] and it ponders how textual consideration and theological reflection may be at work in the common ways that people think about how well they are navigating the life course.

A dialog between faith formation and human development, like any conversation, will not resolve all inherent discrepancies. Differences abound in assumptions between these two areas of inquiry about the nature of personhood, the intended telos of the human experience, sin and its effects, how we discern truth, what we aim to be saved from, and the remedies that are prescribed.[8] Yet, to not engage faith leaders in this conversation is to relinquish the interpretation of the life span to those who, like Cleopas and his companion on the road to Emmaus, have not yet had their eyes opened to the divine presence that is in their midst (Luke 24:13–53).

I began sketching the contents of this book by first gleaning concepts and theories from several human development texts, particularly *The Life Span: Human Development for Helping Professionals*, written by Patricia C. Broderick and Pamela Blewitt. I use this as a standard text for teaching graduate-level counseling students at Asbury Seminary because it serves as a grand collective of the findings I have encountered during thirty years of engagement with

6. Arguments can be made that the life span is not commonly experienced in such discrete stages but lived more continuously or with greater idiosyncrasies. I have chosen to retain the life-stage framework, contending that there are physiological changes that structure development especially in the first two decades of life, age-graded norms are embedded in things like our educational system, and society presents us with developmental tasks at each stage of life that bear resemblance across cultures.

7. Theologians of all stripes of course take culture into consideration. In my experience, however, the methodology of systematics or biblical interpretation commonly addresses contemporary culture at the end of the methodology as an application of a text or doctrine.

8. I was helped in thinking about these contrasts by Hosack, *Development on Purpose*.

the human sciences. Life span development focuses on how people grow and change across the stages of life, especially in physical, cognitive, emotional, and social domains. As a discipline, life span development seeks to integrate fields of research that are of particular value for those serving in ministry, including intergenerational family studies, social history, and life course sociology.

Life span psychology is now required by accreditation bodies in the training of many professions, such as mental health counselors, but it has typically been accessed in a piecemeal fashion by those training for ministry. Why should this understanding not also be requisite preparation for pastors, church staff, parents, and laypersons who work to disciple a congregation? Drawing systematically from life span development insights, I connect felt psychosocial needs that emerge through the stages of life with aspects of discipleship that deepen our understanding of the meaning of the life course. I cite extensively from life span texts, though investigative readers may find it useful to pursue the original resources from which these authors glean their summative material.

Though it may not always be made explicit in the pages of this text, my hope is to function as a sort of double crusader. I want to convert biblical/theological/ecclesiastical communities that have not yet fully discovered that the scientific exploration of the life course offers powerful descriptive insight into the patterns and processes that shape the lives of people. For those in positions of ministry, knowledge about human development enhances our capacity to understand, diagnose, empathize with, speak to, heal, and transform the woes of the human experience. Some of the most transformative ministry I have encountered has come from those few who can weave psychological insight into their pastoral care, preaching, teaching, and leading. On the other hand, I want to influence those who spend their time in social work and the helping professions. I find inadequate what so often seems the establishment position that the truest way to help someone is to tell them to "follow their own heart," or that the highest outcome for human development is adaptation to one's context. Jesus explained the decay of a whole generation of people by telling the story of an unclean spirit that was released from the soul of a man and went in search of a desolate place to find rest. Finding none, the spirit determined to return to the home from which he came. On the way, he gathered seven spirits worse than himself to inhabit the man (Matt. 12:43–45). As a theologian, I am persuaded that the only way social work can bring about the desired healing of the nations is by recognizing that the tree of life, on which healing fruit grows, is watered by the river that flows from the throne of God and of the Lamb (Rev. 22). The human science enterprise falls short whenever it ignores the spiritual dimension of life and the implications of such great revelation. It can deliver people from some maladies, but the human heart is a vacuous hole that is easily filled with compulsions, comorbidities, and misadventures unless we finally discover with Augustine that "thou hast made us for thyself, O Lord, and our heart is restless until it finds its rest in thee."[9]

My attempt is not to straitjacket faith, suggesting that discipleship is limited to or determined by naturally occurring developmental processes. Nor is it to undermine a theocentric focus in the way a person comes to view themselves, others, and the world they inhabit. My hope rather is to give articulation to a life that unfolds according to natural developmental processes and supranatural occurrences that are inexplicable unless God exists and rewards those attentive to his ways. I want to offer ways in which the story of God and a life of faith can reinterpret, re-create, and regenerate the course of one's life. I want to ponder the stages of the life course under the revelation of God as Father and maker of the heavens, the earth, and human beings. I want to consider how Jesus in his incarnation redeems us and re-narrates the story of our lives. I want to promote the Holy Spirit as the sanctifier who mysteriously comprehends the inner groanings of our spirits and transforms human speculation into new plausibility structures of faith.

I write from within a Wesleyan revivalistic tradition that, like other streams of evangelicalism, gives emphasis to punctiliar moments of full surrender. I affirm and give witness to such moments in my own journey, but I often find that these encounters can be so sought after that the quieter and more protracted work of God in the ordinary developmental processes can be overlooked. I appreciate Albert C. Outler's characterization of salvation as an "eventful process" as it holds together crisis moments and crucial processes, the latter requiring intentional and sustained practices through life's passages.[10]

The Scriptures tell us that Jacob spent all night tangling with an unnamed being from whom he would eventually wrestle a blessing that changed his name and transformed his character (Gen. 32:22–31). Yet, the encounter apparently dislocated something in the sinew of his hip, causing him to limp the remainder of his days. I liken my engagement with the human sciences over a third of a century to Jacob's encounter. Sometimes the enigmatic character of what I was receiving from my studies seemed elusive to identify, much like Jacob was uncertain exactly whom or what he was struggling with. There was no doubt that blessing came from a myriad of arrested insights, and yet I was left with an undeniable hobble as I interpreted and evaluated my spiritual and relational life through the lens of human development perspectives that did not always share the presuppositional grounding or telos of my faith.

9. Augustine, *Confessions* 1.1.1.
10. Outler, "New Future for Wesley Studies," 44.

In a recent celebration of its history, the *Christian Education Journal* asked its more prominent scholars to reflect on four decades of educational ministry as well as offer guidance for the future.[11] A recurring theme in the articles that reach across the life span is the perennial human need for Christian teaching that lives "in the tension between text and life,"[12] engaging diverse groups of scholars and disciplines so a more thorough understanding of faith formation is understood.[13]

None of what I write intends to diminish the importance of God's revelation or its primacy as the way to narrate our identity, ethic, and mission. I write assuming that many will read this as a required text for a class that is embedded in a curriculum of biblical interpretation and theology, or it will be read by staff or congregational members embedded in faith communities guided by the Spirit and oriented around orthodox adherence to the revelation of Jesus. Hence, I want this text to be additive and to expand the realms beyond traditional ways of doing discipleship, not subvert them. Whereas most of its readers will have spent years in the conventional methods of moving from text to context—that is, studying a passage of Scripture or a doctrine of the church and applying it to one's particular context—fewer will be adept at moving from context to text—that is, letting the observance of what may be happening in their historical moment or their particular stage of human development serve as the impetus for theological interpretation, reflection, and liturgical formulations.

One of the greatest appeals to me about studying human development is the broad way and the personal way it relates to almost any enterprise seeking to promote human flourishing. Pastors, organizational leaders, educators, mental health counselors, human factors scientists, children and youth service professionals, medical doctors, and social service providers all look to the scientific study of human development for insight and direction. Yet, many of them are also interested in relating their fields and their personal lives to their faith. My hope is that this handbook can contribute to just such a coalescing.

---

11. See also the follow-up issue of *Christian Eduction Journal* titled "Christian Education and the Social Sciences: An Assessment." Note especially the pair of articles by John David Trentham: Trentham, "Reading the Social Sciences Theologically (Part 1)" and "Reading the Social Sciences Theologically (Part 2)."

12. Budd and Bergen, "Adult Ministry in the Church," 483.

13. Larson, "Child in Our Midst," 438.

1 | Womb and Infancy
Origins of Faith and Belief

Why would God choose to have every human being come into the world as a vulnerable baby, the product of two parents? After all, he created the first human prototype by giving his breath to a sculpted mound of earth. So why not just keep insufflating dirt and mass produce the human race? God formed the second human from the rib of the first. Presumably, the first human had another 205 bones that God could have extracted and used to populate a pretty good harem for whatever would have been left of Adam. Why not work with human creation 2.0 as the blueprint for populating the human race?

Dennis Kinlaw answers his own query on this topic by propounding that whenever we encounter a human being, we naturally assume that two others gave it life. Even laboratory methods of fertilization still require a sperm donor and a womb where an egg can be implanted. Hence, every child has a mother and a father and therefore witnesses to the image of trinitarian creation—three persons mutually relating in a familial-like relationship. G. K. Chesterton captures the essentiality of this creation design when he writes, "You can free things from alien or accidental laws, but not from the laws of their own nature. You may, if you like, free a tiger from his bars; but do not free him from his stripes. Do not free a camel of the burden of his hump: you may be freeing him from being a camel. Do not go about as a demagogue, encouraging triangles to break out of the prison of their three sides. If a triangle breaks out of its three sides, its life comes to a lamentable end."[1]

1. Chesterton, *Orthodoxy*, 71–72.

Contrary to popular acclimations, Kinlaw notes, "No human being is self-originating, self-sustaining, self-explanatory, or self-fulfilling."[2] No newborn survives unless someone extends love and care to them, and it is this love that inevitably impresses upon them the very nature of the one from whom their life came.[3] Furthermore, babies come into the world remarkably hardwired to recruit and to receive this kind of care. But what might be the implications of how God designed each of us to be brought into this world and entrusted into the hands of a caregiver? How might we regard the newborn upon their arrival? And what might our role be within the web of relationships that sustains the life of a newborn if we are to help support the origins of faith? In this chapter, I consider what scholars and practitioners have observed about the way we embark on the human journey and what the social landscape might offer if we want that journey to be infused with the knowledge and love of God.

Conception

Research into human development shows that at the very point of conception, when the ovum produced by a woman's body is first penetrated by the sperm produced by a man's body, chromosomes combine and genetic coding begins. The remarkably mysterious and awe-inspiring formation of an immortal being starts taking place. As cells begin to multiply and divide, the genetic code begins determining what the person will look like. Yet, science tells us that the expression of any gene in this coding is dependent on its proximal environment (i.e., the alleles surrounding genes that determine which proteins turn on) and on how it combines with other genes and their coding sequence to determine how and if those particular genes come to express themselves.[4] Hence, cells that carry the same DNA (genotype) may yield very different expressions (phenotypes). The technical understanding of this phenomenon can turn rather complex very quickly. For our purposes, an illustration will suffice. In April 2018, National Geographic attempted to address decades of inequitable publishing regarding race. On the cover of what came to be called "the Race Issue" was a photograph of identical twin girls. Yet, unlike the mirror image of most identical twins, Marcia and Millie Biggs showed rather dis-

2. This was shared conversationally during a series of presentations that Kinlaw offered in 2005 titled "Trinity at the Hill," so named because the site of the conversation on trinitarian theology took place at the Asbury Seminary president's home, affectionately known as Rose Hill.
3. Kinlaw, "Family."
4. Broderick and Blewitt, Life Span, 39–46.

tinct features.[5] The girls were the product of a mixed race couple, sharing the same DNA but with various cells and cell environments turning on different characteristics (for skin, hair, lips, etc.) so that each child favored one parent more than the other. (See the image at https://www.nationalgeographic.com /magazines/l/ri-search/.)

My point here is not to delineate the technicalities of DNA or to enter debates about what *National Geographic* reported but rather to illustrate that from the very inception of a person's life, the environment that they inhabit, even at a cellular level, begins to shape who they are and what they become. There is coaction between heredity and environment, bidirectionality between the person and their social context, mutuality of one influencing the other, internal and external factors that form and transform one as a person.

Temperament and Early Influences of Sense Experience

Some of the earliest theories of human development focused on naming and categorizing temperament dispositions, eventually coalescing around the consensus that five dispositions serve as bedrock aspects of a person's personality and become strong predictors of behavior and outcomes throughout the life course. They are:

- openness to experience: tendency to be curious or cautious
- conscientiousness: tendency toward organization or carelessness
- extraversion: tendency toward having energy or being reserved
- agreeableness: tendency toward social harmony or criticalness
- neuroticism: tendency to feel nervous or confident[6]

Tendencies in these dispositions appear very early in a child's interaction with others. For example, they appear in the manner by which a child seeks attention and care from primary caregivers and the reactivity expressed when they feel discomfort. These early harbingers of personality traits show significant stability throughout the life course, typically moderating only slightly as a person matures. This continuity suggests that individuals carry a genetic component to their personality makeup that exerts influence throughout the life course. A study of one thousand infants in New Zealand, for example, showed statistically

5. This special edition of *National Geographic* celebrating the fiftieth anniversary of Martin Luther King's assassination carried the title "Black and White" and attempted to address what the magazine admitted was "racist" coverage in its history.
6. Lim, "Big Five Personality Traits."

significant associations between the traits of three-year-olds labeled as "under controlled" (impulsive, negativistic, and distractible) and similar temperament traits that identified them at age twenty-six (neuroticism, low agreeableness, and conscientiousness). Similarly, those described as "inhibited" at age three showed high constraint and low extroversion at age twenty-six. In a separate study, girls rated as inhibited at age four to six showed delay in assuming adult roles in their midtwenties.[7]

Yet, what may appear as a simple assumption of genetic determinism becomes much more complex under further scrutiny. First, neurobiology reveals that gene transcription itself is influenced by both environments within the body and ecologies external to the body. Second, most temperament traits are not dictated by single gene candidates but are polymorphic and determined by various clusters of genes and their unique expression. Third, studies of identical and fraternal twins show that nonshared social contexts may account for as much as half of what impacts developmental traits.[8] Fourth, throughout any child's life, they are likely to choose environments that conspire with their unique genetic makeup to develop a personality that will increasingly show gains in stability and consistency into and throughout adulthood. Fifth, our intuition is confirmed by science: some people change more than others.

Theologians writing on human development have maintained that *rationality* and other features of what it means to be human are dependent on *relationality* emerging in its fullest potential.[9] This serves, for example, as the foundational premise in J. O. Balswick, Pamela Ebstyne King, and Kevin S. Reimer's conceptualization of human development characterized as the reciprocal self.[10] Thus, whether we think about temperament, neurological development, or simple cellular functioning, it's the interaction between the human and their environment that becomes key. Grounded in trinitarian theology, this is likewise the foundational premise on which much of my exploration is based. Babies come into the world hardwired for relationality and with the capacity to recruit into their sphere those who will help them survive. When a baby is newly born, their eyes focus at the correct distance to see their mother's face when nursing; a natural sucking impulse brings about nourishment outside the womb; cries allow them to alert caregivers when they are distressed or hungry. Soon babble turns to the first words "Abba," "Da-da," or "Ma-ma," and in months to come crawling yields the capacity to move toward secure attachments.[11] It's astonishing to consider all that developed

---

7. Broderick and Blewitt, *Life Span*, 510.
8. Lykken et al., "Heritability of Interests," 13.
9. Broderick and Blewitt, *Life Span*, 47–50.
10. Balswick, King, and Reimer, *Reciprocating Self*.
11. Hosack, *Development on Purpose*, 128.

in the womb in the making of a human being, all the intricacies of cell division and particular function, that made the child ready to receive care in this world.

James Fowler begins his faith development theory with a stage of faith that occurs inside the womb, before a person is even born.[12] Fowler's theory distinguishes faith from belief. Whereas belief focuses on the contents of a person's confession, faith, at this stage of faith development, is a vague, experienced representation of something trustworthy or mutual.[13]

Science now tells us that neurons begin firing in the brain as early as the fourth month of gestation, even before the eyes are fully formed. By the third trimester of pregnancy, sense organs develop with capacities to perceive stimulation from outside the womb. Hence, the implication that touch is the first of our senses to develop, even before sight.[14] In a study conducted by Anthony J. DeCasper and Melanie Spence, pregnant women recited a nursery rhyme to the fetus inside their body every day for a month during the later weeks of their pregnancy. During the thirty-eighth week, a recorded rhyme was played. Fetal heart monitors recorded a slowing of the heart rate when the rhyme was familiar but an unchanged heart rate if the rhyme was not recognized, indicating a capacity while still in the womb to recognize syncopation.[15] Similarly, a fetus will "turn toward a light source," exhibiting prenatal visual sensitivity.[16] T. N. Wiesel and D. H. Hubel won a Nobel Prize in 1965 for their work with kittens. They forcibly closed one eye of a newly born kitten. When the shuttered eye was opened six weeks later, the kitten was permanently blind in that eye. No amount of intervention proved able to repair what was lost in the absence of stimulation during this critical period.[17]

It is much more difficult to measure the influences on spirituality than sense experience in the womb, but what if this experiment of physical sight has a corollary in the realm of the spiritual? Are there aspects of what Fowler calls "innate pre-potentiation" of faith that might later find cognition to express themselves in belief but that even before birth are awaiting stimulation from one's social and liturgical contexts to awaken?[18] Neurobiology now makes clear that visual and auditory systems begin integrating with other systems in the womb, awakening the foundations of spiritual formation. Erik H. Erikson, in fact, regards the womb as recapitulating our ancestors' Edenic paradise.[19] Unless the mother's

12. J. Fowler, *Stages of Faith*, 117–22.
13. J. Fowler, *Stages of Faith*, 53–56.
14. Arnett and Jensen, *Human Development*, 103.
15. DeCasper and Spence, "Prenatal Maternal Speech."
16. Broderick and Blewitt, *Life Span*, 61.
17. Wiesel and Hubel, "Comparison of the Effects."
18. J. Fowler, *Stages of Faith*, 25.
19. Zhitnik, "Eden and Erikson," 146.

body is traumatized, the womb provides a salubrious, generative environment where everything needed is provided, yielding a world for the fetus that is "good" in all aspects of its creation. As auditory and visual systems awaken in the fetus and begin to interact with and influence each other, what might be awakened in the child that pertains to later faith development and belief?[20] Along with the building of a sensory system, does the quality of care an infant receives set the foundation for their spiritual development?

Karen-Marie Yust uses the beautiful language of "creating a spiritual world for children to inhabit."[21] Calling on the faith community to begin providing things for a newborn that are missing from other arenas of life, Yust challenges the common assumptions that children's ministry is only about (1) providing childcare so parents can be engaged in "real" Christian formation, (2) entertaining kids until they are old enough for religious practices, or (3) equating spirituality solely with adherence to a set of beliefs or specific way of moral decision-making. Instead, Yust commends newborn practices and rituals that replicate the beneficial experience of the untraumatized womb: swaddling with a blanket, rhythmic walking, cradling so the baby can feel the mother's heartbeat, nursing when a baby's cry indicates hunger, and providing a warm bath before rocking a baby to sleep. All these provide an initial answer to what will become faith's most primal question: Is care in this world responsive and trustworthy?

Similarly, Stephanie Paulsell includes bathing, clothing, and nourishing a child as spiritual practices indicative of "honoring the body."[22] Like Yust, she calls us to recognize every human's propensity at any age to have some intuitive experience of the wonder and mystery of God. In the womb and in infancy, an infant is acted upon more than they exercise agency, but as the infant matures, so will their capacity for appropriating aspects of faith. Here our focus is necessarily on precursors of faith and the quality of relationships that give foundation to this journey.

Eugene C. Roehlkepartain and colleagues years ago produced a rather comprehensive handbook on the scientific study of child and adolescent spirituality.[23]

---

20. Some Reformed traditions may express reservation with this view, contending that any person is justified by faith alone. Such a position aligns with efforts to determine when a child is capable/culpable/accountable for faith. My attempt here is not to contend with any faith tradition on theological grounds, though my Wesleyan perspective readily embraces prevenient grace (i.e., the grace that goes before saving faith); rather, I am drawing inferences from developmental science that align with perceiving spiritual openness at very early, even prenatal stages of development. For a good introductory treatment of how this aligns with questions of the *imago Dei* and original sin, see Barfield, "Children and the Imago Dei."

21. Yust, *Real Kids, Real Faith*, xxiii, 21, 22.

22. Paulsell, *Honoring the Body*, 35–96.

23. Roehlkepartain et al., *Handbook of Spiritual Development*, 21–34, 46–72.

Throughout the collection, contributors consistently report evidence supporting a universal sense of spirituality or awareness of the transcendent among
children long before language arrives, what Walter Wangerin Jr. poetically calls
every child's "first dance with God." Wangerin predicts that a child's capacity
to reify these early intimations is either dismissed as fantasy or appropriated
as faith depending on whether the social context provides the language and
experience to "name, explain and contain" the dance the child has already begun.[24] Spirituality, it would seem, is not so much taught to a child as a foreign
import as it is confirmed and directed. One might even argue that it is atheism
or agnosticism that has to be socialized into a child, not the religious impulse.
When we find a child snubbing God, it is almost always accounted for by the
intentionality of an aggrieved parent or the neglect of any religious education
that would have established a child's earliest inclinations.

Perhaps this is best illustrated in the story of Helen Keller, who lost her
sight and hearing at eighteen months of age. She would spend seven tortured
years with her teacher Anne Sullivan before learning language. Throughout her
childhood, Keller was allegedly told that Mother Nature made the sky, trees,
water, and all living creatures. When Keller grew older and encountered alternative ideas about there being a Creator, Sullivan took her to Phillips Brook, the
rector at Trinity Church in Boston. When Bishop Brooks communicated that
God loved her and all his children, Keller responded, "Yes I know Him, I had
just forgotten His name."[25] Years later, having acquired the gift of language and
the ability to keep a journal, Keller penned a poem she titled "Mine to Keep."

> They took away what should have been my eyes
> (But I remembered Milton's Paradise)
> They took away what should have been my ears
> (Beethoven came and wiped away my tears)
> They took away what should have been my tongue
> (But I had talked with God when I was young).
> He would not let them take away my soul:
> Possessing that, I still possess the whole.[26]

Bonnie J. Miller-McLemore asks, "How does one fit children, especially
preverbal infants and unsteady toddlers, into classic Christian understandings
that measure maturity in faith according to the acquisition of reason, the capacity

24. Wangerin, *Orphean Passages*, 20–25.
25. Helms, *God's Final Answer*, 78.
26. Keller, *My Religion*, 9–10.

for verbal confession, and the formation of moral conscience?"[27] Wouldn't such conceptualizations render a misperception of children as "insignificant and incomplete"? Miller-McLemore then presses us to dispense with our notions that spiritual formation is only unidirectional (i.e., moving from adult to child) or forward-looking (concerned mostly with the child making a profession of faith or becoming an adult). She suggests that in a child's smiles, smallness, and freshness there may even be embedded a vocation that provokes care from adults and cultivates responsiveness. In these simple and preconscious acts may lie the harbingers of our first calling—"to call forth a sense of being in our neighbor."[28]

Object Permanence and Its Implication for Faith

But how is it that we come to know the world that we inhabit? Social scientists have long observed the way children utilize and integrate their senses in coming to perceive the property of objects. For example, infants feel with their mouth a pacifier that they connect with what they see their mother or father holding in front of them. This capacity for integrating sensory stimuli witnesses to the remarkable capacity of neurotransmitters in the brain that are developing in the early weeks of one's life. By the first month, babies will focus their eyes more on a pacifier they have sucked on (with certain visual characteristics, such as smooth or ridged) than one they have not. By six weeks, they will reach for the particular object they have been sucking on, "identifying their experience of the pacifier from their tactile experience of it."[29]

Jean Piaget coined the phrase "object permanence"[30] to describe a child's realization that an object has a separate existence apart from its perceiver. Object permanence signifies the capacity to hold a mental representation of an object in mind even when it is out of sight or not currently stimulating one's senses. To assess this, Piaget placed a small object like a ball or a doll in front of an infant and yet within their reach. A cloth was then draped between the baby and the object, and Piaget observed whether the child went in search of the object or appeared to believe that the object had vanished. Studies using this test found that babies from eight to twelve months failed to search for the object despite having the motor skills to do so, but in the later months of the first year, they began developing the capacity for representational thought, realizing the object existed apart from their perceptual action on the object. This capacity for object

27. Cahalan and Miller-McLemore, *Calling All Years Good*, 40.
28. Cahalan and Miller-McLemore, *Calling All Years Good*, 40.
29. Broderick and Blewitt, *Life Span*, 84.
30. Broderick and Blewitt, *Life Span*, 84.

permanence has been related to several observations of children during this formational period. Is peekaboo such a fun game with babies because of their perception that an adult is suddenly disappearing and reappearing? Is separation anxiety linked to object permanence, spiking when a child fears they have been completely abandoned when a familiar adult disappears? Does calm return if and when they can hold a mental representation of mother or father in mind despite mother or father being gone from their line of vision?

James W. Fowler, following Daniel Stern's treatment of Piaget's work, finds in object permanence the genesis of faith.[31] Consider how important it is for us as adults, especially during anxious episodes in our lives, to hold before us a mental representation of God—for example, "The LORD is my shepherd" (Ps. 23:1), "The name of the LORD is a strong tower" (Prov. 18:10), "I lift up my eyes to the hills. From where does my help come?" (Ps. 121:1), "Draw near to God, and he will draw near to you" (James 4:8), "But the Comforter, which is the Holy Ghost, whom the Father will send in my name" (John 14:26 KJV). If the very essence of faith is "the assurance of things hoped for, the conviction of things not seen" (Heb. 11:1), then this capacity for object permanence seems to be a primary ingredient for robust faith.

Attachment

The most important *object* that a baby comes to know is their own mother or father. One of the most generative theories in human development in the last few decades that conceptualizes a link between childhood experience and a relationship with God is attachment theory, most often attributed to John Bowlby. Bowlby's bio-evolutionary view originates from the notion that animals develop a behavioral system that provides them with protection from predators or other dangers. When an animal is threatened or distressed, the system compels them to (1) seek *proximity* to a protector, thus ensuring survival,[32] (2) regain a sense of felt *security*, and (3) use this restored sense of safe haven as an *anchor* from which to explore.

Bowlby and his colleagues hypothesized that through cumulative interactions between an infant and a primary caregiver, an attachment bond begins to form. If the primary caregiver is available and responsive, then secure attachment will most likely form. If the primary caregiver is untrustworthy, distant, dismissive, unsupportive, unavailable, avoidant, inconsistent, or insensitive to the needs of the child, then various kinds of insecure attachments will likely

31. J. Fowler, *Stages of Faith*, 25–43.
32. Kirkpatrick, "Attachment-Theory Approach."

form.[33] Most studies focus on the mother's attachment style, since she typically spends much more time caring for an infant than does the father, but multiple studies found that a father's sensitivity in care also predicts the quality of attachment to him. A child who has a secure attachment to at least one parent is more likely to mitigate an insecure attachment to the other parent than a child who is insecurely attached to both parents.

Over time, from their perceptions of caregiving dependability and sensitivity, the child constructs an internal working model that then begins to direct and influence how they perceive themselves and how they perceive others. A secure bond will most likely create a child who sees themselves as worthy of love and protection, friendly, and good-natured; assumes others are well-intentioned, reliable, and trustworthy; and naturally experiences minimum levels of anxiety when moving close to other people. By contrast, an insecure bond will most likely create a child who experiences themselves as misunderstood and worries that others don't love them or cannot meet their needs. They may be reluctant to open up or slow to seek help when it is needed, or they may exaggerate emotions in order to get attention. Insecurely attached children may feel more inclined to withdraw rather than lean into closeness and may develop coping strategies to avoid recurrence of the distress. Two primary questions that summarize attachment concerns in the heart of the infant/child even prior to their becoming cognizant of them are "Can I count on you?" and "Am I worthy of your love?"

Lee A. Kirkpatrick extends Bowlby's theory, applying attachment dynamics vertically to one's relationship with God.[34] Along with Pehr Granqvist, Kirkpatrick sees a parallel between a child's longing to be recognized and loved—to mean something to a significant other—and the kind of attachment they might develop with the deity. Elizabeth Marquardt, writing about children of divorce, notes a correlation between a child's experience of their parents and that child's feelings about God.[35] Other reports highlight that religious individuals who typically experience anxiety or avoidance in their relationship with God also find it more difficult to trust others.[36]

Theologically then, attachment theory elevates relationality as a central aspect of our formation and identity. This is consistent with current theological views that the image of God is most profoundly recognized in the human capacity to relate to God and to others. The words of John H. Westerhoff are insightful to translate this into a methodology for learning: "The language of instruction does not encourage us to think in terms of interaction. . . . To understand faith

33. Granqvist and Kirkpatrick, "Attachment and Religious Representations and Behavior," 906–10.
34. Kirkpatrick, "Attachment-Theory Approach."
35. Marquardt, *Between Two Worlds*, 1–100.
36. Bradshaw et al., "Attachment to God and Social Trust."

and its content we need to focus our attention on the experiences of interaction between and among faithing persons."[37]

Granqvist and Kirkpatrick hypothesize that two different pathways might exist that link a person's attachment style with a caregiver to the kind of relationship they establish with God.[38] The *correspondence hypothesis* predicts that the kind of bond characterizing one's relationship with a parent will naturally be mirrored in the relationship one has with God. Hence, a securely attached child will socialize easily into a faith community that speaks of a loving and present God who can be depended on and in whose care faith is fostered. The *compensation hypothesis*, by contrast, suggests that when a child's efforts to find security, safety, and love in a parent are unsuccessful, a search will be activated for a more adequate attachment that may be discovered in God.[39] James E. Loder would caution, however, that when a child comprehends God *only* through human images, the spirit of that child is deprived of its natural drive to move beyond itself, turning back toward its own imagination and turning God at best into an aid for social adjustment, potentially deforming the spirit.[40] What is needed is revelation of God's true nature. At every point in the life course, God's revelation of himself mediated through Jesus, the Holy Spirit, and his body the church is critical to correct our misattributions of his character.[41]

One of the more profound social phenomena that pastors and some children's ministry directors are uniquely situated to observe is the intergenerational transmission of attachment styles. Quite often, abusive, intrusive, neglectful, or inattentive parents are themselves victims of adverse styles of parenting. Wounded children far too often become parents who perpetuate their brokenness, replicating their insecure attachments with their children. This seems to be reflected in the biblical foreboding that the sins of the fathers will be visited on the third and fourth generation. Yet, what seems to some a fated and grim reality can be superseded by the promise of steadfast love shown to the thousandth generation (Exod. 20:5–6) when there is the experience of grace-filled interventions. My roles as pastor and campus minister took on new dimensions when I exercised an awareness of family systems at rituals like baptisms, weddings, and funerals. The intergenerational gathering of family members exposed behavioral patterns and abuses that ran across generations.

37. Westerhoff, *Will Our Children Have Faith?*, 80–81.
38. Granqvist and Kirkpatrick, "Attachment and Religious Representations and Behavior," 912–20.
39. Granqvist and Kirkpatrick, "Attachment and Religious Representations and Behavior," 912–20.
40. Loder, *Logic of the Spirit*.
41. Bradshaw et al., "Attachment to God and Social Trust."

Developing an awareness of these patterns yielded understanding as well as possible avenues for healing, extending my pastoral role beyond simply performing a ceremony.

The implications of attachment for faith formation are extensive, as research has linked the quality of one's attachment bond to (1) the formation of conscience, (2) the capacity one develops to cope with frustration and stress, (3) the response one makes to fear and perceived threats, and (4) how easily one finds self-reliance.[42] Attachment theorists further relate attachment to faith, noting that in North America, prayer is the most often practiced form of religiosity as an anxiety-saturated society yearns for security. Brant Wenegrat also notes that attachment imagery pervades the Psalms, encouraging a parental-like attachment to God.[43] What would ministry look like that teaches attachment as a core skill to mothers and fathers even before a child learns language?

Memory

Also closely connected to the emergence of object permanence is the development of our aptitude for remembering. A distinction is sometimes made by human scientists between recognition and recall.[44] Recognition involves seeing the face of a person that we realize we have seen before and hence finding it familiar. Recognition occurs when an experience is repeated and regarded as having been encountered before (such recognition may be assumed in the pacifier examples above). By contrast, scientists see a more advanced process of retrieval in the concept of recall—namely, the capacity to bring to mind a mental representation that is not repeated but is already stored in one's memory. The mental representation now *stands for* the actual experience. Recall becomes increasingly important because it is essential for deferred imitation whereby a child observes the actions of another and then some time in the future summons that memory, enabling them to imitate the observed behavior or choose an appropriate response.[45]

Piaget observed that a child by reflex might accidentally create an interesting effect. For example, bumping a mobile hanging overhead creates a pleasant sound and causes lights to flash. If the effect is interesting, the baby may try to repeat the action to cause the effect to occur again. Piaget calls this "making interesting sights last" and believes that it is the precursor to intentional

42. Broderick and Blewitt, *Life Span*, 135–39.
43. Wenegrat, *Divine Archetype*.
44. Broderick and Blewitt, *Life Span*, 86–87.
45. Broderick and Blewitt, *Life Span*, 86–87.

behavior.[46] Children by the age of eighteen months may even begin to vary their actions to see if new actions result in a different outcome.

Here too are critical and preliminary elements of faith that are often mentioned in the narrative of Scripture. The people of Israel learn who they are through recognition, memory, and recall. As they remember the mighty acts of God, recall his actions in their history, and move toward covenant, more mature and faithful ways of behaving emerge. Israelite children, through enacted ritual, have tacit knowledge of what it means to "do this in remembrance of me" (Luke 22:19).

Play and Caretaker Speech

While object permanence suggests precursors to elements of faith formation, play facilitates development beyond simply learning the property of objects. As infants develop increased motor skills, they begin to sort and organize, learning about numbers and counting, categories, spatial relationships, and memory. Play among preschoolers serves many aspects of socioemotional development, providing multiple opportunities for trained workers in church programs to influence children. Piaget, for example, found that play often creates the context whereby children confront their own egocentrism (more on this in the next chapter). In Western countries, where fathers tend to engage more with infants than in other countries, play is often energetic and rough-and-tumble, whereas a mother's play tends to be ritualized and quiet with lots of vocalization and facial expressions. This variety of interactions provides important social contexts where imitation of adult roles, emotional self-regulation, cooperation, planning a scenario, and turn-taking may develop.[47] Notably, Western parents often enroll their children in preschool to accelerate children's educational advancement and advantage, but in Japanese preschools neither reading nor arithmetic is the focus. Instead, the primary goal is giving children "the experience of being a member of a group."[48]

Parents and adults who talk with children about mental states—for example, what a person feels, knows, or desires—stimulate more rapid progress in children attending to their own emotional states and the thinking and feelings of others. In one fascinating study, researchers made monthly visits for two years to the homes of families representing three socioeconomic levels: poor, working class, and wealthy. They recorded the number of words spoken in a week

46. Broderick and Blewitt, *Life Span*, 89.
47. Broderick and Blewitt, *Life Span*, 115–16.
48. Arnett and Jensen, *Human Development*, 241.

and projected from it the number of words a child might hear by the time they reached age four. The difference between the number of words used in wealthier families and the number of words used in poorer families was thirty million words. Furthermore, families with at least one parent with a high-paying job used speech in an elaborative fashion, soliciting responses from children, offering information, and establishing positive connections. Speech in the lower-income families, by contrast, was often used to regulate and prohibit behavior. Four-year-olds from the wealthier families also displayed far more advanced and expansive vocabularies when compared to the other two groups.[49] An elaborative style of communication that provides lots of details forms children who compose informative narratives of their own lives and show greater comprehension of the lives of others.

It follows that benefits flow from raising children in bilingual households. Whereas historically some pundits thought that speaking more than one language in front of children might confuse them and slow their learning, neurobiology now confirms that bilingual education early in a child's development myelinates together brain circuitry that stimulates understanding.[50] Theologically, how frequently and in what tone we speak to children have profound and far-reaching implications, grounded in the simple affirmation that, like in the Genesis story, words set in motion the creation of a child's world. Further, the value of spoken words is not solely confined to what we hear others say to us. Once language is acquired, many children engage in private speech or verbalizing messages aloud. Internal dialogues may be ways children problem-solve, learn coping strategies, or figure out strategies for anticipated encounters.

Mediated Learning and Intergenerational Ministry

If conversations are so important in the capacity building of preschoolers, it stands to reason that much of development and spiritual formation is mediated by the social context one inhabits. A Russian educationist by the name of Lev Vygotsky extended this thinking and created the concept that the mind is no longer to be located entirely in the head.[51] Vygotsky was convinced that cognitive functioning is not limited by one's biological or maturational development but is largely determined by one's environmental or cultural context. Teaching is largely the product of the collective roles influencing a child.

49. Hart and Risley, "Early Catastrophe," 8–9.
50. Broderick and Blewitt, *Life Span*, 105.
51. Cole and Wertsch, "Beyond the Individual-Social Antinomy."

Vygotsky used the concept of scaffolding as a metaphor for the temporary support structures that are necessary for learning until mastery of a concept has been gained. In the same way that a fragile building or plant needs support (imagine roof trusses on a new home or a stake for a new sapling), novice learners need knowledge structures to grow their reasoning. In fact, Vygotsky thought there is a "zone of proximal development" where a child can grasp a concept or perform a skill only if they have assistance from someone else.[52] Learning new words, tying a shoestring, and making toast may all require a joint effort and shared understanding with a parent. We could also imagine that gender is learned through scaffolding, as are important aspects of faith. How does one learn to worship or to pray or to share or to repair a relationship unless it is scaffolded for them?

Theories of Emotion

Closely related to the notion of how knowledge is gained in the interpersonal spaces a child shares with a parent is the exploration of how emotions are experienced and learned. Evidence supports the established position that a set of basic emotions exists, though some contend that a person must be able to consciously interpret distress or contentment in order for it to rise to the level of being considered an emotion.[53]

Theories of emotion imply that infants are not blank slates but bring innate characteristics into the world. The unique composite of these characteristics within each child causes researchers to explore whether there are infant temperaments, whether these traits show stability over time, and how much these traits are affected by caregiving. Many of these proposed traits, such as shyness, inhibition, or irritability, which are exhibited early in a newborn's life, seem to be based on reactivity patterns with probable biological bases such as thresholds of excitability in the brain.[54]

Carroll E. Izard conjectures that there are innate emotions, as evidenced in an infant's cries of distress, disgust at certain smells, and interest in what grabs their attention. Basic emotions are felt automatically and trigger a set of physiological reactions that typically are exhibited in facial expressions recognizable across cultures.[55] Some theorists surmise, however, that emotions are experienced as only positive or negative distress at birth and then become increasingly

52. Neal, "Power of Vygotsky."
53. Broderick and Blewitt, *Life Span*, 167.
54. Kagan and Fox, "Biology, Culture, and Temperamental Biases."
55. Izard, *Psychology of Emotions*.

differentiated into a more expansive repertoire as they interact with cognitive capacities of attention, persistence, and goal-directed behaviors.[56] For example, distress differentiates into anger, fear, and/or sadness, yet distress can also be mitigated with consistent and thoughtful caregiving. Emotional schemas suggest the integration of cognitive factors (thoughts and images) with emotionality (hormonal shifts) in such things as goal-directed behavior or when the attention of an infant becomes focused. Some conceptualizations differentiate between inborn emotions, such as distress and disgust, and emotions that appear to be learned in a social context and hence require greater self-consciousness, such as empathy, shame, pride, and guilt.[57]

A critical area of exploration for those interested in thinking deeply about discipleship is how emotional schemas develop as memories, images, hormonal shifts, and collective experiences interact through various stages of life, amplifying and moderating these basic emotional experiences. Those who interact with infants inevitably scaffold for them how to regulate emotions, creating synchrony that helps them repair any sense of distress.

Later I will propose that practices of discipleship seek to fasten the emotional life to virtues apart from which we become easily captivated by the sirens of culture. If the emotional life of a child is a product of innate human propensities differentiated through interaction with others, then it is no wonder that the Jesuits have reportedly adopted the maxim: "Give me the child for the first seven years, and I will give you the man."

Early Care of the Child

What is true about the social, emotional, and spiritual influence of families on children also applies to care from others. The effect of day care on preschoolers largely depends on how tuned in teachers are to the emotional lives of the children entrusted to their care. Custodial programs can produce healthy outcomes for both children and their working parents. However, when day care workers are untrained; develop little trust with the children they aim to protect and nurture; have fewer resources to engage children with books, art, or building materials; and are uninvolved with children, the outcomes are likely to be deleterious. Though quality is probably a better metric that quantity, teacher-child ratios in day care centers and schools can also be an important criterion. For three-year-olds, the recommended ratio is no more than nine kids per adult; for four-year-olds, the recommendation increases to ten kids per adult but

56. Sroufe, *Emotional Development*.
57. Broderick and Blewitt, *Life Span*, 152.

cautions against more than twenty kids per group.[58] Bowlby thought it best not to put children under the age of three into day care so that healthy attachment could form with a primary caregiver. When such early noncustodial care is necessary, the American Academy of Pediatrics suggests that the optimal ratio is three infants to one adult.[59] My predecessor at Asbury Theological Seminary, Donald M. Joy, a respected expert on human development, gave the general formula that optimum formation could occur if a child was placed in the care of someone other than a parent for one hour per year of age per day.

I would also hasten to add that in the process of socialization, cultural values come into play in the way adults interact with children and whether care should ever be shared outside the immediate family. In more collectivistic cultures, conversational patterns reflect child-rearing goals of deference to parental authority, the suppression of opposing views, and the elevating of family values above individual desires. In cultures where independence and autonomy are assumed as the telos of human development, kids may be encouraged to express their opinions, negotiate family rules, and seek support for individual desires and goals. An interesting study of different cultural values involves sleeping arrangements. In many non-Western parts of the world, children share a bed with a parent or older sibling. In many Western cultures, family experts recommend getting a child to sleep in their own crib and a separate room (with monitors) as soon as possible.[60] More on cultural value differences follows in subsequent chapters.

The Joyful Mysteries

Throughout this chapter I have emphasized the environments that awaken innate potentialities for faith. From the moment of conception, our genetic makeup begins to be influenced by its surrounding environment. Within the womb, sensory development sets in motion attachment processes between mother, father, and child. At birth, a child enters a world fully dependent on others for their preservation, creating the context where precursors of more conscious elements of faith will soon be formed. Much is at stake in how parents engage their own faith journeys, interpret the spiritual significance of their parenting, and fashion a kind of spiritual world for their child to encounter. It is therefore instructive for us while considering the infancy stage of life that when the Gospel writers tell the story of Jesus, they spend a considerable amount of time narrating events

58. Broderick and Blewitt, *Life Span*, 157–62.
59. Broderick and Blewitt, *Life Span*, 157–62.
60. Mindell et al., "Cross-Cultural Differences."

that occur prior to and during the time that Jesus is in Mary's womb. An angel announces that the child will be conceived of the Holy Spirit (Luke 1:26–35); an angel appears to reassure Joseph about the child (Matt. 1:18–25); a relative who is also pregnant finds her baby leaping in her womb when the mother of Jesus pays her a visit (Luke 1:41–44); a census occurs, dramatically revising the unfolding of the pregnancy and making vulnerable the delivery of the child in anything but a sterile environment (2:1–7). How might these narratives form our awareness of the faith formation of infants and our responses to them?

Protestants are increasingly utilizing *lectio divina*, a spiritual practice that involves Scripture reading, meditation, and prayer. In *lectio divina*, one reads a passage of Scripture several times but does not analyze it as in traditional Bible study. Instead, one enters the context of the passage imaginatively or listens intently for words that speak personally into one's life. Hence, the aim is less on interpretation, though one still trusts that the Spirit is leading one to truth, and more on encountering Christ via placing oneself in the story.

In Catholic tradition, the events of Jesus's life are upheld in prayers that resemble *lectio divina* in repetition, meditation, and attuning to scriptural words that can speak situationally into one's present condition. The episodes of Jesus's life and death are grouped into two sets. Those events associated with the birth of Jesus are called the joyful mysteries; those associated with Jesus's death are called the sorrowful mysteries.[61] One reads scriptural passages using a rosary, says fifty Hail Marys, and frequently repeats the Lord's Prayer. I am not attempting here to bring Catholic practice into Protestant circles by elevating Mary or commending the use of the rosary. Rather, I am attempting to observe a practice, ask what formational value it seeks to bring about, and discern whether it could be appropriated by Protestants.

The five joyful mysteries begin with reading five passages from the Gospel of Luke:

- The annunciation to Mary—1:26–38
- The visitation of Mary—1:39–45
- The birth of our Lord Jesus Christ—2:6–12
- The presentation of the child Jesus in the temple—2:22–32
- The finding of our Lord in the temple—2:41–50

Interspersed throughout these readings are prayers that link aspects of the life of Jesus to a mother's and/or father's experience surrounding the birth of a child.

61. "Joyful Mysteries."

- We pray that "every child be treasured and protected from the first moment of conception as an inestimable and wondrous gift of God."
- "Inspire the hearts of all newly pregnant women with the joy of which you sang at the Annunciation."
- We pray for the "new parents, that the miracle of new life silently growing in the womb will awaken in them a commitment to cherish and protect their child."
- We "intercede for all parents who long to carry a child in their arms."
- "Bless adoptive parents and rejoice with them in the beauty of their child."
- "Comfort expectant fathers when they are afraid."
- "Share your courage with all women who fear the coming birth of their child."
- We "pray for grandparents, that the witness of their joy might be a source of strength to their expectant children."
- We "pray that all our laws may protect and defend the innocent life which lives within each mother's womb."
- We "ask that God gives us wisdom to support those tempted to abort their child's life."
- "Come swiftly to the aid of all those who labor in distress."
- "Give your own courage to mothers who are alone or abandoned."
- We "pray for those who assist with the labor which brings new life."
- "As Christ was consecrated to God at his presentation in the temple, so may we consecrate all children to the holiness, purity, and innocence by which they lead us to God."
- "Bless with your presence the room of each little child."
- "Welcome home to heaven the soul of the miscarried child."
- "As the Christ Child was found in the temple by the Blessed Virgin Mary and Saint Joseph, so we pray for all children, especially those lost and forgotten. May the Gospel of Life impel us to find them when they are most in need and to lead them home to a place where they are treasured, protected, and loved."
- "Deliver the abusive adult from the evil of their actions."
- "Inspire all legislators by your love for us, that they might work for the protection of life."[62]

Embedded in these liturgical acts are several values and perspectives that Protestants share. First, the readings and prayers tell the story of Jesus and apply

62. "Rosary for Life."

it to the real experiences of mothers and fathers today, linking the fears that Mary and Joseph must have felt to the worries and fears mothers and fathers have today. This is no small matter, as the World Health Organization reports that one in seven mothers will experience some form of postpartum depression and that many fathers will abandon children to whom they feel no attachment.[63] Second, these prayers elevate motherhood and fatherhood as sacred responsibilities despite their denigrations relative to other vocations in contemporary culture. Third, prayers are offered for grandparents not only acknowledging their joy but also leaning into the hope of intergenerational care for a child. (Just recently a pastor in New Mexico shared with me that 70 percent of the children in his pastoral region are being raised in homes where a grandparent is present. Quite often, they are the primary caregiver to the child.) Fourth, the barrenness of Elizabeth, the youthfulness of Mary, the plight of the holy family as refugees, and other aspects of the narrative are used as openings to pray for infertile couples, adopted children, distressed labor, single mothers, miscarriages, and abusive parents, creating a sense that these realities are not forsaken by God but are within the realm of his concern. Fifth, the faith community is led to join Mary and Joseph in the search for all children who are lost and forgotten and to become places of shelter and harbor. Sixth, prayers are offered for midwives, doctors, legislators, and even abusive parents.

This practice focuses the attention of the congregation on the unborn child, summoning us to attend to the quality of care and intentional faith formation they will receive when placed in our midst. As parental attachments are being formed to support the infant, the joyful mysteries link the story of Jesus to the cares and concerns of those who, like Mary, are "great with child," and educate a congregation for missional engagement.

Liturgical Practice

Protestants will likely never agree on whether or to what extent an infant can have faith and whether they should or should not be excluded from baptism. Nor will we come to agree on the nature of original sin, predestination, and whether an infant is saved and through what means. We may, however, through the social sciences, come to see more universally what is developing physically, cognitively, emotionally, psychologically, and socially in the life of an infant and agree on the importance of providing a child with safety, nurture, security, and consistent care as a means of establishing the cardinal virtues of faith, hope, and love in their experience.

63. Chatterjee, "What Is Postpartum Depression?"

What would it mean for a faith community to practice promise keeping and blessing when it comes to the words they speak at a baptism or a baby dedication? What if trustworthy men and women journeyed with children through their adolescent years, ready to step in with the conviction they pledged at the baptism to "surround these persons with a community of love and forgiveness, that they may grow in their trust of God"?[64] In this day and age, we should exercise every caution against predators and exploiters of young girls and boys, taking every necessary step in children's ministry with background checks and the avoidance of settings where there is no surveillance. Yet, there is a great need for trustworthy women and men to godparent or sponsor infants into faith.

I have witnessed the power and beauty of a congregation singing at the dedication/baptism/blessing of an infant. I know of families who develop a blessing that they speak nightly over a child and who report that in early adulthood their grown children still call to have the blessing spoken over them. For an example of a baptismal hymn that conveys this kind of blessing, see the United Methodist hymn titled "Child of Blessing, Child of Promise."[65]

CONCLUSION

Pundits throughout the ages have sometimes held the conviction that the worth of any civilization could be determined by the quality of care shown to its children. In this chapter, I gleaned from the social sciences to consider origins of faith. The word *infancy* comes from the Latin compounding of *in* = "not" and *fant* = "to speak."[66] Hence, infancy generally refers to that period of the life course prior to having acquired the tools of speech. In this period, intersensory experience precedes language, or to say it differently, learning depends on community, especially the experiences we have of the primary caregivers who accompany us. Human scientists use the term *synchrony* to refer to the rhythmic patterning of stimulus and response that becomes a coordinated way of interacting between a parent and their child.[67] A baby feels distressed and looks toward the mother; the mother looks back at the child and with her gaze, a gentle touch, and the vocalization of tender words attends to the child's distress and soothes them. At first, the repair attempts made by the caregiver can be derailed. The baby

64. See, e.g., the liturgy for baptism used by the United Methodist Church at https://www.umcdiscipleship.org/book-of-worship/the-baptismal-covenant-i.

65. For more information on this hymn, see https://www.umcdiscipleship.org/articles/history-of-hymns-child-of-blessing-child-of-promise.

66. *Online Etymology Dictionary*, s.v. "infancy."

67. Broderick and Blewitt, *Life Span*, 133.

has no reference for what to make of the mother's words and no experience to know how to interpret her gestures. Nevertheless, when there is consistency on the part of the mother, the baby will most likely come to see the efforts of the mother as reliable and by six months or so learn to find contentment in her response as well as in the father's.

Recognizing the importance of synchrony in emotional regulation, scientists over the past fifty years have conducted various experiments in a mother's contingent responses to her baby. In one of the more salient examples, babies were placed in an infant seat directly in front of their mother. The mother was instructed to engage the baby in a pleasant and playful way, smiling, talking with baby-ese, and touching. When signaled, the mother was then coached to become stoic, still-faced, and unresponsive, as if looking toward the baby but not really seeing them. After a short passage of time, the mother was then permitted to resume her more comforting response to her baby. Interestingly, observers reported that when the mother turned unresponsive, after only a few seconds, signs of heightening distress appeared to show up in the baby. Furthermore, when this continued, many babies seemed to shift their attention from an other-directed coping behavior to a self-directed coping behavior, trying to find some self-stimulating way of finding stability and comfort—for example, rocking, sucking, rubbing their hair.[68] In some cases, babies intensified their signals of distress to emphasis whatever worked to get their mother's attention before. For some babies, even after the mother returned to more responsive care, the negative emotion persisted.

If families and faith communities take a stoic response to babies, making them feel they are not seen, we will likely grow a generation that looks largely to themselves to find succor and meaning for their lives. However, parents, grandparents, teachers, and pastors, made in the image of a loving God, are equipped to create a spiritual world full of grace and truth where the love of God is impressed upon babies even before they learn his name.

68. Broderick and Blewitt, *Life Span*, 133.

2 | Early Childhood
Parenting as Image Bearing

Cathy's childhood years were marked by an early response to Jesus. Her childhood memories are of deeply relational and devotedly warm exchanges with God. Yet, her faith tradition seemed impoverished to recognize the depth or authenticity of her young and salient faith. It emphasized a punctiliar crisis moment of faith, and Cathy could not point to such a marker in her walk with God. There was no available metaphor of a spiritual journey to attach to the affective musings of her own childhood faith, nor was there any persuasion to wait on God's *kairos* timing in the early maturing years of her life. Rather, the compulsion was to get as quickly as one could to the crucial moment of full surrender.

The perception this left in Cathy's teenage, searching mind was not one filled with grace. Instead, it compelled a spiritual struggle marked by a persistent questioning of "Where am I in relationship with God?" Without an experience that matched the radical transformation she heard described, with no language to value the process of her early formative experiences of faith, and without the theological framework to conceptualize ongoing transformation, Cathy found herself questioning the validity of her own journey of faith.

Those spiritual struggles would result in a fitful night in which Cathy, in exhaustion, collapsed on God. She came to the end of her striving and found rest in God. When she awoke the next morning, she felt filled with a sense of joy and peace—a reality that would linger the rest of her days. Further resolution came for Cathy on an Emmaus Walk when she found herself singing, "Jesus loves me, this I know, for the Bible tells me so. Little ones to him belong." In the phrase "little ones to him belong," God gave Cathy a fuller possession of her own story—an appreciation akin to what Marjorie J. Thompson calls the mysterious "innate and untaught" knowledge of God.[1] That realization unfolded later in her life through her work as a professor and is captured in her landmark book, *Joining Children on the Spiritual Journey*.

This chapter centers on the central theme of her experience. It seeks to elevate the reality that long before children enter the grade-school years, and all during those years, they are capable of deep spiritual experience and more often than not sense God's presence. As children begin seeking what they want and avoiding what they fear, the budding of autonomy, the desire for competence, and the capacity for greater relatedness increasingly become part of their experience. Critical social aspects of this developmental season are the way adults handle discipline encounters, the parenting style they adopt, the formation of conscience, representations of justice and mercy, and how these form the character of a child. As Thompson notes, important in the spiritual formation of children are both "natural opportunities and intentional practices."[2]

We begin by exploring what emerges in the biopsychosocial development of the child and then integrate these with foundational aspects of the spiritual.

Executive Functions

Many of the significant changes that emerge first in the toddler years are conceptualized by social scientists as elements of the executive functions. Though often studied independently, the elements of working memory, self-regulation, and cognitive flexibility combine to create the capacity of a preschooler to take charge of their own behavior and develop a sense of agency.

Working memory means that a child is gaining the capacity to remember events in sequential detail. Working memory can be illustrated using a simple span test where numbers are portrayed in sequence on a screen for a short period of time and then determining how many digits a child can recall or repeat in reverse order.[3] Or parents can use a toy and ask a toddler to repeat a sequence of randomly generated lighted buttons.

Early childhood memories can be catalysts for agency in later vocation formation. I have had some interesting conversations with students prompted by the question "What is your earliest memory of God?" or "When do you first recall becoming aware of his presence?" My predecessor and mentor Donald M. Joy recalls being in a field on his farm, finding a somewhat deformed metallic object, and in his childhood reasoning reckoning it was a fallen star. He tried

1. M. Thompson, *Family*, 15.
2. M. Thompson, *Family*, 2.
3. Arnett and Jensen, *Human Development*, 289.

throwing it back to the heavens—an early attempt at what the Jews called *tikkun olam*, or "repairing the universe." Jonathan Edwards resolved early in his childhood to be influential in the cause of Christianity, which might account for his rigorous schooling at home that paved the way for him to enter Yale University by age thirteen.[4]

Self-regulation involves impulse control.[5] High self-regulation indicates an ability to stay focused on what is desired or needs attention while suppressing attention to what is distracting, or a capacity to stop oneself from responding impulsively or automatically to a situation. A toddler with low self-regulation exhibits trouble resisting temptation, waiting their turn, or avoiding aggression. A test of self-regulation is the marshmallow test, in which a toddler is promised two marshmallows if they can resist eating one that is placed in front of them while no one is in the room with them.[6]

A more advanced test that contains elements of cognitive flexibility combines the gestures of "head, shoulders, knees, and toes" with the game Simon Says but requires children to do the opposite of what the leader says. If Simon says, "Touch your head," a person is to touch their toes. If Simon says, "Touch your shoulder," they are to touch their knees. The point is to determine how well a person can shift attention, choosing a behavior that goes against what their impulses are scripted toward.[7]

Although few studies have attempted to link executive functioning to elements of faith formation, it is intriguing to speculate how these capacities, especially during the elementary years, could be significant dimensions of discipleship. Is "taking charge" of one's own behavior a part of exercising faith? Does the virtuous life begin with the Spirit helping us regulate desires? How does the aptitude for shifting attention or goals from one thing to another, resisting learned impulses to the contrary, relate to discipleship?

Joy provides the following diagram of how a parent might scaffold the development of conscience formation in a child. Imagine a child who expresses a desire for a new toy that the parent recognizes has some educational value. The parent first affirms that the desire is legitimate and good (step 1) but then explains to the child that delaying the acquisition of the toy may be necessary (step 2). The parent then creates a calendar for delivery of the toy, possibly adding that delivery is contingent on the child meeting certain expectations, such as doing chores (step 3). During the pause between the expressed desire and the delivery of the toy, the parent maintains positive contact with the child,

---

4. "Edwards, Jonathan (1703–1758)"; Schafer, "Jonathan Edwards."
5. Broderick and Blewitt, *Life Span*, 92.
6. Igniter Media, "Marshmallow Test."
7. Broderick and Blewitt, *Life Span*, 92.

FIGURE 2.1
CONSCIENCE FORMATION

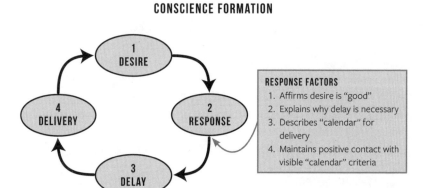

Based on a figure in Joy, *Empower Your Kids to Be Adults*, 17. Used with permission.

reinforcing the established criteria. Finally, once the time has passed and the expectations have been met, the parent makes good on the promised delivery, satisfying the desire of the child (step 4).

What Joy offers in this model is a simplified version of delayed gratification, which is integral to the life of faith.[8] As Thompson so succinctly notes, "A child learns what a child lives."[9] The narrative of Israel as a nation follows the pattern of a promise given that speaks to the desire of every nation (steps 1 and 2); long delays follow with periods of formation, where God abides with the people but tests their capacity to wait on and to trust the provisions of God (step 3); then comes the fulfillment of his promise, revealing his trustworthiness (step 4). Or we can think of an adolescent whose body is awakening to sexual desire. We can affirm that such desire is good and part of God's design for intimacy but that learning to regulate sexual imagination and behavior is critical for moral development. We can help them develop healthy courtship patterns with the promise of sexual intimacy in marriage. Or we can think of spending money wisely to avoid impulsivity and the assumption of debt.

Conversely, numerous biblical examples show the tragedies that occur when this simple pattern is broken. Sarah and Abraham, seeing the promise of a son as improbable in their old age, give birth to Ishmael through a servant, subverting the covenant of promise (Gen. 16–25). Saul loses the kingdom when he fails to wait on the arrival of the prophet Samuel and scrambles the distinct roles of

8. Joy, *Empower Your Kids to Be Adults*, 16–19.
9. M. Thompson, *Family*, 22.

king and prophet (1 Sam. 13). The prodigal son who insists on his inheritance ahead of when it is scheduled to be delivered creates a pattern of living that lands him in a pigpen (Luke 15).

Critical for the model to be formative is the integrity of the parent. They must be trustworthy in the delivery of the promise. One can easily speculate on the various outcomes that might ensue if a promise is made but never delivered on, if the contingencies are unfairly added to, if the parent teases the child during the period of waiting, or if the parent does not respect the child's threshold to wait.

Storytelling

When my son was young, a speech pathologist worked with him in an early start program using story cards. She would relay a short story, illustrating it with the cards. Once finished, she would shuffle the cards and ask my son if he could recount the story, placing the cards in the same ordering as the story. This is the essence of what Jean Piaget calls concrete operational thought. It precedes the kind of scientific logic where every possible factor is tested to establish a hypothesis, but it signals the capacity of the child to understand story, and seeing oneself as part of a story is critical to discipleship. In every Passover meal, an Israelite child would hear again the story that told them who they were.

Diana R. Garland went in search of discipleship practices that families engage in that show high correlation with their children becoming people of faith. In the hurriedness of the contemporary family, she found few families who regularly engage in activities like family altar times, which were sacrosanct in previous generations. What she did find, however, is that families tell stories and that in these stories are embedded narratives of God's character and faithfulness. Garland's conviction became that families do not name things they do to practice faith; instead, they use stories to talk about faith practices.[10] Stories, Garland contends, tell us who we are in relation to one another and tell us what we value and give meaning to in our lives. Families remember what they want to remember. Theologically, by telling a story, a family makes the event happen again. Garland categorizes these stories in a way that encourages families to think about how they might transmit faith through the stories they tell.

- *Beginning and new beginnings.* These stories tell how a family became a family or the significance of how one was named.

10. Garland, *Sacred Stories of Ordinary Families.*

- *Loss and endings.* These stories declare God's presence and faithfulness in the midst of loss. Sometimes this is crucial, as loss and endings redefine a family's identity.

- *Heroes and ancestors.* These stories are sometimes embellished but are so salient in communicating the legacy of a family and the claim that it might make on a person's life.

- *Survival stories.* These narratives convey that when a person is really suffering, they can count on family and on God to get them through.

- *Cautionary tales.* These tales warn relatives and others not to make similar mistakes. They may provide healing as they turn misfortune into a gift to someone else.

- *Funny family tales.* These tell of a vacation or holiday disaster that was unpleasant at the time, but their reciting builds unity around a shared memory.

- *Sacred stories.* These are stories of all the ways God's presence moved in the lives of family members, serving much like the hymn "Faith of Our Fathers, Living Still."[11]

Parents and grandparents can be coached to share stories about their early childhood in a way that avoids lecturing and creates a receptive hearing. These can be prompted by asking, "How does your family try to live its faith?" "When have you felt God close to your family?" "What Bible story do you think of when you think of your family?" I had one doctor of ministry student, Jim Kinsler, who, after reading Garland, realized that many of the parents in his congregation were working, leaving little time for faith engagement with their kids. In his congregation, however, were many grandparents. For his dissertation, he created a model he called Camp Grand. Utilizing concepts from Garland, he coached grandparents on ways to tell their stories of faith and then created a camp setting that combined fun and storytelling in fulfillment of Psalm 71:18: "So even to old age and gray hairs, O God, do not forsake me, until I proclaim your might to another generation, your power to all those to come."[12]

This means of conveying faith to younger generations seems implicit in the Shema in Deuteronomy 6:7: "Talk of them when you sit in your house, and when you walk by the way, and when you lie down, and when you rise." Instructive in the Shema is cultivating teachable moments throughout the flow of a child's day. Ministers often encourage parents to tune into their child's world

---

11. Garland, *Sacred Stories of Ordinary Families*, 19–26.
12. Kinsler, "Grandparenting the Next Generation."

in the natural routines of (1) "when you sit in your house"—creating opportunities around a meal that let a child know that at least once every day there is a time when they can share what they have felt and encountered that day; (2) "when you walk by the way"—talking when bringing children to school or church or extracurricular activities; (3) "when you lie down"—using bedtime routines that send a child to sleep in peace; and (4) "when you rise"—waking children in the morning with gentleness and blessing their day.

There are numerous other ways to incorporate storytelling into the faith formation of a child. Photographs of memorable events in the life of a family can be turned into a faith cube. Whenever someone reaches for the cube to look at the images, a natural opportunity is created for sharing stories of faith. Richard Hardell advocates for creating faith chests whereby symbols representing milestones in a child's faith are stored, creating a collection of memories of God's faithfulness.[13] Missy Griffin turned her faith chest into a sort of family altar. Inside the chest are things like a blanket to establish a bounded, sacred space; a children's Bible and devotional book; a candle that evokes the presence of God when lit; and growing memorabilia to mark the acts of God on behalf of their family.[14] The International Orality Network utilizes an African Bible-story cloth that contains forty-two images of different Bible stories in chronological order. By learning to recognize the images, children and newcomers to the faith gain greater comprehension of the whole biblical story (see fig. 2.2).[15] I have advocated for an ancient technique used by Martin Luther in teaching catechism. Luther sent wooden cutouts of Bible stories home with families who had children they wanted to present for confirmation. A pastor knew a child was ready for confirmation when they could present a coherent narrative of the stories contained in the cutouts. The brilliance of the method was that the best way for a child to learn the narrative of Scripture was by hearing it repeated by a parent, grandparent, or other teacher, thus creating intergenerational conversation and a growing population that knew the story of God.

Parents can use movie nights and fairy tales to generate faith conversations in the family. After they enjoy a story together, they can ask, "What are bad/evil things?" "Why does God allow bad things to happen?" "If you are good, will only good things always happen to you?" "Who did you identify with or like in that story and why?" "What kind of battles did the main character in the story engage in, and how do you face similar challenges?"[16]

13. Richard Hardell taught a seminar in children's ministry at Asbury Seminary in the early years of this century. This information was drawn from that seminar.
14. Missy was a student in my Family Discipleship class.
15. "History Cloth."
16. Wolpe, *Teaching Your Children about God.*

Figure 2.2. African Bible-story cloth

The Formative Value of Embodied Experience and Play

J. O. Balswick, Pamela Ebstyne King, and Kevin S. Reimer chronicle some of
the fascinating gains in development that reveal a child's growing awareness
of the social reality surrounding them during the early childhood years. They
describe the humorous childhood drawings that become masterpieces on re-
frigerator doors as "potato-head bodies with pipe-cleaner limbs."[17] As gross and
fine motor skills improve, commensurate with a child's capacity to understand
the mental processes of others, their drawings begin to reflect more accurate
bodily representations and proportions as well as facial features. Most kids in
the play years, ages three to seven, master handling silverware at meals, dress-
ing themselves, tying their shoes, jumping on a pogo stick, and wrangling with
a Hula-Hoop. These authors report Canadian children ice skating as early as
two or three years of age, becoming adept by kindergarten, and Polynesian
children who swim in waves and navigate climbing rock formations by age five.[18]

Catechesis of the Good Shepherd (CGS) employs the tactile and sensorial
pedagogical method developed by Maria Montessori. Her foundational maxim

17. Balswick, King, and Reimer, *Reciprocating Self*, 145.
18. Balswick, King, and Reimer, *Reciprocating Self*, 145.

that "the hands are the instruments of man's intelligence"[19] propelled the use of manipulative materials to accompany the proclamation of biblical narratives and parables as a way for children to enter holistically into the mystery of God. The aim is the creation of an environment and the presentation of objects (e.g., magi at the manger, a sandbox representing the wilderness wanderings, a structure of the tabernacle, a sheepfold where the story of the Good Shepherd calling the sheep by name is portrayed) that awaken wonder, sparking the child's natural inclination to let the mustard seed of faith grow. Neurobiology shows that some brain structures may not form unless vitalized by bodily experience. Gestures stimulate neural pathways, which become avenues for embodied thought—"neurons that fire together, wire together."[20] Mirror neurons have been discovered that fire equally whether an individual observes another person performing an act or they perform the act themselves. Such motor mirroring is activated first in a child's observance of the parent, and later via others in the faith community, engaging in liturgical acts and the telling of sacred stories.[21] In CGS, age-appropriate participation in liturgies provides mental rehearsals and actual embodied experiences, stimulating neural patterns that anticipate further engagement with the transcendent. I learned a great deal of the Christmas story by having various roles and reciting lines in the annual Christmas pageant my little Lutheran church performed every year. Much of what I currently do as a pastor and teacher can be traced to the early influences of various activities I performed during my childhood years—serving as an acolyte and Vacation Bible School helper, helping mom on the altar guild, playing bingo and visiting shut-ins at the nursing home.

Using child-sized materials that resemble the altar or eucharistic table, playing musical instruments, assembling the books of the Bible as a puzzle, or rolling out a time line of God's events in history give physicality to a child's engagement with God, reifying a sacred world that the child can feel and imagine their way through.[22] I was intrigued years ago reading a book by a Jewish author, David J. Wolpe, in which he advises helping a child gain a feeling of reverence by taking them to a sanctuary at dusk or helping them gain a sense of awe by collecting items on walks that capture their sense of wonder.[23] Further linkages between neuroscience and Montessori's method can be found in evidence that empathic prosocial behavior, as well as virtue, is now thought to derive less from deliberate decision-making and more from habituated interactions with the world.[24]

19. Montessori, *Absorbent Mind*, 37.
20. Hebb, *Organization of Behavior*, 62.
21. Maddix and Blevins, *Neuroscience and Christian Formation*, 162.
22. All of these are aspects of Catechesis of the Good Shepherd.
23. Wolpe, *Teaching Your Children about God*, 5–6, 42.
24. Brown and Strawn, *Physical Nature of Christian Life*, 120–22.

Gretchen Wolff Pritchard reports that in an after-school program she developed for underprivileged children, she was surprised to find how much the kids took to being blessed—that is, the gentle making of the cross on the forehead with words of affirmation spoken over the child. After a few weeks, the children began giving the blessing to each other. Pritchard realized that for many of the kids in her program, the only way they had learned to touch was via fighting. Pritchard also used flannel pieces to tell the narrative of the Bible in an hour-long presentation, then allowed the kids to play with the felt pieces. Along with the originators of CGS, Pritchard contends that "children do their work through play," and that transformative learning and hope emerge not by having everything explained to children in typical Sunday school lessons, but when they can "project themselves into imagined worlds . . . to work out the meaning of the stories for themselves."[25]

Piaget found that play often creates the context whereby children confront their own egocentrism and come to understand the mental processes occurring in others. A young girl who is asked what her daddy wants for his birthday may answer "a dollhouse," referencing her own desire. A child whose playmate begins to cry after suffering a fall may run to their parent rather than the playmate's parents because this would be their natural inclination. In the false belief test, an object is removed from its original location and hidden somewhere else in a room as a child witnesses the relocation. When asked where a second child who was not present might look for the object, children up until age four or five are likely to assume that the second child possesses the same knowledge they have and that the second child will go directly to the new location.[26]

Hence, social play promotes understanding that (1) people can like and want different things; (2) people can have different beliefs about the same thing; (3) people who see something happen will know about it, but people who don't see it happen won't know about it; (4) people do things based on the way they perceive a situation, even if mistaken; and (5) facial expression may hide emotions.[27] Biblical references to play carry deeply spiritual connotations indicating that play is both natural and beneficial (Matt. 11:16–17). Both Isaiah and Zechariah see play as a primary sign of the peaceable kingdom that is to come (Isa. 11:8; Zech. 8:5).

Through playful interactions, children learn that others have thoughts, beliefs, preferences, and desires that are different from their own. Consider the rather complex understandings that a young male exhibits in knowing that the cicada he has caught in the yard might be quite useful to terrorize his sister,

25. Pritchard, *Offering the Gospel to Children*, 18–19.
26. Arnett and Jensen, *Human Development*, 236.
27. Broderick and Blewitt, *Life Span*, 114–18.

who has a phobia of insects.[28] This may also account in part for why the fears of children shift as their cognitive capacities emerge and they become more aware of their own and others' inner dispositions. Young children from about age two to six tend to fear more tangible and immediate threats or issues of personal safety. Children age six to nine may exhibit fears that are more about being alone, imaginary creatures, or the dark.[29] James Fowler discovered that in the stage of a child's journey where "reality and fantasy interpenetrate," children may internalize exaggerated terrors from adult prohibitions and world events that find symbolization in fairy tales.[30] (Consider, e.g., the appeal of Grimms' fairy tales or Maurice Sendak's children's books.) Fowler contended that especially important during these ages was providing children with "ordering images,"[31] precisely what CGS centralizes in presenting to the child the Good Shepherd who leads his sheep through dark and scary places.

Theory of mind studies suggest that children of this age are gaining the capacity to understand the mental processes of others. Implicit in this gain is the emerging capacity to imagine how the self might be seen by God. In the preface to Sofia Cavalletti's pivotal book *The Religious Potential of the Child*, Mark Searle insists that the critical question the catechist (read "minister" in Protestant traditions) must ask is "What is the face of God the child needs?"[32]

Teaching Children to Pray

I recall hearing Scottie May share a transformative moment from her past at a Children's Spirituality Summit. The moment occurred as children's ministry leaders were involved in observing and advocating for a host of ministry curricula, many organized around a heavily programed approach. After some time, someone posed the simple question "But when do your children meet with God?" As I recall, this was a turning-point moment when May, drawing from CGS and its adaptation through Jerome Berryman's Godly Play,[33] turned away from strategies that might be broadly called "edutainment" to ways of creating space where a child could be with God.

I find it meaningful in my children's ministry class to explore with students how they might teach children to pray and how they might honor ways children

28. Balswick, King, and Reimer, *Reciprocating Self*, 145–47.
29. Lyness, "Normal Childhood Fears."
30. J. Fowler, *Stages of Faith*, 129–30.
31. J. Fowler, *Stages of Faith*, 129–30.
32. Searle, preface to Cavalletti, *Religious Potential of the Child*, 10.
33. For more on Berryman's approach, see https://www.godlyplayfoundation.org/the-foundation/our-founder.

can meet with God. Sybil Macbeth invites us to pray in color, allowing one to be free of words.[34] Kristen E. Vincent advocates for using beads to pray.[35] Teresa A. Blythe chronicles fifty ways to pray that include walking, talking, breathing, drawing, and inferring from television and movies.[36] Stuart Hample and Eric Marshall portray the poignant and effervescent statements children can make in journaling and writing letters to God.[37] Catherine Stonehouse and May discovered that when children draw God, they frequently portray elements of light in yellow, red, and orange colors. They believe rays of light indicate a grasp of the glory of God, expressing connection with God's grandeur as a prime attribute of the One they are approaching in prayer.[38] A number of studies regard gratitude as the "parent of all virtues" giving profundity to simply asking a child what they can be thankful for that day.[39] This is the simplest posture of receptivity and the recognition that life can be lived as a gift.

Beyond teaching a child to pray independently, ministry leaders can help parents lead their families in prayer and think about how children can lead prayers in congregational life with some support and coaching. One of my students shared a moment when he felt the Spirit was impressing upon him to invite the children to help him serve communion one morning. He witnessed the formative value it had on them and the congregation. This may not be permissible in some traditions, but churches can think about the roles children can fill during times of worship (e.g., greeters, reading Scripture, ushering, singing in the choir, serving in other ways at the altar, designing the bulletin, giving testimony, engaging children with ritual).

My extended family would often end a mealtime with spontaneous prayer followed by a corporate praying of the Lord's Prayer. Then we would say together a verse written on my office wall: "Oh give thanks to the LORD, for he is good; for his steadfast love endures forever!" (1 Chron. 16:34).

Discipline Encounters

One of the places where the autonomy and egocentric tendencies of the child clash with the will of the parent is discipline encounters. In fact, Martin L. Hoffman reports that children age two to ten experience pressure to change

34. MacBeth, *Praying in Color.*
35. Vincent, *Bead and a Prayer.*
36. Blythe, *50 Ways to Pray.*
37. Hample and Marshall, *Children's Letters to God.* For a tool to aid children in journaling, see S. Peterson, *Let Us Pray.*
38. Stonehouse and May, *Listening to Children on the Spiritual Journey,* 28–31.
39. Wood, Linley, and Joseph, "Gratitude—Parent of All Virtues."

their behavior every six to nine minutes, the equivalent of more than fifty discipline encounters in a day or fifteen thousand per year.[40] No wonder parents sometimes call them the terrible twos and the trying threes!

From a theological standpoint, a great deal is at stake in these discipline encounters because they put in place a child's understanding of how justice and mercy work in the universe and how one relates to people in authority. Henry Cloud and John Townsend capture the essence of the high stakes when they frame their book on raising children using the incarnation. They contend that just as Jesus, the eternal Word of God, became flesh and dwelt among us, allowing us to behold the glory of the Father, "full of grace and truth" (John 1:14), so parents have the glory and the burden to reflect in their discipline encounters with children the delicate balance between grace and truth.[41] M. Scott Peck captures much of what this requires of parents:

> Discipline of children requires time—without which we don't become aware of the subtle expressions that suggest a need for discipline. We often ignore discipline on the grounds that it is easier to let them have their own way. If we are impelled into action by misdeeds and our irritation we will impose discipline often brutally out of anger instead of deliberation—without examining the problem or taking the time to consider which form of discipline is most appropriate. In taking the time to observe and to think about their children's needs, loving parents will frequently agonize over the decision to be made and will in a very real sense suffer along with their children. Internally the message becomes—"if my parents are willing to suffer with me, then suffering must not be so bad and I should be willing to suffer with myself." The time and quality of time parents devote to them indicate to children the degree to which they are valued—without which mechanical words of love or affirmation ring hollow. This knowledge is more valuable than gold—a cornerstone of mental health and self-discipline, because when one feels valuable one will care for the self in all the ways necessary. It is difficult to acquire this disposition as an adult, but when it is learned via the love of their parents it is almost impossible for the vicissitudes of adulthood to destroy the spirit.[42]

One of the more insightful approaches that lends itself to formational parenting practices emerges from Hoffman's theory on empathy.[43] Hoffman rightly recognizes that many of our approaches to control children's behavior rely on

---

40. Hoffman, *Empathy and Moral Development*, 41.

41. Cloud and Townsend, *Raising Great Kids*, 38–49.

42. M. Peck, *Road Less Traveled*, 22–24.

43. Hoffman, *Empathy and Moral Development*. I am indebted to Paul Huber, who first introduced me to Hoffman when he encountered his writings in a doctoral program at the University of Kentucky.

pressure tactics that procure compliance in the child but fail to form the moral conscience of the child. Hence, a child acquiesces to avoid punishment, to be rewarded, or to win favor, but they may never own the value or choose for themselves the good that the discipline seeks to bring about. Ponder for a moment what is learned and not learned when a child is begrudgingly forced to say "I'm sorry," or when a toy is forcibly taken away and given to another child to "teach" them to share, or when a child is humiliated in front of others by a parent's shouting their disapproval. The child may conform to the desire of the parent, but has the child's moral reasoning been formed, or does the compulsion remain external to the conscience of the child?

Hoffman probes how discipline encounters might actually be used for internalizing a sense of what is good. Internalization is achieved when a child accepts and feels obligated to abide by a behavior and attitude without regard to external moral sanctions—that is, the "rule" itself contains a compelling obligatory quality. Children then begin to experience the desired outcome as deriving from themselves, and hence they feel guilt if they act in a way that violates the principle or that brings harm to another. This form of discipline inclines the child to elevate the needs and feelings of others above their own egoistic satisfactions.[44]

Hoffman argues that only by intentional parenting processes can social conscience be formed in a way that it becomes operative when children encounter conflict. The key to this orientation is to help the child become aware of how their behavior affects others. Hoffman calls this kind of discipline "induction."[45] Induction orients a child to feel the distress their action creates in someone else in a way that contributes to moral internalization. Hoffman contends that rather than using induction, most parents discipline either by asserting their own power over the child or by withdrawing love. Both of these tendencies focus on placating the parents rather than helping the child tune into their own behaviors or the consequences of their misbehavior.

Power assertion relies on physical punishment, direct force, demands, constraining, material or privilege deprivation, or threats of such measures: "My child will never get away with doing something like that. I'll make sure of it!" Love withdrawal entails refusing to speak to the child, threatening to go away and leave the child alone, showing strong disapproval and dislike for the child, or withholding a meal from the child: "If you keep acting like that, Mommy is going to go away and leave you alone [or let you walk or find your own way home]," or "You won't get your goodbye hug if you keep whining."[46]

44. Hoffman, *Empathy and Moral Development*, 134–37.
45. Hoffman, *Empathy and Moral Development*, 113–74.
46. Hoffman, *Empathy and Moral Development*, 146–50, with some of my own examples here.

Hoffman, however, does call for moderate forms of pressure to be exerted on a child. Where there is too little pressure, the child too easily ignores the parent; where there is too much pressure, emotions are aroused that prevent the child from effectively processing inductive information. Parents who are too demanding actually interfere with the kind of development Hoffman is aiming to generate. Balswick, King, and Reimer report a study that showed that kindergarteners who were spanked were twice as likely to physically retaliate against peers during a disagreement when compared to those who were not spanked.[47] Other studies have shown that harsh discipline increases aggression and rarely produces self-regulation or desirable moral outcomes. Fifty percent of mothers who first used mild spanking later turned to using an object to spank their children, suggesting that harshness tends to increase when power assertion is the only mode used in disciplining.[48] These studies may not fully dismiss spanking from a parent's tool kit, but they certainly call for a more judicious and limited use of spanking consigned to a particular developmental stage when a child may not yet be capable of moral reasoning. Here it is worth capturing one more insight from Peck:

> There are then two ways to confront—with instinctive and spontaneous certainty that one is right, or with a belief that one is probably right arrived at through a scrupulous self-doubting and self-examination. The first is the way of arrogance and is the most common way of parents, spouses, teachers. . . . It is usually unsuccessful and produces more resentment than growth and other effects that were not intended. The second is the way of humility; it is not common, requiring as it does a genuine extension of itself; it is more likely to be successful, and it is never in my experience destructive.[49]

The key to Hoffman's approach of induction is to put just enough pressure on the child to create active mental processing until it becomes natural for the child to feel compelled to make amends. In doing so, one is building an ally that exists within the child—a proclivity toward empathy. Hoffman believes a moral script can be actively formed within the child whereby a moral motive competes with the egoistic needs that may have prompted the misbehavior or aggression.[50] Induction may sound like this:

- "He feels really bad when you don't let him play your video game, just like you would feel bad if you were not allowed to share his video game."

47. Balswick, King, and Reimer, *Reciprocating Self*, 160.
48. Broderick and Blewitt, *Life Span*, 102–4.
49. M. Peck, *Road Less Traveled*, 152.
50. Hoffman, *Empathy and Moral Development*, 221–50.

- "Can you be quiet and let your sister sleep a little longer? She will feel much better when she wakes up."

As an exercise in parental formation, I have found it useful to put before different groups of people some of the following assumptions that influence how a person disciplines a child, ask them if they agree or disagree, and then talk through the implications. Important in these discussions is acknowledging that cultures may differ in what they regard as good parenting:

- I think it is important to make a child feel sorry for their bad behavior.
- I expect my children to obey me because I am the parent.
- When a child tells a parent no, they are being defiant and should be punished.
- I often fear that I am losing control when my kids misbehave and I have to correct them.
- It's important that my teenage son or daughter learns to follow the rules.
- Children develop best in a home where parents are strict disciplinarians.
- The father should be the one responsible for disciplining children.
- The mother should be the teacher of values to the children.
- A child should be given the freedom to lock themselves in their own room or be given their own space when they want to be alone.
- It is okay for children to keep some things secret from their parents.
- What I most want from my parenting is that my children learn to respect and follow my authority.
- Telling children the reasons why they are being disciplined helps in the learning process.
- Children learn best when there is no interference from a parent.
- Insisting that you always know where your children are is one form of helicopter parenting and should probably be relinquished.
- It's important for a parent to assert their power in discipline so a child knows the parent is the authority figure.
- Threatening to use physical force can be an effective means when disciplining a child.
- Constraint (like holding, picking up, or moving a child aside) is an effective way to change a child's behavior.
- When a child says "please" or stands up to a parent's first demand, like "Turn off the TV," it is okay for the parent to cushion or soften their demand by allowing the child to watch until the next commercial.

- When children ask why they have to clean their room or do their home-work, it should be a good enough reason for a parent to say, "Because I said so."

The following statements—gleaned from Hoffman's illustrations, internet searches, and actual encounters—reveal what is often said to a child in a discipline encounter and may offer points for discussion.

- "I don't like it when you act like that."
- "Big girls don't take toys away from babies."
- "If you run fast while you carry that, you might drop it and break it."
- "If you are not nice to her, she will not be nice to you."
- "You must stay in your room until you calm down and can learn to play nicely with your baby brother."
- "If you have to defend yourself, that's all right, but you may not hit anyone with something in your hand."[51]

These kinds of discussions often open up the space where a skilled teacher can help parents handle discipline encounters by promoting time-outs, withdrawing privileges, exercising control through boundaries, and creating clearly defined rules of conduct that are much more likely to produce desired outcomes in children.

Parenting Styles

Closely related to discipline is the style of parenting that is adopted. And closely related to discipline is the spiritual question "In what ways has my experience with parents or other emotionally significant people in my life colored my view of what God is like and how God relates to me?"[52]

The most-referenced parenting styles in the West over the past several de-cades are credited to Diana Baumrind. Baumrind built on the work of earlier theorists, utilizing the two dimensions of control and warmth to construct a four-quadrant design.[53] The x-axis measures the amount of responsiveness (warmth or hostility) felt in the family, responsiveness being indicative of attune-ment to the child's need for security and the fostering of the child's freedom to

51. See further, Hoffman, *Empathy and Moral Development*, 150–56.
52. M. Thompson, *Family*, 23.
53. Baumrind, "Discipline Encounter."

be uniquely who they are and to feel a sense of approval. The y-axis indicates the degree of demandingness/control parents exercise in the family, reflecting how much focus is placed on the positional authority of the parent and the assertive way(s) they direct the child to behave in a manner desirable to the parent, obediently and in accordance with expectations.[54] The following descriptions reveal how parents differ in their styles of parenting, but these same differences can be ascertained in the intersubjective space between teachers and students, pastors and their congregations, political figures and the populations they serve.

Authoritarian Parenting Style (Low Responsiveness + High Demandingness)

Authoritarian parents attempt to shape, control, and evaluate behavior in accordance with rigidly held values and strict standards of conduct. Authoritarian parents believe children should respect and obey their rules in matters of homework, technology, church attendance, music, dress, etc. If a child questions why they are being told to do something, they are often met with the response "Because I said so." The authority figure makes the rules and enforces them without inviting involvement in problem-solving. When "truth" is conveyed, it is often used to lecture, correct, or critique the perspective of the child. The focus is typically on what a child *ought* to be doing, offering them little choice or initiative except to follow the dictates of the parent. Punishment may be forceful, focused on punishing past behavior more than correcting future behavior. Authoritarian parents often feel it is important to make kids pay for disobeying or failing to meet an obligation.[55] Paul's admonition not to "provoke your children to anger, but bring them up in the discipline and instruction of the Lord" (Eph. 6:4) may have had something like authoritarian fathers in mind. Beneath the surface, authoritarian parents may admit to a fear that they are losing control of their children.

The outcome of this style of parenting is that children do learn to follow rules and be obedient. As they become adolescents, children of authoritarian parents quite typically become highly proficient, but compliance often comes at a psychological price of emotional defection. Buried resentment or frozen rage, especially when it is pervasive but not yet named, keeps kids focused on humiliation or the anger they carry toward an authority figure, preventing a focus on how to do things better in the future. Further, when kids' opinions and voices are not valued, curiosity and spontaneity can become stifled. Children of authoritarian parents are more prone to problems with self-esteem and may

---

54. Baumrind, "Discipline Encounter."
55. Parenting-style descriptions and research are now readily available on the internet. See https://www.apa.org, https://www.parentingscience.com, and https://www.verywellfamily.com.

be more susceptible to peer pressure because they rely on external standards rather than having a developed internal source of self-control.

Particularly germane to the topic of truth and freedom are studies that find a high correlation between authoritarianism and conservative religious beliefs that promote obedience as the cornerstone of character.[56] The linkages to truth in this tradition often run something like this. The doctrine of original sin posits that humans are born egoistic and with natural inclinations to organize their worlds around their own will for survival, power, self-interest, sexual interest, etc. To bring about moral sensibility, socialization must focus on bringing this egoism under control, which may involve breaking the will of the child, ensuring that authority is respected, promoting that children should be seen and not heard, etc.

Scripture no doubt was not written with a framework of parenting styles in mind, and yet we may find illustrative material in its pages. Although she does not have all the characteristics of authoritarianism, Rebekah may exemplify some aspects of an authoritarian parenting style when she directs Jacob to steal his brother's birthright. "Obey my voice as I command you. . . . Let your curse be on me, my son; only obey my voice, and go, bring them [goats] to me" (Gen. 27:8, 13). In this case, the blessing is actually procured for Jacob, but he is estranged from his brother and family for over twenty years and exhibits a way of being in the world in which conniving is the necessary way to secure one's future.

Permissive Parenting Style (High Responsiveness + Low Demandingness)

An alternative approach to parenting is the permissive parenting style. Permissive parents neglect directing the lives of their children, resulting in lots of leniency and leaving children and youth to regulate their own behavior. Permissive parents make few demands and rarely involve children or youth in family tasks. Rather than seeing themselves as responsible for shaping a child's future, permissive parents leave children to find their own way in the world.

Such a lack of involvement communicates to children a lack of being valued. Children and youth of permissive parents report feeling sadness, are likely to struggle in school, and exhibit behavioral problems because they don't appreciate rules or authority. They may rebel when asked to do something that conflicts with momentary desires and lack any affective bonding with parents. Left to themselves, children and teens commonly exhibit impulsive behaviors, leading to poor habits (with food, sleep, dental hygiene, money,

---

56. Baumrind, "Discipline Encounter," 321.

life management), and a lack of persistence. Some become antisocial or even hostile as young adults.

A tradition akin to permissive parenting grounds itself in a doctrine of innate purity, positing that children are innately good but vulnerable to corruption by society. This set of beliefs holds that children contain within themselves a natural propensity toward moral development, and they need no intervention from authority figures for this to unfold. This tradition advocates that children should be given the same civil rights as adults—to be self-determining and free of restraint—at a certain age.[57] A few parents following this tradition resist focusing their children on achievement and seek egalitarian relations with children to avoid placing them at a power disadvantage. Wisdom literature cautions against "sparing the rod," which can lead to spoiling a child (Prov. 13:24).[58] Job, in fact, regards the ostrich as being deprived of wisdom, resulting in the abandonment of her eggs, leaving them susceptible to all that might destroy them (Job 39:14–17).

Neglectful Parenting Style (Low Responsiveness + Low Demandingness)

Closely aligned with permissive parenting and creating similar outcomes, neglectful parenting may be justified in the minds of some parents who want to avoid imposing beliefs, religious or otherwise, on a child, letting the child decide for themselves. For other parents, uninvolved parenting emerges when circumstances make giving attention to a child difficult—mental or physical health challenges, substance abuse, work demands, a lack of confidence to influence right behavior in a child, feeling overwhelmed with the demands of life, etc. Hence, rules and objectives once set may go unenforced, and discipline and unpleasant conversations that challenge behavior are often avoided. Parents may even become invested in helping their children avoid consequences, enabling poor behavior. Sometimes such neglect may inadvertently force children to make adult decisions before they are emotionally prepared.

Adonijah was a rival to King David. In the narrative about Adonijah, we are told that he "exalted himself," wanting to be king, and that Adonijah's father had not rebuked him at any time by saying, "Why have you done thus and so?" (1 Kings 1:6). This suggests that Adonijah knew no constraints to his own egoistic needs, drawing everyone around him into this vortex of self-seeking indulgence.

57. Baumrind, "Discipline Encounter," 325.
58. As noted above, this verse is not justification for harsh punishment and/or justification for authoritarian parenting. It is better understood as a summons to guide and protect via the shepherd's hook.

Authoritative Parenting Style (High Responsiveness + High Demandingness)

Baumrind follows others in seeking a middle ground between the highly conservative, authoritarian style and the liberal, permissive style of parenting. She writes that the choice between tyranny and indulgence presents a false dichotomy and seeks a way to integrate respect for adults with psychological autonomy that would promote prosocial outcomes.[59] Authoritative parenting maintains parental control, but control is not rigid, punitive, intrusive, or unnecessarily restrictive, as in the authoritarian style. Standards are set and expectations maintained, avoiding the perils of permissiveness while still affirming individual qualities—that is, firmness and freedom are held in dynamic tension. Authoritative parents seek to create a context of warmth and communication and respect input from the child. A great deal of time and energy is invested in foreseeing what a child may struggle with and equipping them to overcome these obstacles. Authoritative parents provide reasons for rules and engage in verbal give-and-take with the child, usually avoiding physical punishment. In these exchanges, feelings are validated and appropriate autonomy for the child is retained, while the parents recognize that they carry responsibility for being the adults in the relationship. The system of discipline that emerges seeks to influence more through praise and reward than through constant correction.

Research finds that authoritative parents tend to produce happy and successful children. The interest adults show in social development produces deeper self-perception and self-acceptance in those they parent and guide. This in turn yields teens who show concern for other people, are free from feelings of alienation, feel closer to their families, and are more likely to be committed to religious faith. These youth feel comfortable carrying responsibility, are at ease expressing their opinions, tend to be achievement-oriented, and are usually cooperative.

Seeking to resemble what they see reflected in God in the garden of Eden, authoritative parents grant a great deal of freedom, but this freedom is within certain limits that carry consequences when violated. An example of authoritative parenting may be seen in the example of the father of the prodigal son and his older brother (Luke 15). In this parable, a clear hope and outcome exist in the heart of the father, yet the father chooses to engage with each son contingent on their current circumstances. The children talk with the father, and the father is more concerned with the future orientation of his sons' lives than with punishing their misadventures or nursing a grudge between them.

59. Baumrind, "Discipline Encounter," 321–23.

It should be acknowledged that cultural differences exist in the way parenting roles are understood, how certain functions are regarded as the domain of the father or the mother, and how proper parenting is exercised. Respecting elders without question and showing reverential honor in an elevation of filial piety often govern parenting practices in the East,[60] whereas establishing autonomy and independence encourages children to "speak their mind" to parents more often in the West. In many countries, the father will take the more authoritarian role, while the mother will move into the role of providing warmth and security. I believe there is room for nuance among these parenting styles and adaptations to particular cultural contexts so that each can faithfully capture some aspect of the faithfulness of God's character when enacted conscientiously.

CONCLUSION

Elaine Ramshaw writes, "When you make God's love real to a child by your own deep appreciation and delight in and patience with the child, you are communicating to him or her what it means to be God's beloved."[61] Our primary role as parents and as faith communities in relation to children is to care for children in the manner God would care for them. The axiom underlying this chapter is that parent and child live religious experience together. If we can assume theologically that the fundamental makeup of the child of faith is to love and to be loved, then the quality of the parent-child bond is a critical piece in predicting how a child will relate to the God we seek to image. How we engage a child when correcting their behavior and giving guidance for their life is a critical factor in helping them gain a right comprehension of the faithful character of God—his justice and mercy, his steadfast love, and his formative corrections that operate on their behalf. David Elkind suggests that when children act up, they probably need not a time-out but a time-in.[62] Time-outs take a punitive posture, separating a child from peers and isolating them while dismissing any disclosure of what may have upset them. By contrast, a time-in approach takes an instructive posture, sitting with the child and seeking to understand what provoked them to act the way they did. In an important study of more than a thousand

---

60. Closely related to familial piety in Asian tradition is the high respect given to parental authority in Latin American cultures. Authority is vested in the role any parent occupies and not in the explanation(s) they provide during a discipline encounter.

61. Ramshaw, *The Godparent Book*, 1.

62. Elkind, "Instructive Discipline Is Built on Understanding."

Australian adolescents belonging to the Seventh-day Adventist Church, author Bradley Strahan concludes, "It is important for parents to recognize that *how* they engage children in family religious activity is more important than *whether* children participate in family religion or not. It is quite possible for the *how* of religious practice to be destructive and thus deny what is presumably the real meaning and purpose of religion."[63]

63. Strahan, *Parents, Adolescence and Religion,* 97.

3 | Middle Childhood
New Settings, Skills, and Social Pressures

If one were to take a snapshot of a middle school playground anywhere around the globe, a similar pattern of group interaction would likely be observed. Patricia C. Broderick and Pamela Blewitt describe this universal gender separation: girls on these playgrounds would likely be found in dyads or triads socializing mostly separate from the boys, who would more likely be engaged in some form of rough-and-tumble play focused on one-upmanship.[1] Hence, girls rely more on social skill than on toughness to navigate their social spaces and tussle for popularity. Boys often come together via shared interests in things such as sports, adventure, or gaming; girls choose companions more on the basis of personality. Girls more often use collaborative and affiliative speech that expresses agreement or suggestions, such as "Why don't we both be the mommy sometimes?" Boys tend more toward the use of power-assertive speech, using commands and restrictions. One result may be that women are often less likely to feel that they can influence the outcome of discussions.

I would hasten to add that any of these generalizations can easily turn to stereotyping that mischaracterizes some middle schoolers. Both boys and girls may engage in discourse and behaviors more typical of the opposite gender. Generally, however, gender separation, sometimes referred to as gender cleavage, begins to show up as early as age six. During this stage of life, interaction between the genders is minimal.[2] Juvenile societal norms create taboos evidenced by the fanciful ditties "Boys have cooties" and "Girls' germs, no returns."

1. Broderick and Blewitt, *Life Span*, 311–12.
2. Broderick and Blewitt, *Life Span*, 311.

Gender Construction

The biological origins of sex differences are now rather clear. When a father and a mother both contribute an X chromosome in the twenty-third pair, the genitalia of the offspring are female. When the father contributes a Y chromosome, the genitalia of the offspring are male. From the moment of conceptualization, the role of heredity in influencing sex differentiation becomes apparent, as the pairing of the sex chromosome is replicated in almost every cell of the body. An XY pair of masculinizing hormones, including an SRY gene, produces things like a higher metabolic rate and the formation of the male reproductive system. Females, without the SRY gene and an XX pairing, develop the female reproductive system.[3] But when does a child begin to perceive these differences, and what impact does it have on them?

When looking at pictures of men and women and hearing recorded voices, infants by the end of the first year of life seem able to make some distinction between the sexes.[4] Through both observing themselves and hearing themselves referred to in various ways as male or female, most children by age three can identify others who fit into the gender they ascribe to themselves.[5] In chapter 1, we explored the cognitive capacity of object permanence. This becomes particularly intriguing when applied to gender. How does a child learn that over time their sex/gender stays the same (gender stability), and is there a natural inclination to act according to one's sex/gender (gender constancy)? Are there gender stereotypes that, instead of contributing to gender stability and constancy, are actually harmful to a child in the construction of their gender? My attempt here is not so much to provide answers to the multiple questions arising in contemporary culture regarding gender dysphoria or gender reassignment. Nor is it to address the many categories within LGBTQIA2+ by which people are self-identifying. Rather, I want to propose how faith formation may best work in what appears to be the most natural and common gender segregation patterns that occur in the middle years of childhood.

Descriptive concepts within traditional and conservative ways of thinking about gender can often help us understand what is occurring in the experiences and exploration of children. Yet, we must also acknowledge that some theorists posit more fluid categories for thinking about gender. Situations become complicated when there is not alignment among the following:

- Natal sex = the physical and biological features present that historically were used to determine whether one was male or female

3. Broderick and Blewitt, *Life Span*, 297–98.
4. Poulin-Dubois and Serbin, "La connaissance des catégories."
5. Maccoby, *Two Sexes*.

- Sexual identity (or sexual self-concept) = the perception one has of oneself as a sexual person
- Sexual orientation = the direction of one's erotic attraction
- Gender or gender role = attitudes, interests, and behavioral expectations defined by a particular culture[6]

Decades ago, Eleanor E. Maccoby and Carol Nagy Jacklin reviewed existing literature and concluded that at that time only four gender differences were evidenced in scientific studies: "physical aggression, language skills, math skills, and spatial skills."[7] Since that time, meta-analyses have found others but also nuanced in significant ways what research seemed to be revealing. Boys, for example, often perform near the top in certain math tasks, such as complex problem-solving and using spatially based strategies, especially when the cultural context supports their involvement in the subject. However, more boys than girls also underperform on these tasks. Furthermore, females outperform boys in other mathematical areas, such as computation.[8]

Following are other observations that find support in the research:

- Girls appear to demonstrate slightly more positive expressive emotions but also on the whole experience more internalizing emotions, such as anxiety and sadness; boys demonstrate more externalizing emotions, such as anger.[9]
- When engaging in pretend play, boys act out heroic or warlike themes; girls reenact familial roles or school scenarios. They also mimic princesses or familial gendered behavior involving glamour or romance.
- Girls, more than boys, seem to enjoy the intrinsic value of being together and choose companions who complement their personality.[10]
- Boys tend to use power-assertive or domineering speech in which commands, threats, and restrictions are common, with occasional interruptions or the ignoring of another's remarks (e.g., "Give me that ball!" "Don't move that!"). Girls' discourse strategies are more commonly conflict mitigating, collaborative, and affiliative in nature.
- Boys' interests tend to be more limited than those of girls. Whereas girls may show some interest in traditionally boyish activities, boys are less likely to show interest in traditionally girlish activities.[11]

6. Balswick and Balswick, *Authentic Human Sexuality*, 33–36.
7. Maccoby and Jacklin, "Gender Segregation in Childhood."
8. Broderick and Blewitt, *Life Span*, 308–12.
9. Broderick and Blewitt, *Life Span*, 309.
10. Broderick and Blewitt, *Life Span*, 310–11.
11. Maccoby, *Two Sexes*.

- Some overviews of research suggest that there are fewer behavioral differences between the sexes than is conventionally believed, but there are
  measurable differences in the ways girls and boys spend time.[12]

Theories of human development often carry the assumption, implicit or explicit, that friendship in homosocial groups is the precursor to establishing intimacy and fidelity in the adult years.[13] Yet, there might be other important implications for parenting and ministry as well. Coaching boys engaged in aggressive play toward emotional self-regulation is an important area of discipleship, with implications that reach into future parenthood. Limiting how much girls derive self-worth from adornment or beauty and listening for the messages encoded in self-talk can be foundational to helping girls develop healthy self-esteem.

When I think about my own discipleship in the middle school years, I realize that so much of my faith was forged at important points of intersection with the way I was being socialized as a male—camping programs in the summer, serving as recreation director for Vacation Bible School programs, playing on athletic teams in various church leagues, and doing construction projects in underprivileged neighborhoods. At the same time, common gender lines were also crossed, as Mom involved us in food preparation, playing host and serving tables when the family entertained, decorating wheelchairs and playing bingo in nursing homes with the infirmed, doing household chores in some quarters regarded as "women's work," and sharing the task of childcare when babysitting, all of which oriented me toward virtues of hospitality, giving care, and relinquishing self-interest for the sake of loving neighbors in the human community.

Social science theorists and religious writers, attuned to what children need, have frequently called our attention to formative aspects of the social environment that are powerfully influencing kids in the middle childhood years. Donald W. Winnicott speaks of "holding environments" to describe safe and supportive physical and psychological space important in both parenting and therapy;[14] Heinz Kohot calls for mirroring whereby teens reflect the role modeling they deem worthy of imitation;[15] J. O. Balswick, Pamela Ebstyne King, and Kevin S. Reimer speak of the "reciprocating self," capturing the mutual influence of relationships throughout the life course.[16] Marjorie J. Thompson points to two primary locations for spiritual formation in children: first, in the opportunities

12. Broderick and Blewitt, *Life Span*, 310.
13. See, e.g., Joy, *Unfinished Business*.
14. Balswick, King, and Reimer, *Reciprocating Self*, 75.
15. Cahalan and Miller-McLemore, *Calling All Years Good*, 44.
16. Balswick, King, and Reimer, *Reciprocating Self*.

that occur organically in the relational fabric of families doing life together; and second, in intentional practices that form different aspects of who we are.[17]

Given developmental changes, gender realities, and the accompanying social construction of reality, what is the self-system that is emerging in the child, and how do we think about it theologically? What attributions will a child use to define themselves during this formative period? Where do such attributions come from, and how do they influence character, morality, and social functioning?

A Significant Shift in Social Science Theory

Social scientists are now using decades of scientific exploration to help us understand how personality develops over a lifetime. They largely regard the big five personality traits as the bedrock of a person's personality:

- openness to experience
- conscientiousness
- extroversion
- agreeableness
- neuroticism[18]

Despite a growing consensus that these factors can accurately predict personality, twentieth-century theorists critiqued trait theories for neglecting the role of environment in predicting behavior. Instead of focusing on the big five personality traits, they (Freud, Erikson, Mead, Adler, Horney, Fromm, Rogers, and Bandura) saw motivational and social cognitive constructs as the building blocks of personality. More recently, in an effort to construct an integrated metatheory, Dan P. McAdams and Bradley D. Olson have proposed three developmental layers that contribute to psychological individuality:

- The big five personality traits constituted somewhat by genetics that remain relatively continuous throughout the life course
- Characteristic adaptations that come on board in middle childhood / adolescence that describe motivational, goal-directed behaviors
- The socio-cognitive capacity emergent in young adulthood to narrate one's own life story, providing a third layer of personality development[19]

17. M. Thompson, Family.
18. Lim, "Big Five Personality Traits."
19. McAdams and Olson, "Personality Development," 530.

We will return to the third layer in a subsequent chapter. Here I want to focus on childhood adaptation constructs that include such factors as "motives, goals, plans, strivings, strategies, values, virtues, and schemas" that come to define the self.[20] Prominent in these theories are the questions "How does a person seek out what they want/value and believe is possible?" and "How do they avoid becoming what they fear?" Identity theorists, more typically focused a little later in the life span, conduct research on possible selves and feared selves, exploring these characteristics in greater depth. One particularly salient study considers the impact on self-esteem that occurs when incongruities are encountered between a person's real or now self and their ideal self.[21] A related question is "How do late childhood youngsters internalize expectations from others and respond to conflicts and challenges?"

The important shift in theoretical construction from temperament traits to character adaptations places human agency, rather than biology, at the center of personality inquiry. These theorists posit that beyond simply acting in ways consistent with our genes, we, by middle childhood, begin making choices and exercising greater agency based on desired pursuits during childhood.[22] Theologically, this is anthropology the Christian faith affirms and insists on. Humans are able to exercise choice and to take action apart from being determined by their environment, familial upbringing, temperament, or other biological endowments. As early as the Cain and Abel story, we hear God saying to human beings, "Sin is crouching at the door. Its desire is contrary to you, but you must rule over it" (Gen. 4:7). Quite often, goal-directed behavior seems to emerge via imitating what we perceive others want or want for us and then wanting it ourselves. Growing capacities for autonomy, competence, and relatedness (belongingness) begin shaping us in ways not always equivalent simply to the temperament traits of our genetics. Synaptic pathways wiring together in the brain enable a child to increasingly attune and react to stimuli in their environment.

Thus, motivational objectives, in addition to innate temperament traits, help a child adapt their personality to particular social contexts. For example, a trait of extroversion or agreeableness becomes related to particular social goals; openness inspires economic and religious pursuits. Personal striving, projects, and life longings become more centrally the building blocks or themes that guide personality. A growing need for autonomy emerges amid a parental and social ecology that exerts its own need to constrain and shape behavior and attitudes.[23]

20. McAdams and Olson, "Personality Development," 524.
21. Markus and Nurius, "Possible Selves," 962–64.
22. McAdams and Olson, "Personality Development," 524–25.
23. McAdams and Olson, "Personality Development," 524–26.

Empathy becomes possible, and remarkable acts of altruism can sometimes be witnessed in a child. Yet, just as theologians have historically regarded sin as "humanity turned in upon itself,"[24] the personality of a child may also be observed as inherently egocentric, impulsive, and inclined toward self-gratification. Theories of human development tend to focus on natural, progressive development, rarely taking into consideration any notion of sin or fallenness permeating the human condition. By contrast, Henri J. M. Nouwen, toward the end of his life, allegedly purported that three subtle deceits may be grounded in the early learnings and perceptions of a child:

> I am what I have.
> I am what I do or achieve.
> I am what others say about me.[25]

Historically, religious educators have regarded this as the crucial age when the conscience develops, and if nurtured well, it can become a primary guide to action. Conscience is described as an internalized sense of morality that comes about through identification, instruction, and interactions as the world of the child expands beyond the family into broader interactions of school and society.[26] As I labored to establish in the last chapter, parenting style and the handling of discipline encounters provide the building blocks of conscience and moral formation. The quality of the parent-child relationship, even more so than parenting practice, may affect how middle-aged children learn to externalize or internalize emotions as they exhibit morality or feel inhibited in its expression. The study of how conscience functions is sometimes segmented into (1) the judgments one makes about what is right and wrong (an evaluative and cognitive aspect) and (2) whether one prefers to act in ways that are judged to be right (a dispositional or obligatory aspect). Closely related are aspects of self-control and whether a child will stop themselves from a proscribed act like stealing, cheating, or hitting *and* whether they can perform an act they don't really feel like doing—putting duty ahead of pleasure, fulfilling a commitment, inconveniencing oneself.[27]

Erik H. Erikson regards the primary tasks of the childhood years to involve autonomy, initiative, and industry while recognizing the possibility of their accompanying deformations of shame, guilt, and inferiority.[28] Critical

---

24. A. Johnson, review of *The Gravity of Sin*.
25. See, e.g., Nouwen, "Being the Beloved."
26. Broderick and Blewitt, *Life Span*, 194–96.
27. Hoffman, *Empathy and Moral Development*, 9–12.
28. Erikson, *Childhood and Society*.

developmental tasks confront the school-aged child, creating challenges to achieve in many domains:

- Learning and education. Recall your own emotional experiences with the spelling bee.
- Physical education. What feeling accompanied the hour of physical education in school when things like dodgeball, softball, and dance were taught?
- Extracurricular activities. What clubs were you involved in, and were they sources of belonging and accomplishment?
- Peer leadership. Could you influence others as a follower or leader?

To frame these developmental tasks in religious terms, a child's spiritual character is being shaped in profound ways during the middle childhood years. Embedded in the growing character adaptations are what Rabbi Howard I. Bogot calls "liturgical ingredients"—wonder, joy, love, drama, and natural spontaneity.[29] Whether these natural inclinations turn Godward, however, may depend on whether a child acquires the religious language to verbalize an awareness of God. Writing about this, Karen-Marie Yust summons us to recognize how critical involvement in a faith community is, as it becomes the best means whereby the meaning of religious language is felt and learned.[30] Just as children in educational settings need to memorize vocabulary lists in order to acquire the language of a culture, so too do children need to learn the grammar of faith to transform their budding desires and aspirations into declarations to and about God. Yust calls this "helping children name God's presence in their lives."[31] Imagine the concern we might have for an eight-year-old who has not yet grasped the basic foundations of language, hindering them from vital social connections needed for growth. Put this into the religious dimension, where without language the shared reality of faith conveyed through worship, liturgy, preaching and teaching, fellowship, and mission is forfeited. Bonnie J. Miller-McLemore notes the emerging capacity a child has for (1) acquisition of reason, (2) verbal confession, and (3) formation of moral conscience,[32] all of which likely factor into the historic practice, in both Catholic and mainline churches, of confirmation being positioned during these years in the life course. These faith traditions recognize that this life stage is prime for inculcating the pillars of the faith. Through the creeds, a middle-aged child learns the basics of what the church

29. Bogot, "Making God Accessible."
30. Yust, *Real Kids, Real Faith*, 70–75.
31. Yust, *Real Kids, Real Faith*, 69–92.
32. Cahalan and Miller-McLemore, *Calling All Years Good*, 41.

believes (doctrine); by memorizing the Ten Commandments, they learn how God followers pursue holiness and set their lives apart; the Lord's Prayer is a practice that directs them to hallow God's name, see his goodness as their daily bread, and find consolation when they feel guilt, anxiety, or doubt over temptation or badness/evil in themselves or others; and through the sacraments, they find a means of grace and a lexicon for dying to sin and living as new creations.

An interesting exploration, involving both faith traditions and our legal system, addresses when a child is regarded as culpable or accountable to God for their own behavior. This may become especially salient as virtual reality creates simulations of lived experience that make the border between what is real and what is imaginary more difficult to determine. How is sin nature conceived in children, and how is it affected by the waters of baptism? Aligning with moral development theory, some faith traditions see the development of conscience taking place at the onset of formal schooling, setting the age around six or seven. Hence, the Jesuit maxim: "Give me the child for the first seven years, and I will give you the man." Other traditions believe the development of conscience takes place around puberty, roughly age eleven to thirteen. These traditions more typically focus on a candidate making a profession of faith either through believer's baptism (e.g., Southern Baptist) or through confirmation (e.g., Catholic and mainline denominations). Support for this may be found in Jesus being among the religious leaders at what was apparently his bar mitzvah (Luke 2:41–52). Still others turn to the exodus story and the fact that it was anyone twenty years of age or above who was refused entrance into the promised land for their disobedience and distrust of God after experiencing his great deliverance (Num. 32:11).

Yet, despite our fallenness and bent toward organizing the world around our own ego, most theological systems would also acknowledge that whether the image of God remains in a child (constitutive grace) and/or is restored in a child (restitutive grace), intentional parenting and/or socialization in a faith community can mediate the grace of God to produce character that bears resemblance to that of the child Jesus, described by Luke as growing "in wisdom and in stature and in favor with God and all the people" (Luke 2:52 NLT).

The Self-System

Theorists now use the language of "self-system" rather than simply "self" because it offers a more multidimensional view of the developing person. In the foundational work of William James, Charles Cooley, and George Mead, a distinction is made between the I and the Me. The I is regarded as the active agent, the self as knower, that which is subjectively known and part of one's self-awareness. The Me is the self as object, what others observe about the self, or the part that is known. Temperament traits and self-directed activity are likely part of the I, and the I is often evaluating itself based on the Me. The I and the Me create self-awareness of our distinctiveness from other human beings. The social self, or the Me, is recognized by others but also contains spiritual qualities of character, such as beliefs and values.[33]

This I-Me framework allows theorists to make subtle but important distinctions between things like a person's self-concept—a person's knowledge of their personal attributes—and a person's self-esteem—their positive or negative valuation of those attributes. Thus, William James, for instance, regards self-esteem as being constructed from more than an accumulation of achievements. Rather, he posits that self-esteem is determined by the "number of successes we enjoy relative to our aspirations or pretensions."[34] A person who equates success with winning as a star athlete will view completing a mile run much differently than the person who sees it as a milestone in their aspiration to lose weight. How well or how poorly we perform in a particular area may impact our self-esteem only if we deem that area of personal importance. I may be poor at painting with watercolor, but if handling a pastel-soaked paintbrush is unimportant to me, then my inability to create a flower arrangement of purple hydrangeas will have little effect on my self-esteem.

However, it should be pointed out that young children have not yet developed the capacity to integrate many appraisals into their self-concept, so various social self-descriptors ("ugly," "nice," "mean," "beautiful") may not register the same way they will in the adolescent years.[35] A good axiom from human development is the Thomas dictum: "If a perception is real, it is real in its consequences."[36] Hence, it is always important to try to see with the eyes of the child and to understand how they have been affected by a negative appraisal.

As a child grows, so will the structure of their self-concept. Adequacy in a task and support for engaging in a task both contribute to the self-esteem one feels. Lev Vygotsky regards transmission of knowledge as occurring within the "zone of proximal development" (ZPD).[37] ZPD contains concepts and/or skills that a child cannot master independently but could master if given the appropriate level of support or scaffolding. Good examples are how a young child learns to tie their shoes, how an older child learns to crack open and scramble an

33. Broderick and Blewitt, *Life Span*, 174.
34. Broderick and Blewitt, *Life Span*, 175.
35. Broderick and Blewitt, *Life Span*, 255.
36. For a good treatment of the Thomas dictum, see "Thomas Theorem."
37. Arnett and Jensen, *Human Development*, 185.

egg, and how an early adolescent learns to knot a necktie or to apply makeup.[38] What can be awkward and likely failed explorations when attempted on one's own become rather manageable and even enjoyable when accompanied by a more capable parent or peer.

What if we regarded faith as operating like this, unlikely to be mastered or even begun unless there is someone further along to scaffold what learning and practicing the faith looks like? We build scaffolds around structures that are too unstable to stand on their own, adding necessary reinforcements until they can support themselves. It is not hard to draw an inference to the human domain and imagine the problems that can occur when a child is over- or under-scaffolded. The former is deprived of the exulting feeling of "I can do it myself"; the latter is left with a foreboding sense of "Where were you when I needed help?"[39] Many facets of Christian experience are acquired through scaffolding. Think of practices that are learned in this manner, such as how to pray, how to confess sins and receive forgiveness, how to sing from a hymnal or follow an order of worship, how to take communion in a given tradition, how to perform the *lectio divina*. Or consider how unlikely it is for one to learn the virtues of hospitality, stewardship, generosity, mercy, and humility apart from a community that gives articulation to them. It is no coincidence, then, that the early church gave great gravitas to those who sponsored candidates for baptism, the vestiges of which can still be found in the naming of godparents in some traditions. Other parallels can be made to the importance of "other mothering" in African American communities[40] and "fictive kin" in ancient Israel.[41] Consider also how children can be scaffolded as they learn about their sex/gender and femininity/masculinity.

Self-esteem appears to follow three trajectories: consistently high, chronically low, and a U-shaped pattern that bottoms out around eighteen years of age before rebounding.[42] Attribution theory adds nuance and explanation to self-concept by focusing on elements such as locus of control, stability, and perceived agency. According to this theory, depressed people tend to attribute bad events to something inside themselves, predict that what creates anxiety/despair is likely to reoccur, and express a lack of control over outcomes. Nondepressed people, to the contrary, tend to attribute bad events to external circumstances, perceive they have more control over outcomes, and expect more fortunate unfolding.[43]

38. For a touching treatment of this, see the Father's Day commercials created by Gillette ("This Father's Day, Go Ask Dad").

39. Balswick, King, and Reimer, *Reciprocating Self*, 183–84.

40. See T. Brown, *Can a Sistah Get a Little Help?*

41. See Sandra Richter's treatment of fictive kin in *Epic of Eden*.

42. Broderick and Blewitt, *Life Span*, 259.

43. Broderick and Blewitt, *Life Span*, 284–85.

Carol S. Dweck enhances our understanding by contrasting fixed and growth mindsets.[44] Children, teens, and adults who operate from a fixed mindset regard intelligence, talents, and abilities as set in stone—that is, capacities some people possess and others do not. Fearing they do not have enough of these gifts to achieve, they will tend to avoid challenges and withdraw from engagements that they perceive will set them up for failure or cause them to look deficient. Trying to avoid negative attributions about the self and feeling threatened by the success of others lead them to make excuses, place blame elsewhere for shortcomings, and take on a defensive posture. Problems are regarded by those with a fixed mindset as too difficult to solve, an entrapment that can make them see cheating or lying or bullying as the only way to succeed. A person with a growth mindset, by contrast, takes the perspective that with effort, perseverance, and tenacity, most tasks can be accomplished and most competencies acquired. This is similar to what Angela Duckworth writes about grit. She notes that excellence in most any field—writing well, preaching, mastering an instrument—takes ten thousand hours of investment.[45] Those with a growth mindset equip themselves with a framework to overcome obstacles when they are encountered and to see mistakes as opportunities to improve rather than impediments that stagnate growth. Where a fixed mindset feels threatened by the success of others, a growth mindset finds excellence in others inspirational. Dweck and those who follow her framework suggest that parents, mentors, and educators can adopt certain behaviors to help foster a growth mindset in children. These include praising effort rather than results; giving feedback that communicates "not yet" rather than "fail"; and creating formative evaluations rather than summative evaluations so that students are given the chance to remedy and address gaps in knowledge rather than grow discouraged.[46]

Carol Gilligan[47] and Mary Pipher,[48] among others, gained attention for their studies purporting that girls "lose voice" as they approach and move through adolescence. Their carefree, authentic, and willful self goes underground, and rather than speaking for themselves, they suppress their voice in the service of retaining connection to important others around them. Suppressing their own voice, these authors claim, could lead to disassociation from their true self and a loss of awareness of their own feelings and opinions. Gilligan began her work decades ago in a much different social context than many experience today. Subsequent research has found that losing voice is not a phenomenon

44. Dweck, *Mindset*.
45. Duckworth, *Grit*.
46. See, e.g., Armstrong, "Carol Dweck."
47. Gilligan, *In a Different Voice*.
48. Pipher and Ross, *Reviving Ophelia*.

only girls experience. Regardless of gender, the level of voice among young girls *and* young boys largely depends on whether they feel support for self-expression, with girls actually faring better when in the presence of close friends and classmates.[49] Lawrence Steinberg and Kathryn C. Monahan actually found that girls were "less likely to change their behavior to conform with peer pressure than males."[50] A composite of other studies indicates that for both genders, self-esteem follows an inverted S-shaped pattern—declining in late childhood, leveling during adolescence, gradually increasing through the sixth decade of life, and then declining again.[51]

A similar myth exists regarding ethnic minorities. It is often assumed that African Americans have lower self-esteem than whites. Yet, large studies reveal that minorities typically show slightly higher levels of self-esteem than whites. Those studying this phenomenon posit several reasons. It may be that when minorities receive negative feedback, they can deflect some of its damaging effects by attributing it to societal prejudice. Further, the standard for social comparison that they value may reside within their own minority group rather than in groups of privilege. Finally, domains in which members of their ethnic group excel are given greater salience—for example, the role of a mother, athletics in some minority groups, academic excellence in other groups.[52]

Cultural values also create differences in the self-system. In cultures where the aim of development is autonomy and individuality, the social script encourages decision-making according to personal interests. Becoming exceptional and distinct is praiseworthy. By contrast, in cultures where the aim of development is to accept one's place in the social collective, deference to elders and to tradition is prized, for it maintains social harmony and interdependence. In honor cultures, more common in the East, diminishing the self in the presence of others is more esteemed than taking pride in the self. There may also be high expectations to conform to the expectations of others and remain loyal to one's in-group.[53]

A Few Models of Children's Ministry

In light of the self-system of the child, scaffolding faith development, and how faith takes on the shape of the community one is embedded in, I want to elevate

49. Broderick and Blewitt, *Life Span*, 260–62.
50. Steinberg and Monahan, "Age Differences in Resistance to Peer Influence."
51. Broderick and Blewitt, *Life Span*, 261.
52. Broderick and Blewitt, *Life Span*, 260–63.
53. Broderick and Blewitt, *Life Span*, 265.

several contrasting models of children's ministry because of the emphasis each gives to particular elements of a child's faith formation.

The Matthew Initiative. Directed by a mother-daughter team, Sharon Yancey and Jordan Yancey Black, both graduates of Asbury Seminary, the Matthew Initiative is unique in the way it focuses first on the children in a community. Elevating the values of joy, hospitality, and hope, participants begin by assessing the needs of children and families in the community where a church is located and create launch events outside the walls of the church. The preparatory work often causes under-resourced and underserved congregations to find renewal by seeking to realize Jesus's command in Matthew 19:14: "Let the little children come to me and do not hinder them, for to such belongs the kingdom of heaven."[54]

Saint Anthony on the Lake. This is a Catholic parish that aims to gather families together to create a viable community to catechize children. Staff and leaders develop the curriculum for the weekly gathering of families. They provide all the needed resources, but parents become the actual teachers to their children. On alternate weeks the children break into same-age groups while parents receive teaching or have conversations about family discipleship. The conviction is that religious socialization is most effective when families know each other. Hence, joining families over mealtime is also a large part of their program.[55]

Godly Play. Directed by Jerome Berryman, this adaptation of Maria Montessori and Sofia Cavalletti's Catechesis of the Good Shepherd catechetical model centers stories, symbols, and ritual in the religious training of a child. Beyond traditional pedagogy, this methodology builds on a child's innate capacity for wonder, play, and imagination to help them experience the presence of God.[56]

Faith-Forward. Founded by David Csinos, Faith-Forward is unique in its ethnic diversity and prophetic approaches to the shaping of children, storytelling, and style of singing. The diversity means broader theological perspectives that may challenge those traditionally minded but may also be the catalyst for reimagining what children's ministry might address.[57]

Awana Clubs and Orange Curriculum. Awana was founded by Lance Latham and Art Rorheim. Though different in style and content from the Orange Curriculum developed by founder and CEO Reggie Joiner, I link them together because in my judgment the predominant emphasis in both is a Bible-based curriculum that church and parents partner together to use to shape the faith of a child.[58]

---

54. See https://thrive.asburyseminary.edu/sharon-yancey/.
55. See https://www.stanthony.cc/family-program.
56. See https://www.godlyplayfoundation.org/.
57. See https://www.faith-forward.net/.
58. See https://www.awana.org/ and https://thinkorange.com/.

Technology and the Self

It would be virtually negligent (pun intended) to address the self-system in younger generations without considering the impact of social media. So much has been written on the culture of comparison, anxiety, depression, and fear of missing out (FOMO) created by social media platforms that it is rather common knowledge now that there are deleterious effects to the average of nine hours of screen time and thousands of touches to smartphones that constitute our typical day.[59] I will not regurgitate statistics and effects of social media here. But I will say that a Barna study awakened me to the reality that the number one source of conflict in families today is children's use of media and that I was not offering students help in how to address this with families in their congregations.[60] Following are ideas that have come from my efforts to redress my negligence and begin to build ways to understand and navigate the new media landscape.

Angela Williams Gorrell suggests first examining our own posture toward the new media landscape and how our own affinity for or dismay over technology may be affecting our responses to children. She notes that there can be several misdirected tendencies.[61] When we vilify new media, we easily dismiss the good it has for extending our human capacity to see and relate to each other in new and broadening ways. We also neglect the potential it has for communicating the gospel and discipling the next generation. For example, the Protestant Reformation was deeply dependent on the new medium of the printing press to disseminate tracts, to put the text of the Scriptures into the hands of laypeople, and to reform the church. At the same time, we can be naively indiscriminate in regarding technology as a neutral tool, utilizing it without examining the embedded values and narratives that reflect a fallen world. On the micro scale, users of technology should recognize the built-in rewards that marketers and news sources use to habituate us to their sites. On a more macro scale, Jonathan Haidt has likened social media to Babel in the way it has confounded us so that we do not understand one another, polarized us so that we are inhospitable to cooperation, and led to the fragmentation of many things in our democracy. Social media platforms typically attract the 10 percent of people most polarized and who speak the loudest, leaving the more moderate views of 80 percent of the population misrepresented or unaccounted for. Haidt quips that technology did not give everyone a voice as promised but instead handed them a dart gun for shooting at others in a

59. "Impact of Media Use on Children and Youth."
60. Crouch, *Tech-Wise Family*, 25–41.
61. Gorrell, *Always On*, 11–46.

way not likely in face-to-face communication. This has made much of social media toxic.[62]

For younger generations, technology is not something they simply use as a communication tool. It is better conceptualized as the world they inhabit. Therefore, we have a critical need for discernment and discipleship regarding their media consumption.

Andy Crouch's *Tech-Wise Family* found great traction among Christian families. Instead of suddenly imposing restrictions on children's use of technology, almost inevitably creating an adversarial relationship between parents and children, he recommends a values-based pathway toward setting limitations on cell phone use. By asking, "What is technology displacing in our lives?" "What do we value as a family?" and consequently "What place do we want to give technology in our lives?" we can determine the role we want technology to have in our lives and families.[63]

I found great practical wisdom from the Axis group, which provides a thirty-day reboot for families.[64] Particularly helpful is their focus on building high-trust relationships in the family to create the right climate for having conversations. They quote the axiom "Relationship precedes and determines influence," crediting it to Kara Powell from the Fuller Youth Institute. If your kids are not yet immersed in social media and you are just establishing boundaries, there are a number of helpful steps you can take that will make navigating this space in future years much easier. First, elementary-aged children can use devices that have limited functionality, like phones that are used only for calling. Or at the least, use trackers to record how much time is being spent on a device. Corporately decide with your church youth group or child's friendship group the appropriate age for having certain devices. We needed a way to contact our kids to coordinate rides and schedules for extracurricular activities at about age thirteen. However, I wish in hindsight that we had not purchased smartphones or iPads until they were about age sixteen. As the Axis group accurately notes, too much freedom before a teen is ready inevitably leads to bad choices. We don't allow children to drive before age sixteen or to purchase firearms until age eighteen because we recognize what is at stake. How much more is at stake when smart devices allow anyone, including musicians, marketers, predators, extremists, and makers of pornography, direct access to the hearts and minds of our children.

For some years, we were active in a Mennonite faith community. Kids raised in that community were accustomed to being different, eschewing the wearing

---

62. Haidt, "Why the Past 10 Years of American Life Have Been Uniquely Stupid."
63. Crouch, *Tech-Wise Family*.
64. Find them at https://axis.org.

of makeup, sharing adult work in families, being homeschooled, and spending much of their social life in youth group activities. Cultivating a sense that we are a peculiar people (1 Pet. 2:9–10)—a people set apart (a helpful description of holiness)—raises the awareness of being on mission for the God who saved us, is for us, and has a meaningful purpose for our lives together.[65]

Instead of buying children their own cell phone, which implies that they have sole authority over how it is used, retain ownership of the device and communicate that it is on loan for their use. Retain the right as parents to determine how it is put to use. That makes applying filters, requiring your approval for adding apps, and setting limitations on use much easier. Some families find that contracts their teens sign provide accountability. These contracts typically spell out how smartphones are to be used, caution against the dangers of divulging personal information, and specify the consequences when misuse or overuse occurs.[66]

Other practices can be followed as well:

- Engage in the interests of your children and learn about their culture as a means of showing interest and care (Axis has a free weekly newsletter that can help immensely). Remember that one of the "habits of highly effective" people is that they "seek first to understand, then to be understood."[67]
- Help your teen develop their own conscience and the capacity to make moral choices rather than simply prohibiting behaviors, which leaves them dependent on an authority to monitor every decision.
- Enter into the flow of your child's life rather than insisting that they enter the flow of yours. In other words, you may not find a good reception if you start barking directives at your child when they are intensely focused on "mortal" combat in a video game or navigating the intricacies of social life on their phone. Respect their personal space and look for a time when they are free from distraction to talk.
- Set the right tone for engaging in conversations about technology by creating an environment of trust and respect where good memories are made, positive emotions are shared, interest is shown in another person's interior world without passing judgment, and warmth is established.
- When addressing technology use in the family, lead with questions about what they love about their smartphones. Ask about their top three favorite

65. See the conversation between Andy Crouch and Jonathan Haidt, sponsored by the Murdock Foundation, in The Trinity Forum, "After Babel."
66. My gratitude again to Axis for these insights (https://axis.org).
67. Covey, *Habits of Highly Effective People*, 237.

apps. Give reasons for setting limits on the use of technology: we value being present to each other as a family, we practice Sabbath and rhythms of nonuse, we find joy in building community and appreciating God's creation. Discuss the research that shows that excessive technology use leads not to greater connection but to depression and loneliness. A preference for the safety of virtual communication can result in the diminishment of real involvement and the displacing of shared activities.

- Share your own vulnerabilities with technology and experiment together with ways to overcome them, such as turning off notifications on your phone, setting colors to grayscale, using an alarm clock to eliminate the need to keep your phone on as your bedside companion, respecting Sabbath and unplugging for several hours or a full day every week to break the compulsivity of always being plugged in and online.

Moral Development

As the self-system develops and children experience more inculcation of adult values, and as their cognitive functioning matures, great gains are made in their moral reasoning. Research shows that children progress universally and sequentially through early levels of moral reasoning but show increasing diversity across cultures and among individuals at higher stages of moral reasoning.[68]

Critical to this discussion is an axiom upheld by Sofia Cavalletti that is as true at any stage of life as it is for children: encounter with God is foundational and must precede the presentation of moral principles. After God has been trusted and enjoyed, then the ethical life can properly unfold.[69] The biblical/theological justification for this is clearly evident in the exodus story and in Jesus's reconstituting of the people of God in the Sermon on the Mount (Matt. 5–7). In the former, after God establishes his might over the pantheon of Egyptian gods through the plagues and leaves the Egyptian army as carcasses on the shores of the Red Sea, he gives the emerging nation the Ten Commandments. Even then, the prologue reminds them, "I am the LORD your God, who brought you out of the land of Egypt, out of the house of slavery. You shall have no other gods before me" (Exod. 20:2–3). In the Sermon on the Mount, the people Jesus has just healed of various diseases, afflictions, and torments, those counted as spiritual zeros who would never have been seen as worthy to be consulted about spiritual matters, Jesus now stunningly declares are "blessed" (Matt. 5:3–11). They are not subject to a fated condition because the kingdom of God and all

68. Arnett and Jensen, *Human Development*, 363.
69. Cavalletti, *Religious Potential of the Child*, 24–25.

its future hope are bestowed on them. It is then that he summons them into an ethical and virtuous life. Glory!

Jean Piaget studied children and how they become oriented to the rules of a game.[70] It was his premise that morality is a governing system of rules and that just as a child has to learn the rules of a game to play it well, so we have to learn the rules of a society to function at an optimum level.

Piaget observed that children's egocentrism initially prevents them from the social reality of rules—for example, try playing the game Jenga with a three-year-old and you quickly learn that they are more interested in seeing the tower of blocks tumble than following the rules of the game. In a transitional phase, children imitate the actions of older peers. Children believe they are engaged in the play of the game, but they are not yet fully oriented to the rules of the game. Consider the child who pushes pool balls around on the table with a pool cue but has no comprehension of one player being responsible for the striped balls. Eventually, however, a child accommodates to the rules of the game, an essential act if there is to be a contest in which everyone agrees on the terms of engagement and how a winner is determined.

Most helpful from Piaget's work are the two types of morality that he came to see as reflective of two forms of respect.[71] Younger children operate out of unilateral respect. Unilateral respect is built on the child's perspective that older, smarter, and bigger people carry the authority to impose rules and to require obedience. Rules in this stage are sacred, untouchable, and not to be changed. They may even be reinforced by immanent justice—namely, God or nature itself will punish you or ensure that rules are not violated. A child gains this perspective from experiencing the consequences of an action and reasons that the consequences determine the greatness of the offense. The way to undo the consequences of bad behavior is through punishment, and the harsher the punishment, the more likely it is to restore order and re-create harmony with authority. Piaget found that unilateral respect can actually be reinforced by parents when they use constraint or insist on obedience solely to appease the parent. The theological equivalent of such an orientation may be the notion of expiation: to win God's approval, punishment for a crime must be imposed, and the harsher the punishment, the more likely it is to appease God. The ultimate expression of this was sacrificing one's own children to Molech, as did the nations inhabiting Canaan (Lev. 20:1–5).

At about age nine to eleven, Piaget observed a change occurring in most children from unilateral respect to mutual respect.[72] Instead of rules being handed

---

70. Piaget, *Moral Judgment of the Child*, 13–23.
71. Piaget, *Moral Judgment of the Child*, 109–94.
72. Piaget, *Moral Judgment of the Child*, 109–94.

down arbitrarily from powerful authority figures, the relinquishment of adult constraint allowed a child to begin to see that rules serve to protect and enhance the social bonds in which we live. Rules can be changed if people together determine that there are better ways to play a game or to serve societal interests. An important shift occurs in a child's moral reasoning whereby they gain the capacity to judge an action based not simply on its consequences but on the intentions of the actors involved. With this deepened understanding, a child turns from a concern for harsh punishment to appease an authority to a concern with punishment being equal to the crime or misbehavior and eventually to a concern for the preservation of the community. A growing sense of injustice is heard in a child's rebuttal, "That's not fair!" or "Why am I being punished when I didn't do anything wrong?"

Piaget found a methodology to test his theoretical assumptions. He made up two stories contrasting these different forms of respect and listened to how a child processed the outcomes.[73] For example, he told a child that there were two children, Nick and Violet (I've changed his French names to make them more readable). Nick is called to supper by his mother, and as he is responding to her wishes, he races through a swinging door that knocks over a tray of cups, breaking fifteen of them. Violet was told not to get into the cookie jar, but she reached for it anyway. In doing so, she hit one cup that was on the counter and caused it to break. Piaget asked the child to repeat the stories to make sure the child understood them and then asked, "Who is the naughtier child?" Quite often, younger children, prior to having a grasp of intentions, would answer that Nick was the naughtier child. When asked why, the answer for younger children was simply, "Because he broke more cups." When a child begins to take into account intentions, they flip and judge Violet as the naughtier child because her intent was to disobey the parent. Piaget predicted that as a child's understanding expands, so will their concepts of justice in relation to how punishments should be administered. While younger children judge on the basis of expiation, older children judge punishment as fair only if it is in proportion to the crime—that is, rather than thinking "the more severe the punishment, the more likely it is to set things right," they begin thinking more akin to restitution or an axiom like "an eye for an eye." With further maturity, they may even judge that inflicting additional punishment only increases suffering and come to consider how punishment might be commuted if it serves a redemptive purpose for those involved.

Similar to a child's developing ideas about punitive justice, Piaget observed a child's growing understanding of distributive justice—that is, how should

73. Piaget, *Moral Judgment of the Child*, 109–94.

Figure 3.1. Equality versus equity in Piaget

resources or opportunities be portioned out?[74] Young children operating under unilateral respect and adult constraint judge based on whether one is conforming to the favor or disfavor of the authority figure. Only when a child begins to be influenced by mutual respect among peers do they begin to judge on the basis of equality—everyone should be treated the same. As they mature, a child may even arrive at an understanding of equity whereby what is "equal" may have to take into consideration many factors, such as the capacity of an individual, the history of the relationship, the situational context, and so on. To see the difference between equality and equity, consider this example. Taxing everyone a flat sales tax of 6 percent represents an attempt at equality—treating everyone the same. Taxing everyone instead based on the amount of their income—the rich have a greater ability to pay—represents equity whereby what is fair takes into account how one is situated and utilizes resources relative to others.

Of course, these early conceptualizations of justice in the formation of a child's moral reasoning have far-reaching implications, as illustrated in figure 3.1, which compares equality and equity.

74. Piaget, *Moral Judgment of the Child*, 263–75.

Let's set aside considerations of distributive justice and return momentarily to concepts of retributive justice. Piaget again offers stories to children to distinguish the difference in their reasoning. He suggests considering two sisters, one slightly older than the other. To celebrate one of their birthdays, the mother takes the girls to the park. She gives each a balloon and tells them to hold onto the strings, because if they do not, the balloons will fly away. The younger girl disobeys and lets go of the string on her balloon, and it flies away. When the mother later cuts the birthday cake, how big of a piece should each girl get?[75]

In Piaget's theorizing, children ages six through nine are likely to judge that the youngest daughter should not get any cake because she disobeyed her mother and lost the balloon; these children place retributive justice above equality. Older children, ages ten through thirteen, are at the stage of reasoning that puts equality above retributive justice; they would judge that the daughters should get the same amount of cake because that is only fair. If, however, children have progressed to reasoning with equity, they might suggest that the younger daughter should be given the same amount or even more because she was sorrowful for not being able to fulfill what was intended.

Research has generally supported the trends Piaget observed. Younger children do show a proclivity to judge moral culpability based on consequences more than intention. Younger children also focus on equality in distribution, while older children try to balance equality amid a complex set of concerns. However, research has also found that many children exhibit a capacity for recognizing the role of intentions earlier than Piaget hypothesized.[76] Furthermore, Piaget's assumption that all rules are essentially the same in the mind of a child has been challenged. For example, the following distinctions might be made:

- Moral rules address foundational concerns of justice and individual rights.
- Rules of convention are more arbitrary and vary from culture to culture—that is, customs that function as the outcomes of explicit or tacit social agreements.
- Personal rules constitute areas of functioning in families or among individuals.[77]

Inconsistent with Piaget's idea that children's moral judgment is based on their capacity to understand a set of rules, children display differences in how

---

75. See Piaget's discussion of this story and what it reveals of a child's conceptualization of retributive justice in *Moral Judgment of the Child*, 262–76.
76. Broderick and Blewitt, *Life Span*, 270.
77. Broderick and Blewitt, *Life Span*, 271.

they judge violations of rules in each category, recognizing as early as age three that violating a moral rule is more consequential than violating a conventional or personal one. Important for those working with children is recognizing that parents and their children, especially as they become teens, may differ as to which category they think a rule belongs. For example, is dress, spending, or friendship a rule of convention or a moral issue? Is getting a tattoo or determining whom one dates a matter of personal choice and hence solely in the domain of the teen, or is it a matter of morality and one that parents have legitimate concern to influence?

CONCLUSION

The formation of our self-system brings deep impressions of autonomy, competence, and belonging. The I and the Me become more organized as competencies are formed and social comparison causes us to wonder whether our own assessment of ourselves is congruent with the appraisals of others. Foundational in the middle childhood years is how a person experiences a sense of their own goodness and self-efficacy. Feeling worthwhile and generally satisfied funds a sense of hope, will, purpose, and competence as one enters the crucible of adolescence. With insufficient emotional deposits in the self-system, a child may find themselves engrossed in a compensatory search to find ways of feeling better than others.

In 2011, Lisa Pearce and Melinda Lundquist Denton published a book addressing the religiosity of American adolescents titled *A Faith of Their Own: Stability and Change in the Religiosity of America's Adolescents*. These authors utilized the image of tile mosaics to describe distinct profiles of adolescent religious engagement.[78] To employ their useful metaphor, think of two-by-two-inch pieces of colored tile of various shades and colors that one is using to construct a piece of artwork, in this case representing a person's emerging self-concept. One shade of tile might represent a person's understanding of their gender, another shade might represent their race or ethnicity, another shade might represent their faith. A shade may not appear at all if it has not been made available in the person's social context or if it has little importance to them at this stage of life (e.g., political viewpoint or sexual orientation). Imagine that the importance a person gives to any particular dimension of their self is depicted by the number of tiles and the intensity of the shade. Further, imagine that the

---

78. Pearce and Denton, *Faith of Their Own*, 20–21.

tiles can be moved and some can even be replaced, indicating that the person can continually modify their tile portrait in relation to their social context. Finally, imagine that the landscape for the artwork can expand, adding more and more dimensions to the tile mosaic. This image of a mosaic may help us grasp with wonder the myriad ways a self is being formed and made distinct as a person shapes with the divine artist all the various ways he creates his workmanship (Eph. 2:10).

4 | Adolescence
Sharing the Power of Creation

About a decade ago, I attended a conference on family ministry. Ordinarily, my introversion and insecurities kick in at such venues and I turn solitary. But recognizing that it does not serve me or my students well for me to miss the chance to discover the possible resources in the room, I reached across the aisle and met Larry Fowler, who at that time was serving as executive director of global training for Awana. Larry told me about a conversation he had on a plane with a business owner who was adept at making long-term plans. Recognizing the man's strengths, Larry asked him what he had done to plan for the spiritual health of his children. Crestfallen, the man admitted he had done little and had little idea how to do so. For all the things we give to children, financially and educationally, we do not seem equipped to provide what is most essential. We want to, but we're not sure we have anything to offer and the adolescent world seems a bit foreign.

Larry went on to tell me about a book he was writing titled *Raising a Modern-Day Joseph* that centers on what he calls the "most difficult moment" (MDM) in the life of a parent.[1] Here is a paraphrase of how I recall the conversation: "Whenever we bring children into the world, we are eager to hold them and the embrace is wonderful. But at the same time, as soon as our children are born, we also begin a process of letting go. We notice it perhaps at first when we wonder if the baby is strong enough to sit up—and we let go for a moment to see if they will totter. It's kind of like we let go with one of our ten fingers. And then shortly after comes that moment when they are almost walking, and they hold on to get steady until they let go to walk on their own. And suddenly

---

1. L. Fowler, *Raising a Modern-Day Joseph*, 13–22.

we realize that we now hold on with eight fingers instead of ten. Then there comes learning to ride a bike, and we take a whole hand away—five fingers. Next, there's the letting go when they ask for the car keys."

Larry portends that the most difficult moment in any parent's life is when we let go with that last finger. For many, that moment comes outside a dorm room when their child enters college; for some parents, it's when their child gets on a bus for boot camp; for still others, that most difficult moment occurs at their son's or daughter's wedding. We do not leave their lives forever—we will always have some influence—but there is a relinquishment of the control and closeness that have been, a letting go.

That was enough to hook me, and so I asked Larry more about his book. In it he compares two stories from Scripture—one is historically real, the other is a parable Jesus told. Both are stories of a father letting go of his son; both involve a betrayal, a coat, a foreign land, brother(s), and an inheritance; and both contain an aspect of the most difficult moment.[2]

The first story is of Joseph in the Old Testament (Gen. 37–50). At age seventeen, he is sold into slavery to the Ishmaelites, and his departure is propagated by a lie: his brothers say that their father's favorite son has been torn apart by a wild animal, leaving only his bloody coat. We are told in the text that "Jacob tore his garments and put sackcloth on his loins and mourned for his son many days" (37:34). This was no doubt for him a most difficult moment.

But the reality was that even though his father thought him dead, Joseph lived. Stripped of all systems of support; bereft spiritually, socially, financially; betrayed by his brothers and unknowingly followed by a lie that dismantled any hope of pursuit, he is transplanted to a foreign land. If ever someone had a reason to manipulate a way to survive, it would be Joseph. Yet, tempted by a woman who held his fate in her hand and later given power that he could corrupt and use to avenge his wrath on his brothers, he maintains his purity and rises time and again to use power for the sake of saving many nations, finally fulfilling part of the blessing that was promised through Abraham.

Where did such character come from? What was it about Joseph's relationship with God and with family that kept him pure and that focused him beyond himself? What did the family give him that originated and sustained such a faith?

Contrast this with a story in Luke 15 about another son who has a father who is forced to let go. This father also loves his son, but they are separated not by tragedy but by the son's own initiative. The prodigal insists that he receive his inheritance early, essentially wishing his father dead, and rides off with more money than he can responsibly handle. His immaturity costs him, and

2. L. Fowler, *Raising a Modern-Day Joseph*, 45–52.

he squanders all that his father tried to instill in him. Another most difficult moment.

The question that serves as the premise behind Larry's book is this: In the most difficult moment, what do I want my teenage son or daughter (or the youth graduating from my ministry) to know, believe, and carry with them as they are released into the world? Or to pose it another way, How do I avoid sending out a prodigal and instead raise a modern-day Joseph?

Origins of Adolescence and Its Meaning

Stanley Hall is often credited with coining the term *adolescence* around the turn of the twentieth century.[3] Prior to this, Western society was like much of the rest of the world whereby kids moved from childhood directly into adulthood through marriage or through taking on adult work roles (e.g., working the fields in an agricultural society). J. K. Balswick and J. O. Balswick note that prior to

Figure 4.1. Giotto, *Madonna and Child*

3. Balswick and Balswick, *Family*, 125.

the Industrial Revolution, children were in fact regarded as little adults and were often treated as such, for example, by being made to sit still for long periods of time during services of worship.[4]

We may see this illustrated in medieval artists' paintings of the Madonna and baby Jesus, like the one in figure 4.1 by Giotto. Eager to ensure that Jesus was pictured as perfect and unchanged, and influenced by the philosophical notion of the homunculus or small human, artists avoided painting Jesus as a baby, which might signify immaturity or something incomplete and lacking.

Renaissance art offered more realistic portrayals of children, but it was largely the Industrial Revolution that brought about change in the understanding of the life course.[5] Prior to this time, apprenticeship served as a rite of passage into adulthood. A child learned a craft or mastered the trade their family was engaged in. Readiness to take on the work of the family signaled passage into adulthood. With industrialization, adolescents were co-opted into factory roles that required little skill. As these children were housed in slum apartments in cities separated from their families, adolescent subcultures began to emerge.

During the Industrial Revolution social scientists grew interested in the experiences of children. Developmental theory began to articulate qualitative differences between children, teens, and adults in their cognitive thinking, psychological makeup, social perspective taking, spiritual centering, and more recently neurobiology. All of this led to the conceptualization of the life course as including a period between childhood and adulthood, now commonly regarded as adolescence, that commences with puberty and ends with entrance into adult roles, especially employment and marriage.[6] Today, social media and pop culture have helped create an adolescent subculture that is a "tribe apart."[7] Adolescent identity is established less by imitation of exemplary adults and more by peers and marketing that dictates what is fashionable, what music to listen to, what movies constitute the canon of correct affiliation, and even what gender designations are in vogue with the culture. The Balswicks observe that the greater a person's sense of insecurity about their own identity, the more susceptible they are to relinquishing identity formation to what a peer group sanctions.[8]

Education in industrialized societies also became one of the major drivers of change to the life cycle. As high school became mandatory, churches began hiring pastors/ministers who specialized in this particular segment of the life

4. Balswick and Balswick, *Family*, 158–59.
5. Kett, "Reflections on the History of Adolescence in America."
6. Balswick, King, and Reimer, *Reciprocating Self*, 168.
7. Hersch, *Tribe Apart*.
8. Balswick and Balswick, *Family*, 161.

journey and bore titles specific to this particular age group. Yet, little biblical material specifically addresses adolescence. Most likely, references to "the
young" could refer to anyone from about age thirteen to thirty or until they
married. In fact, in many parts of the world, "youth" still refers to the age range
eighteen to thirty-five. Some have rued changes in Western culture, observing
that today many teens are relieved of familial and community responsibility to
pursue individual achievement goals. No longer taught to become an asset to
the home, they are treated as guests to be entertained, consumers of goods and
technology at an increasingly rapid pace.[9] Sadly, many youth programs seem
to encourage this bent toward self-absorption by trying to compete with the
culture to entertain and indulge teens in fun to keep them involved, offering
little to stir their imagination toward anything beyond themselves.

Some theologians and social scientists, however, have helped us to see with
clearer eyes the deep longings of adolescents in these pivotal years. Erik H. Erikson, for example, focused attention on the quest for identity during this stage
of life.[10] Kara Powell and her team at the Fuller Youth Institute expanded the
developmental tasks, naming identity, belonging, and purpose as three critical
needs for adolescents.[11] Kenda Creasy Dean drew from the remarkable witness
of Mary the mother of Jesus to summon teens to become "God-bearers," saying
yes with the same simple fidelity—"let it be to me according to your word."[12]

In the following sections, we explore what is happening with adolescents by
looking at various domains of development.

Physical Development and the Power of Creation

Developmental theorists like Erikson often claim that their theories are universally applicable and observable across cultures. This claim rests on the assumption that physical development is largely driven by biology. Erikson uses
the term *epigenetic* to signify that the normative pattern for human growth follows an innate blueprint that gradually unfolds with only moderate variations
across the life course.[13] Indeed, if we simply measure physical growth rate, we
will find a common pattern across cultures. The head of any newborn is about
one-fourth the size of their body, and the head of an adult is about one-eighth
the size of their body. During the first two years of life, the body and the brain
develop at a remarkable pace, as noted in earlier chapters. After about two years,

9. Joy, *Empower Your Kids to Be Adults*, 1–28.
10. Erikson, *Identity*.
11. Powell and Griffin, *3 Big Questions*.
12. Dean and Foster, *Godbearing Life*, 48.
13. Kroger, "Epigenesis of Identity."

however, this accelerated growth levels off to a gradual, fairly linear progression until adolescence. At adolescence, the body mimics the rate of growth that was seen in childhood.

Puberty is signaled in the brain by kisspeptin (so named because it was discovered in Hershey, Pennsylvania, headquarters of the Hershey Kiss). Kisspeptin stimulates the pituitary gland, launching the further development of the body's reproductive system. An estrogen hormone is released in females, producing estradiol at a rate eight times more pronounced than in males. An androgen hormone is released in the male body, producing testosterone at a rate twenty times more pronounced than in females. Puberty on average begins just prior to thirteen years of age, with girls typically hitting puberty about two years earlier than boys. Over the next four years, height increases ten inches on average. Gender differences also appear, such as pelvic spread for girls and a broadening of the shoulders for boys. Males also generally develop larger heart and lungs, thicker bones, and more muscle tissue. During this period, girls add an average of thirty-eight pounds to their body weight; boys add forty-two pounds.[14] Growth in different parts of the body is not always symmetrical in timing, leading to clumsiness and awkwardness during this period. The ratio of white to gray matter in the brain increases, and accelerated myelination allows faster processing speeds. Such monumental physiological changes create moodiness in teens that may account for increased strife with parents, the negative emotions associated with adolescence, and some risk-taking behavior.[15] However, the characterization of adolescence as an inevitable time of storm and stress between parents and teens may be overstated.

The arrival of puberty appears to be governed primarily by genetic factors, but it is influenced by environmental factors as well. A daughter's age at first menarche correlates highly with her mother's age at first menarche, and identical twins tend to start menstruating within a couple months of each other.[16] Research indicates, however, that the onset of puberty may be gradually dropping (in 1850, it was approximately three years later). Researchers believe that a higher intake of fats, malnutrition for some, family conflict and/or other sources of stress, and ethnicity may account for this earlier onset of puberty. In one particularly intriguing finding that is somewhat dated but still relevant, an unrelated man in the home seems to hasten puberty in girls.[17]

Ronald L. Kotesky was one of the first to note that the age of first menstruation has decreased, sliding downward from around age sixteen a couple centuries

14. Broderick and Blewitt, *Life Span*, 343–45.
15. Arnett, *Adolescence and Emerging Adulthood.*
16. Broderick and Blewitt, *Life Span*, 344.
17. Broderick and Blewitt, *Life Span*, 344–45.

ago to just under thirteen on average today. At the same time, the average age at marriage has steadily increased from the early teen years to the late twenties today.[18] This creates a crucible for religiously oriented youth whose bodies indicate sexual ripening a decade before they are likely to be in marriages, where engaging in sexual intimacy is permissible.

Of particular psychological impact is whether individual maturity arrives "on time"—that is, if it is consistent with the maturity rate of one's peers (though maturation rates in boys relative to girls and indications of maturation differ somewhat across cultures). Generally, the more extremely "off time" one is in their maturation schedule, the more prone they are to depression. However, some gender differences come into play. Girls who mature early are more prone to depressed mood, negative body image, and eating disorders, often due to attracting the romantic and sexual interests of males before being psychologically equipped to navigate these relationships well. In Western culture, sexual debut (first intercourse) is regarded as early at age fifteen, normal between age fifteen and nineteen, and late after age nineteen. I would hasten to interject here that it is critical for ministers to be discerning in broadcasting such statistics. Teens who have chosen to maintain chastity can be perceived as bucking conventional norms and being regarded as prudish or judgmental when living by a different standard.[19]

In contrast to girls, early maturation in boys is likely experienced as an advantage, moving them toward a favorable height, voice, and build. Late maturation may be felt more negatively by boys. Girls, however, may feel that puberty moves them away from the thin, slim-hipped ideal elevated by their culture.[20] But ethnic differences are also at play, as the ideal body type is regarded differently by different cultures. In one interesting experiment, professional marketers from different countries were sent a male and a female image and asked to airbrush them to match what they regarded as the ideal body type, revealing that ethnic differences sometimes affect what is considered desirable.[21] Nevertheless, ideals of female attractiveness are often punishing to young women, despite some cultures' greater success at promoting body images free from unrealistic Barbie-like models of beauty.

Issues in Sexuality

Children begin to show sexual interest just before puberty, triggering a desire to begin moving out of segregated gender groupings, which permeated much of

18. Koteskey, *Understanding Adolescence*, 12–13.
19. Broderick and Blewitt, *Life Span*, 354.
20. Arnett and Jensen, *Human Development*, 335.
21. Alexander, "Ideal to Real."

the discussion in the last chapter. The earliest activity, being driven to a younger age by media culture, is sexual fantasizing, which may begin as early as age ten. This is often followed by masturbation for boys as early as age eleven but more commonly accompanying the teen years. Masturbation for girls is less common but is becoming more prevalent with more education about how their bodies function and greater gender equality.[22] Religious groups commonly frown on self-release, and sexual fantasy is often accompanied by feelings of guilt. Social sciences, unconcerned with divine injunctions, often suggest that such explorations lead to greater self-awareness and more satisfying partner relationships.[23] To further complicate matters, Christians themselves may hold very different views of what a "sex education" curriculum should address and what practices it should promote. For example, if STDs and/or pregnancy are the risks to be avoided more so than promiscuous behavior, masturbation (solo or mutual) might be regarded as a necessary concession in a sexually saturated culture. From this perspective a person might also support condom distribution and birth control. Alternatively, arguments might be made that discourage masturbation, if not on biblical grounds, because it causes one to (1) focus on getting to orgasm rather than cherishing a partner, (2) narrow the means by which arousal occurs, (3) release the emotional bonding hormone oxytocin without a person to attach to, inevitably leaving one feeling bereft, and (4) diminish self-respect by losing a sense of regulating one's own impulses. Early church fathers taught that because of our sinful, fallen state, we are wired for excess.[24] Desires that when rightly ordered under the direction of our will migrate to the center of our lives because the pleasure and immediate relief they offer us soon entrap us (cf. Rom. 6:12–14; 1 Cor. 6:12). A critical component of discipleship is the ordering of desire, the practice of wedding (pun intended!) one's emotional life to virtues like patience and self-control to gain mastery over compulsivity.

Sexual debut may occur on a more protracted schedule in Christian communities where sex outside of marriage is taboo and abstinence is elevated as a virtue. Religious belief is one of the few factors correlated with restraint, though this too is increasingly challenged by patterns of cohabitation. Early sexual activity, especially when it is not protected by the permanence implicit in marital vows, quite commonly promotes insecure attachment that increases as the relationship progresses, predicting a defective bond.[25]

22. Broderick and Blewitt, *Life Span*, 355–57.
23. Broderick and Blewitt, *Life Span*, 356.
24. Hall, *Living Wisely with the Church Fathers.*
25. For more on the effects of passing sexual thresholds without deliberate and explicit communication of commitment, see the section titled "How Far Is Too Far? The Trajectory of Physical Intimacy" in Setran and Kiesling, *Spiritual Formation in Emerging Adulthood*, 198–203.

Adolescents who take a virginity pledge may not count certain behaviors such as oral sex or mutual masturbation as "sex" to maintain their pledge and consequently use less protection. Hence, those who take the pledge have STD rates as high as those who do not take the pledge.[26] Oral-genital stimulation as an alternative to penetration may also reinforce girls as givers and males as receivers.[27] Many in Christian communities fear that sex education and birth control encourage early sexual activity. The predominance of research, however, indicates that informed youth are not more prone to early sexual behavior but instead make better decisions when they do engage sexually.

A double standard of sexuality/gender is well documented in the messages that parents and culture send and in the reported experiences of young people traversing the waters of adolescence. Female sexuality is judged more harshly than male sexuality. Girls with multiple sexual partners may receive pejorative labels, whereas boys are lauded for their conquests. Girls can feel a drop in self-esteem at pubescence, attributed in many cultures to an awareness that female roles are less valued than male roles, projecting lower expectations of success. Teenage girls often acquire a more cooperative conversation style compared to boys, who are often socialized into a more domineering and direct style of communication. Girls may inadvertently "feel as if they are less likely to influence the outcome of a discussion" and feel dismissed or overlooked in educational, familial, or professional circles. Girls also tend to internalize their emotions.[28] Directing attention to negative feelings through rumination or talking repeatedly about a negative experience may deepen and prolong a sense of depression. Some studies show that depression is relatively equal for boys and girls prior to adolescence but that being female puts one at greater risk for all types of depression in adolescence.[29] I would hasten to add as a precautionary note that this should not preclude us from taking seriously the mental health challenges of teenage boys.

The Centers for Disease Control report that among high school seniors surveyed in 2021, 30 percent reported having had sexual intercourse.[30] About half of high school students in the United States report that their sexual contact is "only heterosexual."[31] Western culture seems increasingly bent on adolescent identity exploration, including experimentation with hetero- and homosexual partners. It is important to regard these dalliances as explorations and not as conclusive

26. Broderick and Blewitt, *Life Span*, 356.
27. Broderick and Blewitt, *Life Span*, 356.
28. Arnett and Jensen, *Human Development*, 247.
29. Arnett and Jensen, *Human Development*, 381.
30. Centers for Disease Control and Prevention, "Sexual Risk Behaviors."
31. Broderick and Blewitt, *Life Span*, 357.

indicators of one's sexual orientation. Less than 20 percent of adolescent girls and less than 4 percent of adolescent boys who reported same-sex contact in their teenage years identified themselves as something other than heterosexual in their twenties.[32] A teenager who identifies as or is labeled "same-sex attracted" may be more inclined to regard their sexuality as a behavior/inclination to be managed than a teenager who self-identifies as or is labeled "gay" or "lesbian" and becomes inclined to adapt this as an identity to be lived.

Gallup reports that in the decade between 2012 and 2022 the percentage of Americans who reported as LGBT or other than heterosexual doubled to a new high of just over 7 percent. About 86 percent reported as straight/heterosexual, and 6 to 7 percent offered no opinion.[33] The bulk of research presently available suggests that there is little empirical support for environmental causes being responsible for sexual orientation. In others words, Freud's notion that sexual orientation hinges on identification with one's parents is disconfirmed by research. Neither do teens appear to become same-sex attracted through seduction or the modeling of homosexual love. Evidence supports biological influence as primary in directing one's sexual orientation, and most sexual minorities report that their sexual orientation is not experienced as something chosen.[34] Several studies have shown that many gay and lesbian adults had cross-gender interests as children—preferences for the toys, clothing, and activities of the opposite sex, along with wishing they were of the other sex.[35] Another discovery is that a mother's body begins to develop antibodies to male proteins such that the more children she has, the slightly greater chance one of her later children will be homosexual.[36] Conservative Christian communities wanting to demonstrate understanding and compassion are divided on whether to acknowledge that there is a "gay Christian identity" and whether one should be encouraged to disassociate from this orientation.

According to the Heritage Foundation, nearly two-thirds of teens who reported they had engaged in sex wished they had waited longer, and those who were sexually active reported being depressed all or most of the time three times more frequently than those who were not sexually active.[37] The younger adolescents are in their first sexual experience, the more likely they are to have more sexual partners during their teenage years. The opposite is also true—those

32. Broderick and Blewitt, *Life Span*, 357.
33. J. Jones, "LGBT Identification in U.S. Ticks Up to 7.1%."
34. Broderick and Blewitt, *Life Span*, 358.
35. Broderick and Blewitt, *Life Span*, 358.
36. Broderick and Blewitt, *Life Span*, 358–59.
37. K. Johnson, Noyes, and Rector, "Sexually Active Teenagers Are More Likely to Be Depressed and to Attempt Suicide."

who wait the longest to have sex report the fewest number of partners and lower rates of STDs or other problematic outcomes.[38] For Christian communities, carefully discerning what virtue(s) they build a sexual ethos around is imperative. When virginity is elevated as the only reward in the Christian life, many feel they are already excluded from the economy of grace. When abstinence is the only virtue taught, the focus tends to be on behavior, which misses the deeper motivations of the heart. Chastity and modesty go deeper but can put the weight of restraint primarily on females. Purity may be more equal in its summons, but while purity pledges have led some down a pathway to faithfulness, they have led others to hiddenness and shame or to frigidity difficult to overcome when they marry.[39]

There may be ways other than a purity pledge to acknowledge a rite of passage into adulthood. A decade ago, I became acquainted with a liturgy embedded in a Leader Resources initiative called J2A, an acronym for journey to adulthood. Their thoughtfully designed curriculum for the teen through the young adult years begins with rite 13, a liturgical celebration acknowledging pubescence. Theologically, the ritual is based on Psalm 139, that one is "fearfully and wonderfully made" (v. 14). With the arrival of pubescence, a person is given the power of creation, a gift bestowed by their Creator, with whom they now share a sacred entrustment. The power of creation, of course, extends beyond the sexual domain to touch vocational choice, stewardship of resources, and use of one's energy for the common good. At the culmination of the journey to adulthood, students are sent on a pilgrimage to a destination of their choosing and instructed to customize the trip in a way that they might encounter God in a personal way (i.e., not a vacation or a missions trip). They are also asked to discern what their spiritual gifts might be and how they hope to use these gifts in the service of the faith community. Upon returning from the sponsored pilgrimage, young adults are invited to give testimony to the community of their encounter with God and their anticipated adult involvement in the faith community.[40]

Cognitive Development and Imagined Possibility

One of many physiological changes brought about by pubescence is a change in cognitive functioning, especially the capacity to generate possibilities of a world

38. Broderick and Blewitt, Life Span, 357.

39. For more on virtues associated with a curriculum for sexuality, see Setran and Kiesling, Spiritual Formation in Emerging Adulthood, 161–83, esp. 179–81.

40. "Journey to Adulthood."

that could be. Changes in the brain lead to enhanced selective attention, more complex memory strategies, and greater executive functioning.[41] Jean Piaget characterizes this cognitive enhancement as the arrival of formal operational thought, or hypothetical thinking. To illustrate this advancement consider this problem-solving illustration drawn from Broderick and Blewitt's *Life Span.*[42]

Several pendulums that can be manipulated in a variety of ways are put before a high school student. They can change the amount of weight the pendulum is holding, lengthen or shorten the string holding the weight, change the height from which the pendulum is dropped, and even vary the amount of force that sets the pendulum in motion. The task is to determine what factors account for some pendulums swinging faster than others.

One student might try to solve this problem by trial and error, changing one of the variables to see if it has any effect and reaching a conclusion when they notice that changing the length of the string affects the swinging rate of the pendulum. An adolescent displaying formal operational thought would test every possible combination of weight, length, force, and height before reporting that only the length of the string can account for changes in the pendulum swing. Whereas the first student relied on concrete operational thinking, the second student, who generated and tested all possibilities, demonstrates the arrival of hypothetical thinking.[43] This capacity for generating all possibilities bestows on adolescents a new and needed competency for self-development: the ability to construct ideals and begin to organize them systematically.

To further illustrate this difference, scientists asked children and teens to ponder what the world would be like if all the people in it did not have thumbs. Preadolescent children tended to answer in ways reflecting concrete realities: "No one would be able to write," "We couldn't give each other the thumbs up," and so on. Teens who were developing hypothetical thought could ponder all the possibilities. One student, for example, commented, "It would change everything" and referred to a left-handed friend who bemoaned that the whole world seemed made for right-handed people, from the way door handles turn to the way school desks accommodate leaning only one direction.[44] The arrival of hypothetical thinking enables one to ponder a variety of possibilities and hence to make comparisons and contemplate what the ideal might be.

One developing area of research seeks to understand how one's "possible self" and one's "feared self" function in personal and relational development. For example, does imagining and enacting one's possible self help one reach

41. Arnett and Jensen, *Human Development*, 345–46.
42. Broderick and Blewitt, *Life Span*, 361–62.
43. Arnett and Jensen, *Human Development*, 344.
44. "Abstraction and Hypothetical Propositions."

toward authenticity? How does the discrepancy between one's actual self and one's possible self lead to feelings of failure and depression? How might a romantic partner or spouse encourage a person to become their possible self? Why do some fall prey to becoming their feared self? Research indicates that when the possible self that people imagine is an unattainable fantasy rather than a reasonable expectation, effort and performance diminish in that domain.[45]

Pondering self research some years ago, I was intrigued reading E. Stanley Jones's devotional book on the Sermon on the Mount.[46] Jones's interpretation of the Beatitudes—the "blessed are . . ." statements from Jesus in Matthew 5—indicates that by grace no one is subject to fate. In our culture, which promotes self-made life trajectories, we may not realize the significance of Jones's statement, but early Greek literature interacted frequently with the question of whether human life was subject to fate. In the stories of the Bible, over and over again, the grace of God opens a pathway through the wilderness. He is the great way maker who frees us from being fated regardless of difficult childhoods, poor choices, misadventures, or besetting psychological tendencies.

A related area of research has been called want-should conflicts. "Wants" are associated with that part of the self that focuses on immediate gratification. "Shoulds" are what is best for the self but may require restraint or discipline as a means of acquiring a more favorable outcome. The challenge becomes devising strategies that increase a person's ability to act more often on their shoulds and overcome the temptation to give in to their wants.[47] For a humorous but striking illustration, recall Walter Mischel's marshmallow test in which a child is given the choice of eating a single marshmallow placed before them now or obtaining a second marshmallow if they can wait to eat the marshmallow until an adult returns after stepping out of the room for several minutes.[48] At the level of a child, this seems rather inconsequential, but raised to the level of an adolescent enticed toward sexual activity, stealing, cheating, drug use for the sake of acceptance, or violence as a distorted way of gaining respect, it is highly salient. Training in delayed gratification, refusal skills, problem-solving, and coping as part of comprehensive education programs has proven more effective than programs that focus on changing behavior alone.[49] Take, for example, sex-education programs. When the intervention includes contraception discussions, on-site clinic services, and personalized health counseling with trusted and trustworthy advisers, much better outcomes are achieved when compared to simple presentations

45. Bybee and Wells, "Development of Possible Selves."

46. E. Jones, *Christ of the Mount*.

47. See Bitterly, Mislavsky, Dai, and Milkman, "Want–Should Conflict," 245–46.

48. Igniter Media, "Marshmallow Test."

49. Broderick and Blewitt, *Life Span*, 417–18.

about abstinence.[50] It should also be noted that the quality of relationships that surround a teen, especially with parents and peers, may be the most determinative factor influencing choices and outcomes related to sexuality.[51]

Both through natural means and through means of grace, adolescents improve their executive functions, growing the ability to suppress already learned information to allow for new understanding and selective focus of attention on relevant information. This forecasting of possibilities is essential for vocational and relational discernment as teens develop the imaginative capacity to place themselves in a variety of work and romantic roles and alliances, vicariously considering what life would be like if they pursued such a pathway through adulthood. Faith communities that produce young adults who continue to serve the church are those that create multiple opportunities for exploration in ministry roles. As Reggie Joiner, CEO and founder of Orange, regularly reminds leaders, "A kid may get over what I teach them, but they will never get over what God does through them."[52] The capacity to project possible scenarios into the future is reflected in the writer of Hebrews as he characterizes faith as "the assurance of things hoped for, the conviction of things not seen" (Heb. 11:1). Implicit in this delineation is the realization that faith banks on the promises of God, imagining a future that human resources alone cannot create. The nation of Israel is established by just such a promise when God makes a covenant with Abraham and promises that he will bless him and make of him a great nation (Gen. 12:1–3). Abraham's challenge, looking at the stars (15:5) and counting grains of sand (22:17), is to entrust his future to God and avoid taking things into his own hands . . . which he does with his concubine Hagar (Gen. 16).

The tendency toward idealization also comes with liabilities. Idealizing what one's life or the world could be often makes current reality feel imperfect, shabby, and inadequate by comparison. Awakening an aptitude for idealization can create a zeal in young people that fuels reform movements, protests, and societal change.[53] Yet, ideals, by definition, are not real, and social systems often prove quite resistant to move from homeostasis. Youthful idealism needs the wisdom of elders just as elders need the enthusiasm of youth. Institutions need the constant reforms pushed by visionaries just as new movements need the wisdom and resources of established institutions, without which they will most certainly lose momentum or become institutionalized themselves.

On a more personal level, idealizing can turn not only to grandiosity but also to toxic criticalness toward others and toward oneself, intensifying mental health

50. See, e.g., "Comprehensive Sexuality Education."
51. Broderick and Blewitt, *Life Span*, 355–57.
52. Powell, "How to De-Stress Your Family's Pandemic Holidays."
53. See, e.g., White's treatment of this in *Practicing Discernment with Youth*.

issues or self-criticism that sometimes leads to eating disorders, depression, or stagnation. The cure for being overly critical may come from experience, but for the teenager, because so much of life is a first-time experience—from finding their locker at school, to determining whom to sit with in the cafeteria, to going on a date, to having a first period or a nocturnal emission—it is no small wonder that this period of life is often accompanied by a great deal of moodiness, meandering, uncertainty, and confusion.

Os Guinness wrote a helpful book some years ago originally titled *Doubt* and later titled *In Two Minds*. His premise is that doubt is not the same as disbelief. Whereas belief is to be decidedly for a position, and disbelief is to be opposed to a position, doubt is to be "in two minds." Guinness claims that whereas Jesus often did not respond to disbelief—for example, "And he did not do many mighty works there, because of their unbelief" (Matt. 13:58)—he actually responded to authentic doubt by revealing more of himself to people—for example, saying to doubting Thomas, "Put your finger here, and see my hands; and put out your hand, and place it in my side. Do not disbelieve, but believe" (John 20:27). (I use "authentic" to suggest that not every question asked of Jesus was authentic; many were ruses to trap him.) Discerning how doubt is functioning in a person's journey of faith may be critical in offering wise spiritual direction.[54] Sharing vulnerably one's own faith struggles often gives teens permission to attend to and honor their own questions. Religious clichés or answers that seem dismissive discourage making faith one's own. Are you comfortable with doubt having a place in the journey of faith, or do you respond to people's doubt by pronouncing, "You just have to believe"?

In terms of adolescent cognitive development, David Elkind posits that forms of egocentrism persist into adolescence, leading quite often to thinking errors. Intense self-focus can dissuade teens from planning ahead, it can prevent them from seeing that their thoughts and experiences are not unique, and it can lead to risky behaviors if probable consequences are miscalculated to favor imagined social rewards.[55]

Social scientists follow Elkind in giving names to some of these patterns of thought:

- *Imaginary audience.* Teens engage in a great deal of self-conscious thought, pondering how others may respond to them. This is likened to being on stage with critics constantly assessing their performance. The imaginary audience induces acute self-consciousness—everyone is watching me, aware of my inner thoughts and emotions.

54. Guinness, *In Two Minds.*
55. "Cognitive Development during Adolescence."

- *Personal fable.* The need for an ideal leads adolescents to see themselves as unique or possessing something that is special. Setting before youth winsome role models, introducing curriculum that tells the stories of biblical characters who conquered through faith, and exposing teens to narratives that help them identify with those fighting epic battles for the common good are critical facets of youth ministry programs.
- *Invincibility fable.* With lack of experience in the school of hard knocks, teens often feel that they can avoid probable and statistical outcomes. "That will never happen to me!" leads too often to escapades in risky behavior.[56]

Adolescents vary widely in the way they reach for greater autonomy and recoil back into places of dependency, seeking greater freedom but still needing emotional shelter and provision from adults. Growth and change yield volatility in self-representations, often creating inconsistencies in commitment or a retreat into indecision until greater stability at the core is gained. Rapprochement—learning how to make amends, repair relationships, and promote a harmonious state of affairs—is an important competency to acquire during the adolescent years but one that is likely only caught if it is demonstrated by significant others during one's adolescent journey. The response parents and ministers make with youth when expectations go unmet and monumental disappointments occur may be the bricks that pave a return road for prodigals in years to come.

Identity Development and Experiences of the Self

This brings us to the developmental task that pervades the adolescent years and follows us through the rest of the life course. Erikson is credited with naming this the identity crisis of adolescence centered around the quest to discover "Who am I?" or perhaps better phrased in Erikson's conceptualization as "What do I want to make of myself and what do I have to work with?"[57] Erikson sees the task as a psychosocial reality that asserts itself subtly but in a variety of ways:

- Can one become consistent in one's definition and sense of self across various social contexts—that is, unique in terms of roles, attitudes, beliefs, and aspirations—despite pressures to conform to expectations?

56. Arnett and Jensen, *Human Development*, 346–47.
57. Broderick and Blewitt, *Life Span*, 366.

- Identity may be constructed from a consolidation of earlier identifications. If so, how does one imitate role models while yet becoming authentic?
- Is there a "funding" of earlier developmental resolutions that fosters feelings of trust and self-worth (stage 1 in Erikson's model), confidence and an absence of shame in taking initiative (stages 2 and 3 in Erikson), and joy in being industrious (stage 4 in Erikson), or is healing needed that may come about only through therapeutic and supportive social contexts like youth groups and/or foster families?
- Identity for Erikson functions as a forever-to-be-revised sense of self within a social reality.[58] Hence, identity is deeply shaped by the feedback we receive about ourselves, which makes the choice of our social contexts critical through the adolescent years.[59]

The incapacity to construct a viable identity Erikson calls identity diffusion or role confusion. This default pathway might be characterized by mind-numbing bouts of video games or watching TV; seeking identity through brand-name clothes, styles, or tattooing; jumping from one romance to another in the hope of finding a relationship that defines oneself; and disorganized thinking, procrastination, or avoidance of issues and actions.

The most predominant operationalization of Erikson's theory of identity development over the past fifty-plus years has relied on the work of James E. Marcia.[60] Marcia studied identity formation by examining the following domains of identity:

- personal (ideological)
  - politics
  - religion
  - vocation/occupation
  - lifestyle choices
  - philosophy
- social (interpersonal)
  - friendship
  - dating
  - gender roles
  - recreation

58. Arnett and Jensen, *Human Development*, 25.
59. For additional work on identity constructs in Erikson and their linkage to spirituality, see Kiesling, "My Sense of Spiritual Self."
60. Marcia, "Development and Validation of Ego-Identity Status."

Marcia hypothesized that in each of these domains youth may or may not engage in some form of ideological or behavioral exploration, trying on what it feels like to adopt a particular role for oneself with various levels of experimentation. He also hypothesized that commitment to a role could come simply by conforming to the expectations of those around one, or it could emerge as a deliberate choice one makes to become a certain kind of person. Marcia's design contains four quadrants or categories of identity status:

- Diffused—characterized by an absence of both exploration and commitment. Diffused teens often find too few psychological resources within themselves needed for identity formation. Defaulting on the task of identity construction, they may situate themselves in highly controlling contexts or relationships in the unexamined hope that they might dictate identity to them.

- Foreclosed—defined by commitment based on parental or societal imposition of values without a period of exploration. Foreclosed teens, with little reflection, step into a preordained role ascribed by family obligation or constrained by circumstance. Finding security in parental authority, they structure life according to parental authority and seek to replicate cherished childhood memories in the family they create with a spouse. Foreclosing may reduce the anxiety of encountering a plurality of ideas, but it may seem as if they have never left home and can articulate values only by parroting the say-so of an authority figure.

- Moratorium—indicative of involvement in active deliberation without yet having arrived at sustained commitments. Those in moratorium exercise agency in identity deliberations but may still make frequent shifts vocationally, relationally, or ideologically. Though such teens are transitory and inconsistent in provisional commitments, their exploration, unlike that of the diffused, typically leads toward a personally constructed identity. Sometimes exploration comes with a dramatic departure from one's family of origin, leaving scars of guilt and self-doubt.

- Achieved—determined by clear commitments that follow an active period of searching, resulting in internalization and an owning of commitments. Achieved teens have reworked their childhood selves in self-satisfying ways, often relinquishing being the "ideal" son or daughter maintained by the foreclosed. The internal quest is often driven by a desire for autonomy and authenticity.[61]

61. Broderick and Blewitt, Life Span, 366–68.

Jane Kroger found that moratorium often peaks at about age nineteen, suggesting that much identity work occurs in the latter adolescent and young adult years, facilitated by colleges/universities and other mentoring communities.[62] Research supports a progressive movement over time from diffusion or foreclosure to identity achievement, though it is estimated that about half the population will show little change in their adult life course and that 10 to 15 percent may actually regress.[63] Progress may also differ according to various domains of identity—for example, a person may have explored a great deal of diversity in friendship but given little deliberation to politics. Consistent with attachment theory, families that provide a secure base and offer support for teens as they move into the broader world optimize identity development. Adolescents characterized as identity achieved generally have warm and open communication with parents and the freedom to voice their own opinions.[64]

A good deal of research correlates identity status with other factors—for example, identity achievement and moratorium correlate with higher levels of adaptability, reflectivity in decision-making, and satisfaction in relationships. By contrast, a foreclosed status correlates with lower levels of anxiety, a higher need for social approval, and more occurrences of authoritarianism. Further, identity diffusion correlates with higher levels of compulsivity and lower levels of moral reasoning and autonomy.[65] Michael Berzonsky proposes that identity statuses may be thought of as information processing styles that predict such things as (1) how likely a young person is to seek out new information, (2) whether they will search for a community of like-minded people or those who offer new perspectives, and (3) the kind of mentor and/or mentoring community they will want to foster in their educational and professional journeys.[66] Similarly, research points to mechanisms for change as those things that disequilibrate one's present way of thinking and being—that is, meeting new people or having a sustained relationship with someone who sees the world differently; having new experiences, like immersion in a cross-cultural setting; or undergoing a major life change, like a loss, illness, or nonnormative life event.[67]

Theorists who work with identity status research have sensed a need to nuance some of the statuses, realizing that there may be important distinctions between those who engage in exploration for breadth (trying out different religions, political affiliations, romantic/sexual partners) and those who engage in

62. Kroger, *Identity Development*.
63. Broderick and Blewitt, *Life Span*, 370.
64. Berk, *Development through the Lifespan*, 390.
65. Broderick and Blewitt, *Life Span*, 366–67.
66. Berzonsky, "Identity Style," 268–72.
67. Holcomb and Nonneman, "Faithful Change."

exploration for depth (concerted study within one's religious tradition, questioning of one's family system, undoing of a previous commitment).[68] Some commitments may also resemble a "closed posture," a kind of acquiescing because
teens feel they lack influence. Hence, they fall into an oppositional or negative
identity, like a gang member.[69]

The implications of this research for those in ministry are far-reaching. The
outcome of an identity crisis may be predicated on whether there was good
resolution to preceding stage tasks, whether a teen is exposed to good role
models, and whether personal and/or institutional support exists for exploration.[70] Furthermore, the importance of commitment for arriving at identity
achievement resonates well with the evangelical emphasis on making a decision
for Christ, if this is not a forfeiture of growth, questioning, or making faith one's
own.

Critical questions emerge when considering how things like gender, ethnic
identity, and sexual orientation intersect. Are certain domains of identity more
important to women than to men (e.g., interpersonal)? Some theorists believe
that women's successful identity resolution in many countries has long depended
on maintaining connection or establishing intimacy, whereas men achieve identity via separation from others. Others find inequity in such socialization. When
does ethnic identity or sexual orientation become important? How central is it
to one's sense of self, and how positively is it regarded? Is being white a characteristic of race or one's sociocultural reality? How is ethnicity a nonissue for
many Caucasians? For some biracial adolescents, whether they identify with
a minority category may depend on what social context they are currently in.
Code-switching and style shifting refer to linguistic shifts many teens make as
they navigate between different social contexts.[71]

It is an interesting exercise to consider what kind of preaching, practices,
and people within churches align with each of these identity statuses. It is also
important to note that the identity status framework is clearly biased toward
autonomy as the end goal of development—which comes about through greater
locus of control, self-chosen values, charting one's own path, etc.—with the
clear implication that identity is something one has to achieve. These aspects
may resemble movement toward a more mature faith, and yet more conservative believers may also find their pathways diverging from these conceptual

68. Broderick and Blewitt, *Life Span*, 368.
69. Broderick and Blewitt, *Life Span*, 456.
70. For more on how faith communities foster a particular identity status, see the chapter
titled "Identity Formation: Internalization, Refusal and Embrace" in Setran and Kiesling, *Spiritual
Formation in Emerging Adulthood*, 55–80.
71. Broderick and Blewitt, *Life Span*, 371–75.

itineraries as they alternatively seek centeredness in God as the telos, look to his revelation as a source of guidance, and follow ancient and established means whereby Christian identity is bestowed rather than achieved.[72] It may also be the case that those living in more collectivist cultures will encounter the expectation that their identity journey involves taking on responsibilities within the extended family. This is quite different from achieving an identity via increased independence and separation from family, as implied in Western theories of identity construction.[73]

Social Development and Rites of Passage

Research indicates that parents remain the primary influence on their teenager's faith development through the adolescent years. This suggests that, much like with parenting styles, a middle ground that avoids the pitfalls of overcontrol and undercontrol and that takes into consideration the unique characteristics of the adolescent is best.[74] In other words, becoming independent and personally responsible does not exclude emotional connection to a parent and may even be best facilitated by such closeness.[75] I also want to add that nonparental adults can act as surrogates. Numerous are the testimonies of teens whose religious belief was sourced not in ideology but in youth groups where they found belonging and where adults for the first time liked them and wanted them to be part of the "family."

Foster Cline and Jim Fay coined the term *helicopter parents* to describe parents who are overinvolved, overfunctioning, and overprotective, always assessing possible risks and seeking to mitigate them for their teens.[76] A preferred metaphor might be satellite parents. Instead of hovering, they provide a safe and secure haven to which teens can return while also granting increasing amounts of freedom. Conventional research purported that knowing where your kids are at all times is a key factor in preventing delinquent behavior. More nuanced research is discovering that the underlying key factor associated with healthy outcomes may actually be the willingness of adolescents to disclose information about their behavior based on their perception of their parents' understanding. In fact, too much monitoring can impede disclosure rather than encourage it.[77]

72. Kiesling and Sorell, "Joining Erikson and Identity Specialists."
73. Kiesling, Mucherera, and Gatobu, *Tri-Level Identity Crisis.*
74. Broderick and Blewitt, *Life Span*, 398.
75. Broderick and Blewitt, *Life Span*, 394.
76. Fay, "Are You a Helicopter, Drill Sergeant, or Consultant Parent?"
77. Broderick and Blewitt, *Life Span*, 398.

Other styles of parenting have been offered, making for playful presentations:

- Lawnmower (or curling) parents mow down (or sweep) a path by removing all obstacles or struggles for their teens.
- Tiger parents expect excellence in academics and carefully choose extracurricular activities to optimize a child's future.
- Elephant parents value emotional security and connection above achievement and stick close to their teens. They may even delay independent sleeping quarters during the childhood years.
- Dolphin parents seek collaboration, flexibility, and balance. Coined by author Shimi Kang, this style encourages POD—play/exploration + others + downtime for rest/exercise/sleep.[78]
- Free-range parents offer anything from freedom to walk to school or ride public transportation to wide-open play in the country on bicycles or motor bikes.
- Dry-clean parents drop off teens at youth group, exporting the task of faith formation and hoping that when they pick them up, they will have been cleaned and pressed into shape.

Though statistically parents remain the primary influencers of their teens' beliefs at least for several more years, family as an institution seems to be on a downward slide in the West in (1) the functions it serves for a society, (2) the social power it has to create a sense of obligation toward parental expectations, and (3) its power relative to other social institutions and influences.[79] Peer groups and online affinity groups become increasingly influential in the lives of adolescents for both good (e.g., mitigating stress, caring for the vulnerable, reengaging the de-churched) and ill (encouraging risky behavior, cyberbullying, regrettable affiliations).[80]

It is important to note that at the very time teens are experiencing the identity crisis of adolescence, their parents may be undergoing midlife crises and experiencing ruptures in their self-evaluations, with accompanying feelings of "powerlessness, rejection, and personal regret."[81] We will explore this is greater depth in a later chapter, but midlife often presents parents with the sobering realization that they have not arrived at the pinnacle of professional success they imagined for themselves at this stage of the life course. Parents may feel

78. Kang, The Dolphin Parent.
79. Popenoe, "American Family Decline."
80. Powell, "Can Social Distancing Reinvent Youth Ministry?"
81. Balswick and Balswick, Family, 157–69.

that their best years have passed and that the important roles they filled for their children are now being occupied by others. A double insecurity can be felt by middle-aged parents who are witnessing their teenage daughters and sons physically growing in beauty and strength at the same time their own bodies are sagging and showing signs of frailty.[82] As adolescents individuate and seek autonomy, parents can internalize the sense that they are being marginalized in the lives of their children as other mentors—such as teachers, coaches, and pastors—replace them as primary sources of wisdom and guidance.

For the adolescent, family structure deeply influences their development during these years. Enmeshed families have low thresholds for allowing teens to think differently. More differentiated families respect a teen's growing interiority, leading to freedom for independence. At optimum levels, families cultivate cherished, shared life experiences that foster visions for interdependence. In some family constellations, like the single-parent home, it is critical that teens feel "responsible to" the authority placed over them without feeling "responsible for" their parent's emotional well-being.[83] Quite often, parents bearing the wound of a divorce, carrying stressful work or familial anxiety, or feeling emotional vulnerability for a host of other reasons easily "parentify" their children. Roles become reversed, and the child carries the burden of the emotional well-being of the parent—serving as a confidant, becoming the family hero who carries the honor for the family, ensuring that nothing upsets the parent, or curtailing their own development to be present for the adult.

As teenagers individuate from their parents, peers become increasingly salient as coconstructors of identity. It is an interesting paradox that at the same time youth are attempting independence from parents, they become more dependent on peers.[84] Vivian Seltzer uses the term *frameworklessness* to signify the absence of clearly defined ways of behaving and thinking.[85] Lacking a framework leads adolescents to "feed off of the beliefs and actions of their peers," borrowing from others an identity they regard as glamorous.[86] Often the imitation of others through wisecracking, passing on advice without consideration of the context in which it was given, assuming a role of spiritual director or counselor with a friend, displaying a talent that is not yet refined, or delivering a movie line in the hope that it produces the same enchanted moment creates episodes of awkwardness and embarrassment. Yet, such acts likely serve as harbingers of movement toward greater wisdom and understanding.

82. Balswick and Balswick, *Family*, 157–69.
83. Balswick and Balswick, *Family*, 163–69.
84. Broderick and Blewitt, *Life Span*, 390–96.
85. Seltzer, *Psychosocial Worlds of the Adolescent*, 17–18.
86. Broderick and Blewitt, *Life Span*, 390–96.

In studying the influence of peers, scholars sometimes make a distinction between cliques—small, cohesive social groups of three to twelve people who share common interests and know each other well—and crowds, which are larger groups that include those not regarded as friends but who nonetheless give definition to one's identity via social location. A meta-analysis of crowd studies found that typical crowds tend to exist in most schools:

- elites: popular students and "preppies" distinguished by high social status
- athletes (or "jocks"): known for their affiliation with a particular sports team
- academics: those striving for good grades and sometimes regarded as socially awkward, known as "brains, nerds, or geeks"
- deviants: those marginalized from the school environment and regarded by others as "druggies or burnouts" for suspected use of contraband or engagement in at-risk behavior
- others: run-of-the-mill students who do not stand out in a particular way and hence get ignored as "normies or nobodies"[87]

Of great interest, but more difficult to research, is determining *how* one comes to belong to a particular group, especially since some teens belong to more than one group. Various theories suggest that affinity for a group may be a function of personality, shared interest like music, shared values like religious commitment, shared pain from divorce of one's parents or mental health challenges, types of groups available, or even the indirect ways parents manage teens' associations by affecting the accessibility of peers.[88]

As teenagers affiliate with peers, the values of youth pop culture often clash with the parental value system. Regardless of one's culture, when parents and adolescents agree that a particular issue is of moral consequence or involves safety, parental intervention is regarded as legitimate. Conflict is more likely to emerge when parents impose rules, seeing them as moral or conventional in nature when their teenage son or daughter regards them as personal.[89] Consider whether the following are moral/conventional issues needing parental monitoring and control or personal issues that should be left up to the young adult to decide: fashion and dress, use of social media, curfew, music, movies, youth group attendance, spending habits, sexuality and gender, friendships, hygiene, politics, work. Complicating this interpersonal space are trends showing that behaviors considered deviant in previous generations have increasingly become

87. Arnett and Jensen, *Human Development*, 371.
88. Broderick and Blewitt, *Life Span*, 392.
89. Broderick and Blewitt, *Life Span*, 394–97.

part of the experimental repertoire of teenage years—that is, same-sex attractions, use of previously banned substances, vaping, explicit and violent media, use of weapons, YouTube challenges, etc.[90] These can become explosive topics, and self-report data indicates that adolescents who perceive their parents as controlling, cold, and rejecting tend to tell more lies and conceal more information from their parents.[91] When parents subvert a teen's effort at psychological autonomy by invalidating feelings, constraining verbal expressions, becoming overly critical, physically or psychologically dominating, or withdrawing love, teens often feel resentment and withdraw.[92] A good place to start with teens who are acting out is to probe, What does this behavior serve in the functioning and perception of this adolescent? What is the pain that is leading to the compulsive behavior?

Yet, despite these many areas of conflict, meta-analysis of research suggests that the characterization of the teenage years as a time of major conflict—storm and stress with parents—has been overexaggerated.[93] Furthermore, research has consistently established that parental faith practices protect against both minor and more serious forms of delinquency.[94] A fascinating and far-reaching area of research is the exploration of how various cultures, particularly through rites of passage, have structured pathways toward adulthood with elders carrying the responsibility for directing the constructive use of adolescent energy and prosocial interactions. Richard Rohr contends that men will inevitably abuse power unless they are validated by older men, usually through a rite of initiation. Western culture sets young men, and often women, on frantic journeys devoid of opportunities to get in touch with what Rohr calls their "father hunger." Rohr created retreats that gave men space to learn vulnerability, where they could admit sadness, suffering and pain and so encourage the awakening of their inner worlds.[95] Women also need wisdom to transform their pain, but because they begin in most cultures from an inferior status, their pathway entails ascent and discovering inner strength.[96] In a book written with two colleagues titled

90. In contexts where high levels of individual freedom of expression are valued, some level of antisocial behavior can be regarded as adaptive in the way it promotes individuation and self-determination. An intriguing research question is to parse out whether any moderate forms of social deviancy can be regarded as reaching otherwise acceptable developmental outcomes.

91. Broderick and Blewitt, *Life Span*, 394.

92. Eating disorders can sometimes result from such family system dynamics. The family often misjudges anorexia as a problem with eating and tries to force the patient, usually a daughter, to eat more. This misguided attempt fails to realize that anorexia is most often more about maintaining control.

93. Balswick, King, and Reimer, *Reciprocating Self*, 167.

94. Regnerus, "Linked Lives, Faith, and Behavior."

95. Rohr, "Growing Up Men."

96. Rohr, *Men and Women*.

Tri-Level Identity Crisis, I present a chapter on rites of passage titled "ITAV Camps" (It Takes a Village). In this chapter, I detail work I largely inherited from my predecessor, Donald M. Joy, that takes a classic model of a rite of passage and from it creates a trail camp experience for initiating youth into adulthood. The chapter draws heavily from rites of passage practiced in various cultures and faith traditions. It distills critical elements that might allow us to recover a process that ascribes value to youth, transmits faith through creative ritual processes, instills a healthy understanding of what it means to be a man or woman, and initiates adolescents into having meaningful roles and status in our shared faith lives.[97]

In what many regarded as a landmark study crafted by the National Institute of American Values at the turn of the century, a group of thirty-three children's doctors, research scientists, and mental health and youth service professionals concluded that the rising rates of mental health and emotional distress occurring in youth could be attributed to the diminishment of "morally authoritative communities" in society.[98] These authors note that a misattribution often occurs in our work with adolescents—namely, that we far too often locate the problem within the individual instead of recognizing that the "identified patient" is the product of larger systemic deficiencies. The remedy sought is then too often pharmacological, using medicine to bring an adolescent's behavior into acceptable conformity. Although often helpful and necessary, the pharmacological solution can divert attention away from the broader familial and societal systems that have put teens at risk.

One place where science proves quite helpful is in program evaluations that help identify effective interventions. Several treatments that have been proven to be ineffective include (1) using scare tactics that sometimes curb immediate behavior but do not have effective long-term outcomes and may actually increase other vulnerabilities, (2) providing factual presentations (talking at youth) without providing the attendant support of skill building in real-life social contexts, and (3) segregating at-risk teens into punitive platforms (though sometimes separation of an aggressor is necessary).[99]

Helpful alternative approaches, as promoted in this book, are developmentally sensitive interventions that connect information and skills/practices to real-life social contexts and build toward broad-based communal support. This is represented well by the asset-building model promoted by Search Institute. Search identified forty positive supports and strengths every young person

97. Kiesling, Mucherera, and Gatobu, *Tri-Level Identity Crisis*, 123–39.
98. Commission on Children at Risk, *Hardwired to Connect*.
99. Broderick and Blewitt, *Life Span*, 422.

needs to succeed. About half of these assets are external supports needed from family, school, and community; the other half are internal competencies that need to be nurtured within youth. The asset model has both a diagnostic and a guide to help families and communities determine strengths and gaps in their care of adolescents. Similarly, peer mediation is showing some good results, as it, like good therapy, may provide "better than average" social support and a second family for troubled youth.[100]

CONCLUSION

In my early years of ministry, I had the privilege of serving with Sean Gladding, noted author of *The Story of God, the Story of Us* and other important texts. Sean shared with me a story that has been attributed to the Himba tribe of Namibia, where the mother of a newborn crafts a birth song to be sung whenever a child is born into the tribe. If the young person ever wanders so far off into the world that they lose touch with their identity, commit a crime, or are lured by the sirens of the world away from the childhood dreams that once resonated in their heart, the tribe will not shame the person but will simply sing over them the song about who they are.[101]

I began this chapter asking about the anchoring convictions we hope to plant in the hearts and minds of our adolescents before we launch them into the world. If we do this well, our parenting and ministry work provides an anchor that youth carry with them so that when the gales of culture blow the strongest and the winds of adversity threaten to blow them off course, teens will remember the songs we sang over them and find a way to drop anchor and avoid being lost at sea.

100. "Developmental Assets Framework."
101. The origin of the birth song has been hotly contested and even criticized as Western romanticization of African culture (see, e.g., Manduley, "The Real Origin of the African Birth Song"). Nevertheless, its value may be that it opens us to imagine a circle of restorative justice where "mercy triumphs over justice" (James 2:13).

5 | Young Adulthood
The Script to Narrate One's Life

My first appointment as a pastor after completing seminary was serving as director of two college campus ministries while pastoring a small congregation in rural Arkansas. To this day, I count the little church in the wildwood of Manchester, Arkansas, as my most enjoyable pastoral experience. The people in that church knew how to love and grow a pastor. My role directing the campus ministries was largely shaped by my own transformation as a student at the Texas Tech Wesley Foundation under the leadership of my lifelong friend and mentor, Steve Moore. Steve had created a program called Lunch and Last Lecture whereby professors, pastors, civic leaders, and other influential people in the community shared over a luncheon what they would say if this was their last lecture. Students were given a glimpse of the social visions and the values that governed the way these people lived their lives.

"James" was a student who episodically attended these luncheons. It was pretty evident in our informal conversations afterward as he was scuttling out the door that James's real interest was not in wrestling with the spiritual or philosophical meaning-of-life questions that were offered as low-hanging fruit in the table discussions. He was there for the hot meal that many United Methodist women's groups so often provided, often made with produce from their own gardens.

On one particular Monday, however, this all seemed to change. James found me before the meal and asked if we could talk afterward about this Christianity stuff. He reported that he was suddenly interested in finding out if the Christian faith "worked," and so I opened space that afternoon for further conversation. I asked James what had prompted his exploration. He explained that over the weekend he had gone with a friend to the marketing convention of a company

that operated much like a pyramid scheme. He was enamored with the testimonies of those who had acquired success through the selling of household products.
Many of them testified to their faith in God, who they believed had helped them
gain prosperity in their lives and secure a good life for their families. Connecting Jesus to this version of the American dream, James was enchanted with the
possibility that these testimonies offered a way out of his floundering academic
life. He wanted to figure out how he could make Christianity work for him.

James illustrates what this chapter seeks to convey. Developmentally young
adults acquire the ability to author their own lives, reconstructing their past and
imagining a future. Often this occurs by identifying with characters in social
media or seeing something favorable in someone they have met, and trying to
emulate characteristics and outcomes associated with their lives. Critical for
our consideration are the social visions offered to young adults and whether
the compass of their internal lives get pointed to true north.

Narrating One's Life

In chapter 3, we saw how Dan P. McAdams and Bradley D. Olson used social
science conceptualization to create a life span framework. The early layers of
this framework suggest the following:

- A constellation of dispositional traits evident in the early childhood years
  and governed primarily by genetics will remain relatively continuous
  throughout the life course (the big five personality traits).
- Around the period of middle childhood, adaptations come on board that
  add motivational, goal-directed behaviors to a child's growing competencies and interests.

A third layer is introduced in the young adult years:

- In young adulthood, a sociocognitive capacity emerges that helps a
  person narrate their own life story. This is the flowering of personality
  development.[1]

Around the 1980s, social psychologists in particular began developing personality theories that credited young adults with emergent capacities that enabled them to begin authoring their own lives. Gains in executive functioning,
moral reasoning, and hypothetical thinking, discussed in previous chapters,

---

1. McAdams and Olson, "Personality Development," 526–28.

endow a young adult with the capacity to see coherence between earlier events and their current sense of self, creating the gist of who they perceive themselves to be. At the same time, this sense of self is interacting in powerful ways with specific mores, expectations, and opportunities embedded in the particular location and time in which they live. Added to innate temperament traits and motivational adaptations is an evolving story about the self that the young adult begins to mull over internally as they strive for unity, purpose, and meaning.[2] According to Jeffrey J. Arnett, many of the students he interviewed experienced early adulthood as the first chance to reconstruct their past and imagine a future for themselves,[3] a task made probable when at least one person cares about and is not willing to give up on them.

In McAdam and Olson's theoretical framework, a person moves from actor to agent to author, appropriating resources along the way while working within social, political, ideological, and economic realities. Elements in the narrative of a person's life that influence their sense of what is within their reach may include the formative experiences of their family, how they have navigated gender and ethnic role expectations, personality characteristics, and a host of other adaptations.[4]

McAdams and Olson describe the identity process within an individual as akin to a storyteller drawing from the social visions made available to them. Characters from movies, books, and familial and social gatherings capture a young adult's imagination and consciously or unconsciously serve as main characters the young adult comes to see something of themselves in.[5] Intersecting plotlines develop as they interpret the milestone moments in their own journey. Inadvertently, the young adult is moved to emulate stories, hoping they might obtain a similar outcome of happiness, financial success, physical prowess, or status as these characters, regardless of how embellished their stories might be.[6] This was certainly the case with James, as Christianity became co-opted into a version of the American dream being used to solicit more sellers for a marketing scheme.

Narratives of Love

Robert J. Sternberg is probably best known for his theory of love triangles.[7] In this theory, love consists of three primary ingredients: intimacy, passion, and commitment. In the same manner that the outcome of a recipe can be changed

2. McAdams and Olson, "Personality Development," 526–29.
3. Arnett, *Emerging Adulthood*, 189–90.
4. McAdams and Olson, "Personality Development," 526–27.
5. McAdams and Olson, "Personality Development," 526–27.
6. Setran, "Living a Better Story in Emerging Adulthood," 71–74.
7. Sternberg, *Triangle of Love*.

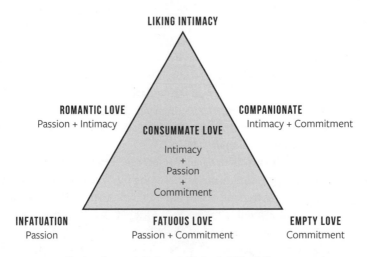

Based on a figure created by Lnesa. Public domain. Wikimedia Commons.

by altering the amount of certain ingredients, a relationship can be changed by altering the amount of each of these ingredients. A relationship of infatuation that is just budding is high in passion but low in commitment and intimacy. A relationship of companionship may be high in commitment and intimacy but low in passion. The various combinations of these ingredients reveal several types of love relationships. Figure 5.1 seeks to capture the possibilities. The names at the points of the triangle signify when a solo ingredient is high in a relationship; the sides capture relationships in which two ingredients are high. Only in the center of the triangle, with consummate love, are all three ingredients high. While this center love is ideal, it is difficult to attain and harder to sustain in the course of a committed relationship. When none of the ingredients are present, no love exists or the absence/death of a relationship may occur.[8]

Less known is the way Sternberg further developed his theory of love triangles to include a focus on love stories. Love stories seek to explain how we develop a personal sense of what or who we love based on the needs we have (e.g., to care for others or to be cared for, to be strong for another or to let them lead, to be socially engaged or to live quietly) and the stories we encounter in entertainment venues or by observing others. We may be highly conscious or largely unconscious of the story or stories that have come to influence how

8. For a succinct summary of Sternberg's eight kinds of love, see Broderick and Blewitt, *Life Span*, 527.

we think about what love is, how we interpret possible romantic encounters, and/or how we choose to act as we seek to influence relationship outcomes.[9] Yet, we can quickly get a sense of how powerfully a love story can shape a whole generation by recounting the popularity of such dramas as *Romeo and Juliet, Gone with the Wind, The Bridges of Madison County, Titanic, Beauty and the Beast*, and *The Notebook*. If we were to probe for more spiritual stories that have shaped Christians over the last few centuries, we could likewise name Sheldon Vanauken's *A Severe Mercy*, Mike Mason's *The Mystery of Marriage*, Walter Wangerin Jr.'s *As for Me and My House*, and C. S. Lewis's *A Grief Observed*. Sternberg seeks to raise our awareness of what stories may be influencing our perceptions, actions, and interpretations. His theory predicts that the greater the correspondence or complementariness between two people's love stories, the more likely they are to find happiness and satisfaction. Further, if a couple has tension in their relationship, identifying their independent love stories may help them determine how to write a love story together that blends and honors both of their intended outcomes. A couple of examples may prove helpful.

Daisy has internalized a house and home story from her childhood. She cherishes her childhood with parents who were highly involved in their children's lives. Weekends were spent doing things together as a family, including going to lunch with the grandparents after church on Sunday. Daisy's circle of friends is relatively small because most of her relational needs are met by her immediate family. Her ideal evening now involves the family quietly being together, sharing a meal and playing music. Daisy married Cash. Cash's vocational calling is to be a pastor, and his ideal love story is for his wife and children to be on mission, especially to those in need. Though he loves his family, he envisions Sunday as the best opportunity he has to be involved in the lives of his congregational members and those not yet reached for Christ. It is not uncommon for Cash to be the last one to leave the church building on Sunday, and quite frequently he is eager to visit further with people after finding out that morning what has been happening in their lives. Daisy finds herself often cajoling Cash to stay home and honor time with his family. She feels like she is in a tug-of-war with God over Cash, but whenever Cash does stay home, he feels anxious, as time that could be spent advancing God's kingdom on earth seems to be passing by.

Or consider Jalen, who in his love story resembles a police officer or coach. He wants his family and wife to be the very best they can be, and so he carefully

9. For a good treatment of Sternberg's love stories, see "Love Stories Influence Your Partner Choice." See also Sternberg, *Love Is a Story*.

monitors their appearance, how they speak, and the way they comport them-selves in public. Jalen married Taylor, whose love story is a version of being swept off her feet by a prince who loves her in the honor-bestowing way a knight would grace his princess. Taylor perceives Jalen's attempts to correct her speech or fix her appearance as deeply cutting and personal, tapping into deep suspicions that she never measures up to Jalen's high standards or to those of his family. Jalen contends that he is only trying to help her become even better than she already is.

Although there might be an infinite number of love stories, Sternberg identi-fied some of the most common:

- Art. One's partner is to be aesthetically beautiful, a work of art, lovely to behold.
- Autocratic. One partner controls the other.
- Business. A relationship is a strategic partnership that leads to increased wealth or power for everyone involved.
- Cookbook. Love needs to follow a certain recipe. Deviations from what is prescribed are unwelcome.
- Democratic. Partners act as equals.
- Fantasy. The valiant knight swoops in to save the princess, and they live happily ever after.
- Game. A relationship is played like a game or a sport.
- Gardening. A loving relationship requires upkeep and care, continual nurture and tending.
- Government. A relationship runs smoothly when it is well governed.
- History. The backstory of the relationship is the most salient aspect of how the love story is being written.
- Horror. You know you're in love with someone when you terrorize them or are terrorized by them.
- House and home. Home is where the heart is. Household maintenance, decorating, and nesting behaviors are important to a relationship.
- Humor. Love is funny and wacky.
- Mystery. Because love is mysterious, couples should remain mysterious to each other. Knowing each other too well diminishes romance.
- Police. It's important to monitor your partner's every move, ensuring they're not up to something untoward.
- Pornography. Love is carnal, and the aim is erotic satisfaction.

- Recovery. Love is helping each other recover from whatever trauma each has experienced.
- Religion. What love is and what it should look like are prescribed by religion.
- Sacrifice. To love someone is to make sacrifices for them.
- Science. Love is something that can be analyzed, dissected, understood, and guided.
- Student-teacher. Love is a relationship between a student and a teacher. One partner learns from the other.
- Theater. Love follows a script. There are lines, acts, and scenes that all unfold in a predictable manner. Lovers are playing roles.
- War. Just like Pat Benatar sang, love is a battlefield.[10]

Sternberg's theory is a useful way to identify the scripts that may be influencing a person's relationship, and it may provide a means of coauthoring a story that increases happiness when it is shared. To fashion this perspective as a discipleship question, however, we must ask, "What might it mean for our love lives to be narrated by the gospel story?" Volumes could be written and have been written in this regard, but here we can at least offer foundational plotlines and roles for the characters to play.

Craig R. Dykstra made the stunning observation years ago that "family is constituted by promises." Promises make family before family makes promises.[11] How is it that people become family? The most common way is through blood, yet many who share bloodlines hardly relate as family members. Conversely, how do those who don't share any biological heritage become family? Dykstra offers that it is through making promises—that is, taking vows. What links us together, whether we are biological kin or marital partners, is the promises we make and keep with one another. Why might this be the case? Because promises declare intentions. They state a mutual acceptance of responsibility for the other person's welfare, identity, and future. A promise declares to another person and to all those who witness the promise that I am now seeing you in a certain way and in a certain role and you are seeing me in a certain way and in a certain role. The covenant that God makes with Abraham to bless him so he can be a blessing to all nations (Gen. 12:1–3) suggests that making covenant with another indicates a unilateral commitment to bless—spiritually, emotionally, financially, sexually—and to extend this to all who are born from this union.[12] For those

10. This summary of Sternberg's twenty-six love stories is adapted from "26 Love Stories."
11. Dykstra, *Growing in the Life of Faith*, 98–99.
12. I gleaned this insight from reading von Rad's *Old Testament Theology*.

wanting to enact a Christian marriage, an ineffectual, namby-pamby sliding into a cohabiting relationship simply will not do. Critical to the plotline of Christian marriage is the public act of promise making before God and a community of those who pledge to support and uphold the union.[13] Lewis contends that it is not so much that we impose a promise on such an act of commitment but that implicit in the act or marriage itself is this commitment.[14] Lovers naturally commit themselves to each other. The act of intercourse likewise implies a promise to any potential offspring of that personal act. Permanence changes the nature of a relationship because it provides the attachment security whereby a person is most free to be fully vulnerable and fully known. Once we start withholding ourselves from another, the mutuality of blessing turns into a reciprocating feedback loop of holding back and restraint. To cite Dykstra, "It is promise-*making*, not promise-keeping, that constitutes the family. . . . As a matter of fact, the promises that constitute the family are difficult promises to keep, and we all continually fail at doing so. . . . What destroys families is the collapse of promise-*making*. It is when the very making of promises is no longer believed in that families die."[15]

A second critical element in authoring a Christian love story is implicit in the first: sacrificial love. "Husbands, love your wives, as Christ loved the church and gave himself up for her," writes Paul to the Ephesians (Eph. 5:25). Lewis, writing about this verse, states that a Christian marriage looks like a crucifixion.[16] Mike Mason was on his journey to becoming a Trappist monk when he fell in love. Already approaching age thirty, he likened himself to a densely populated city. If there was going to be any room for a spouse, demolition of what had been so carefully constructed would have to begin. Love asks all of ourselves, Mason discovered, and it keeps on asking. We become broken either at the place of love itself or at the place of the self. We are in a recurring Gethsemane, where we surrender to what love insists.[17]

One of the most common illusions about marriage, suggests Mason, is that it provides us a sanctuary, a haven against the harsh world, an oasis where one finds refreshment from the heat of the journey. This is illusory because it inclines us to think of home as a place where change and challenge are minimized, where the bruisings of the world are abated. Married life is expected to be a comfort station where a person can be lazy, selfish, and an ogre with those living next to them. Rather than thinking of marriage as a sanctuary, Mason contends, we

13. For an excellent treatment of this, see Stanley et al., "Sliding versus Deciding."
14. Lewis, *Mere Christianity*.
15. Dykstra, *Growing in the Life of Faith*, 100–101.
16. Lewis, *The Four Loves*, 105–6.
17. Mason, *Mystery of Marriage*, 14–16.

would be much better off if we thought of it as akin to a monastery—an entrance into the taking on of holy orders.[18] To think of marriage in this way is to regard marriage as a systematic and loving program that allows us to deliberately examine our own self-willfulness and be persistently reminded of our need for repentance and self-denial. In a monastery, through vows of chastity and poverty, one voluntarily pledges obedience to a superior and fidelity to a community. In marriage, through vows of self-sacrifice and faithfulness, two people voluntarily pledge obedience to the Lord and mutual submission to each other. People who succeed in narrating a Christian marriage are those who accept the conditions of this struggle—what Mason calls the "wild, audacious attempt at an almost impossible degree of cooperation between two powerful centers of self-assertion, . . . a crucible in which these two self-wills must be melted down and purified and made to conform. . . . One's own self cannot and must not emerge as the winner in this struggle."[19] What turns Christian marriage into something sacramental is the love that loves when the beloved can't give back.

Authoring a Christian love story may be nuanced in many different ways, but one more element that cannot be edited from the story line is shared mission. In the United Methodist liturgy, a marriage ceremony often ends with a sending forth of the couple with these words:

> Bear witness to the love of God in this world,
> so that those to whom love is a stranger
> will find in you generous friends.[20]

This signifies a centrifugal movement of marriage—a movement away from gazing at each other to facing outward. Adam and Eve are charged with sharing dominion over all creation as co-regents in Eden (Gen. 1:26–28). The marriage between Jesus and his bride the church is also grounded in the *missio Dei*. To be married is to find ways to be missional as a couple and eventually as a family.

Narratives of Work and Vocation

Sigmund Freud identified love and work as the two great themes of the adult life.[21] When I first encountered this observation, I turned to the moderate library I had accumulated during seminary and the first five years following and wondered how many books I had purchased that addressed these pervasive

18. Mason, *Mystery of Marriage*, 137–43.
19. Mason, *Mystery of Marriage*, 167.
20. Service of Christian Marriage I.
21. Broderick and Blewitt, *Life Span*, 462.

influencers in the adult life cycle. Truth be told, I could count the number that focused on a person's professional work life using my earlobes. No wonder I struggled to come up with an insightful message when my mother asked me to bless the opening of her new real estate office or when a parishioner honored me by asking if I might toast his graduation from medical school.

Though I was slow to think about what discipleship of one's work life looked like, Jesus was not. He learned the trade of carpentry from his father. Os Hillman notes that out of more than 130 episodes recorded in the New Testament of Jesus's life, over 90 percent occur in the marketplace. In addition, over 80 percent of his parables assume a market context.[22] A quick recall of Jesus's teaching reveals the pervasiveness of marketplace settings: the merchant who leaves tenants in charge while he travels abroad, fishermen discarding some fish and holding on to others, a sower casting seed, the overprivileging of pleasures in this life. Over and over, the kingdom of heaven is illustrated with stories of debts being forgiven, land being returned, or the poor receiving the good news. W. Jay Moon and Frederick J. Long comment that Jesus's teaching portrays a keen awareness of financial matters and the practice of managing resources well.[23] Jesus summons his twelve disciples not from the Roman centers of Socratic dialogue or the ecclesiastical centers of renown chief priests and elders but from the seaside and the tax office. This consciousness of Jesus of the marketplace suggests an influence in sectors of society that holds remarkable possibilities if reclaimed for Christendom today.

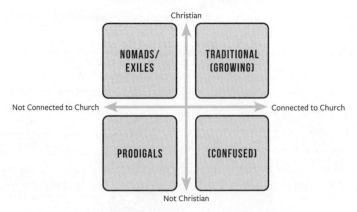

FIGURE 5.2
KINNAMAN'S YOUNG ADULT CATEGORIES

Based on a description in Kinnaman and Hawkins, *You Lost Me*.

22. Hillman, *9 to 5 Window*, 23.
23. Moon and Long, *Entrepreneurial Church Planting*, 37–45, 65–66.

Using the work of David Kinnaman in *You Lost Me*, I developed a schema to describe young adults based on two dimensions: an x-axis signifies how connected they feel to church—a dimension of belonging to a faith community—and a y-axis signifies whether they still regard themselves as Christian. As with many social science models, these dimensions yield a four-quadrant design (see fig. 5.2).

Traditionals are active Christians who are growing in their faith.

Prodigals are those who have left the church and left the faith altogether.

The confused are those who are uncertain of why they are alive.

Nomads/exiles are those who no longer affiliate with a church but who still see themselves as Christian. Kinnaman further divides this category:

- ○ Nomads are those whose faith has faded, who see the church as optional, and who are exploring (perhaps these fit the newer designation of deconstructing faith).
- ○ Exiles are those who are still committed to the faith but whose primary domain is now located outside the Christian community.[24]

This model becomes especially interesting when thinking about narrating vocation. Reading a bit perhaps into Kinnaman, this model seems to suggest that just like persecution dispersed Christians away from Jerusalem and into the rest of the world in something like a forced fulfillment of the Great Commission, the current ecclesial malaise may be akin to a new diaspora whereby Christians are immersed in work roles in almost every sector of society. If they are awakened through something like marketplace evangelism and discipleship, a new harvest could result.

What many experts of modern work culture have observed is that today's young adults, more so than previous generations, seek to find purpose primarily through their vocational roles, regarding what they do professionally as an extension of their identity, values, and beliefs. So how do we think about and support narrating a vocation, narrating for and with young adults how their work lives steward God's giftings in them and afford them unique places for mission?

The most popular approach to career counseling from the social sciences begins by taking into account a person's personality characteristics and then matches them to the characteristics of a work environment. John Holland's model, for example, classifies six ways a person interacts with social and

---

24. Kinnaman and Hawkins, *You Lost Me*.

FIGURE 5.3
HOLLAND'S THEORY OF VOCATIONAL DEVELOPMENT

environmental tasks.[25] Figure 5.3 shows six types of work environments clas-
sified according to personality attributes such as interests, attitudes, beliefs,
abilities, and values. Once a person's temperament is discerned, it is used to
predict the kind of job environments in which that person is likely to meet
with success, stability, and satisfaction. Holland's approach aims to bring high
congruence between a person's own expression of personality and the environment in which they work. The shades on the chart suggest that a person works
best with others who are of the same type or a complementary type closest
to them. For example, artistic types are likely to find the most satisfaction in
a work culture with other artistic types, but they may bristle if placed in an

25. Holland, *Making Vocational Choices*. For a succinct discussion of Holland's theory, see
Arnett and Jensen, *Human Development*, 470.

environment that insists on the conventional. Within each domain are career clusters that allow the noted attitudes and values to be expressed.

A similar assessment is CliftonStrengths. This assessment claims to measure one's "natural patterns of thinking, feeling and behaving."[26] Marketed more as a way to discover one's strengths, unlock potential, and aid in building effective teams, CliftonStrengths represents another way of shaping the work story of a person's life.

More grounded in biblical categories are spiritual gift inventories, based on passages such as Romans 12, 1 Corinthians 12, Ephesians 4, and 1 Peter 4, that help believers discern what Spirit-bestowed endowment they may have that equips them to contribute to the building up of the body of Christ. Spiritual gifts move beyond natural giftings to extraordinary divine enablement. Spiritual gifts are not always directly related to one's professional work role, but they often can be.

Clearly, there are more factors to consider than a simple inventory when determining a vocational choice. Guides that accompany these inventories will often direct a person to both subjective confirmation (the Spirit's witness within of what the inventory reveals) and objective confirmation by a community or others (the bearing of fruit when the gift is employed).

A second reality of modern work culture, inflated by the pandemic, is the likelihood of multiple changes to one's work role through the adult life stages. First, this is quite different from previous generations, whose members often stayed with a work role and a particular organization for much of their vocational lives. Second, it suggests that work for a lifetime is less and less the by-product of an education curriculum or at least that lifelong learning may be necessary. Third, vocation may become more of a process than a destination where one feels they can put down roots.

A good complementary theory to Holland's focus on personality that might find resonance in this new vocational landscape is Donald Super's Developmental Self-Concept theory.[27] Super's theory regards vocation not as a static point in time but as an ongoing process keyed to the development of one's self-concept. Just as the self evolves over time, so will social learning, personality, needs, values, and abilities. Super uses five stages in his model (see fig. 5.4). However, he acknowledges that movement through the rainbow is not always linear and that one can go through mini- or maxi-cycles that repeat stages of exploration, establishment, and maintenance. The common pattern, however, is that as one's

26. "Learn How the CliftonStrengths Assessment Works."
27. Super, "A Life-Span, Life-Space Approach." Super's model is presented in a concise way in Arnett and Jensen, *Human Development*, 469.

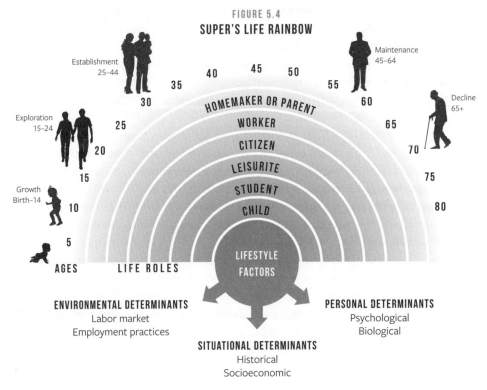

FIGURE 5.4
SUPER'S LIFE RAINBOW

Based on a figure from Super, "A Life-Span, Life-Space Approach."

self-concept becomes more realistic and stable, so will one's vocational choice and behavior. Hence, Super's theory provides an avenue for realizing that crisis points in the vocational journey offer opportunity for further self-authorship in an ongoing refinement of vocational discernment.

Still, there are challenges to the sanctification and meaning of work today. David F. White, in *Practicing Discernment with Youth*, focuses on the challenge of orienting adolescents to work roles that are aimed at something more than just making money.

> Embedded in the media of our technological and commercial culture are mes-
> sages that anything of value can be bought, must be sensational, can be done
> alone, must be simple to understand, requires little effort, involves immedi-
> ate gratification, and does not have a history that began before her or extends
> beyond her in space and time. Furthermore, industrial factory work focuses
> the attention of workers on wages, distracting them from the common good of
> the community, from creativity or the intrinsic value of work. Modern adult

work has become identified with alienation from our most creative, caring, and responsible selves.[28]

White observes that today's young are relegated to schools and media-driven peer culture that largely disconnect them from adult guidance and from concern for the common good. The cultural pressure to succeed also leads to a lack of participation in a faith community, resulting in a subtle shift from love of God and neighbor to love of or desire for something else. Entertainment sound bites create a habit of inattention and shape cultures with the "expectation of titillation."[29] Churches capitulate with a simplistic gospel as an easily consumable product so that the whole of the Christian life comes to be ascertained as attainable in full once a person prays the sinner's prayer. This may not be too far away from the precaution Miroslav Volf issued, warning that evil is capable of generating ideational environments in which it can thrive unrecognized.[30]

By contrast, the book of Proverbs summons young adults to wisdom that pertains to a sense of order, regularity, and recurrence and is gained through prolonged engagement with and awareness of the world via reasoning and meaning making. Walter Brueggemann contends that this requires the cultivation of habits of the heart around such things as "fascination, imagination, patience, attentiveness to detail, and observation of the regularities that seem to govern."[31]

White's proposal is for educational and ecclesial communities to bring the experiences of woundedness in the world into educational and ecclesial settings. With adult care and guidance, active experiments with physical, political, and social problems can tap into innate curiosity, critical thought, and creativity that foster a habitus for loving God and loving neighbor through work roles. White sees such acts as crafting not a culture of passive consumers but vocations oriented toward the common good.[32]

Reconnecting this to narrative, White maintains that when we fail to orient young people to an alternate story, we relegate them to a culture that tells its own story. Leaning on Brueggemann, White regards community as preceding the individual.[33] Critical is the telling and retelling of foundational stories through preaching, teaching, testimony, and ritual that capture God's mission in the world and invite people into it. The power comes, suggests White, when a young person can envision themselves as part of a movement of God stretching

28. White, *Practicing Discernment with Youth*, 178.
29. Mahan, Warren, and White, *Awakening Youth Discipleship*, 32.
30. Volf, *Exclusion and Embrace*, 12.
31. Brueggemann, *The Prophetic Imagination*, 72.
32. White, *Practicing Discernment with Youth*, vii–xii.
33. White, *Practicing Discernment with Youth*, 144.

back to creation's beginning and into a future in which all creation finds fulfillment in God's redemption. The best curriculum for forming young adults in
these vocational pathways involves seeing and experiencing the mission/story
of God unfolding in the corporate life of a vital faith community.

The seminary where I teach is located near historic Shakertown in Har-
rodsburg, Kentucky. The history of the Shakers is a fascinating theological
excursion into one utopian society that eschewed procreation, worshiped for a
time with choreographed dancing, and was sustained by agricultural practices.
The American leader of the Shaker movement was Ann Lee, who is credited
with coining the phrase "hands to work and hearts to God." The phrase signified a vocational spirit that permeated all of life in the Shaker community. It
is evident in their practice of hospitality and in the craftsmanship that gave
shape to all the community created. A Shaker table, for example (see fig. 5.5),
is easily distinguishable by its simplicity, sturdiness, and utility—all of which
were values of the Shakers, signified as well in their style of dress, speech, and
manner of community.

Sarah Archer was particularly intrigued by the phrase "hands to work and
hearts to God" and the connection it has to "craft" as a way of thinking about
work, contrasted with the commodities we manufacture today that are focused
primarily on securing profit margins. By "craft," Archer wants us to see what
emerges from and connects us with generations of skill and knowledge. Craft
gives shape to objects that reflect the culture and community from which they
come.[34] What does vocation look like when it is similarly formed by immersion
in the gospel story, when its values are embedded in faith communities,
and when it is shaped by continuity with intergenerational wisdom?

I was once invited into a Wabash Center colloquium for midcareer
faculty that had us adopt a craft as a hobby and then reflect on how our
teaching might change if we thought of it as craft. I chose the art of wood-
working, as there was a craftsman of wood in the first congregation I
served who caught my imagination in the toys and furniture he produced for underprivileged kids and friends in
the community. In my reflections through that colloquium, I kept coming back

National Gallery of Art. Wikimedia Commons.

Figure 5.5. Rich Winslow, *Shaker Table*, 1937

34. Archer, "Hands to Work."

to the contrast between the macro institutional pressures a teacher faces to optimize class size, manage multiple delivery systems, and offer resources universal
enough that students of many different stripes can access them and the micro
approach of the craftsman, whose aim is not mass production but using cultivated
skills to produce a single, unique work of art never intended to be replicated.

Thinking about craft and community may be one pathway of reclaiming the
value of work, but this may also be easier for those who work with their hands.
Are there other things we might glean from church history about the sanctification of work and the shaping of vocational narratives?

The early catechumenate reveals that candidates for baptism were scrutinized
and that some were turned away if their profession failed to signify a Christian
life. Newcomers to faith were taught lifestyle practices that shaped what they
did in their work in addition to being taught what to believe.

Christopher A. Hall finds ancient wisdom in the teachings of Gregory of
Nyssa, who issued caution that distraction is our fundamental human problem,
stopping us from seeing what is of eternal value.[35] Sounding remarkably contemporary, Gregory observed that in the routinization of our days, we let the
urgent overtake the important. The particular temptation of the tradesman was
the tendency to placate anxiety via competitive marketing—that is, displaying
wares before others could get to customers. It is not hard to draw parallels in our
digital age to the frequent checking of the market, strategies to upstage competi-
tion, and FOMO tendencies that drive the marketplace. Gregory recognized
that in our perpetual surrender to urgent tasks, we become increasingly vulnerable to cultural idols. The way to break this compulsion, Gregory thought, was
through the simple act of having prayer that preceded work so that the tasks
of work and the values of the marketplace did not supersede what God firmly
established in the heart during the time of prayer.[36] Justin Whitmel Earley, in
The Common Rule: Habits of Purpose for an Age of Distraction, contemporizes this
practice in the simple habit of kneeling in prayer before checking one's phone.
Earley realized that when the first thing he did in the morning was check his cell
phone, he surrendered the start of a day to others' agendas, and he immediately
felt the rush and anxiety to meet their expectations. By posturing his body in
prayer and naming with words what is desired for the day, Earley joins God
in an act of creation that sets the emotional and spiritual contours of his day.[37]
The ancients knew this regularity of prayer would be difficult to sustain, and so
they prescribed short breath prayers that could be embedded in liturgy but then
practiced throughout one's daily affairs to help one sustain spiritual attention.

35. Hall, *Worshiping with the Church Fathers*, 146–47.
36. Hall, *Worshiping with the Church Fathers*, 143–72.
37. Earley, *Common Rule*, 34–41.

The most commonly cited prayer was Psalm 70:1, a prayer that appears in the Anglican practice of daily prayer: "O God, make speed to save us; O Lord, make haste to help us."[38] Short prayers prayed repeatedly throughout the day, as if in a single breath, even at the beginning or in the midst of conducting a business meeting, can order the heart so that God is not sidelined by our self-absorption.

John Cassian offered criteria for testing thoughts to determine whether they move a person toward good or evil, criteria that we can use to search the heart in our professional enterprises.

Is the thought filled with what is good for all?

Is it heavy with the fear of God?

Is it and the feelings that underlie it genuine?

Is it aimed at human show or prized for being novel rather than grounded in truth?

Has the burden of fame or glory lessened its merits or diminished its luster?[39]

From my own faith tradition, I could add John Wesley's dictum, "Gain all you can, save all you can, give away all you can," a summons to stewardship of one's possessions with a concern for the poor.[40] Wesley recognized the persistent threat wealth posed to the vitality of Christianity, and hence the third piece of his counsel was especially important. Usually interpreted as a directive toward personal stewardship, if generalized, it would have important implications for larger economic enterprises. "The directions which God has given us, touching the use of our worldly substance, may be comprised in the following particulars. . . . First, provide things needful for yourself. . . . Secondly, provide these for your wife, your children, your servants, or any others who pertain to your household. If when this is done there be an overplus left, then 'do good to them that are of the household of faith.' If there be an overplus still, 'as you have opportunity, do good unto all men.'"[41]

The Process Model

In the sections above, I tried to offer important theological plotlines to help young adults disentangle from cultural scripts and fashion lives more attuned to

38. See, e.g., the opening prayer for the daily office: https://www.dailyoffice2019.com/.
39. Cassian, *John Cassian.*
40. This dictum summarizes Wesley's sermon "The Use of Money."
41. Wesley, "The Use of Money."

the gospel story, especially in regard to the two largest themes of the adult life according to Freud, love and work. In this section, I want to enlarge narrative perspectives to address the prevalence of mental health issues. McAdams and his colleagues are keen on contrasting redemption narratives with contamination narratives.[42] In their simplest form, redemption narratives move from negative to positive, whereas contamination narratives move from positive to negative. An example of a redemption narrative might be a young adult who grew up with a shattered home life or who lived in abject poverty but who, upon leaving the home, found a footing in college and set their trajectory on a healthy life course. An example of a contamination narrative might be a young adult who earned good scholarship money, but the campus party scene led to a toxic relationship that dominated the narrative of their college years. Here I want to attempt to deepen and broaden an understanding of how young adults can forfeit the capacity to author their own lives or become captive to things that are self-destructive, or, conversely, how they can find traction in authoring pathways to freedom and thriving.

Texas Tech University was one of the first colleges to offer a full addiction recovery program in its curriculum. Instrumental in its development were Carl Anderson and Kitty Harris. Harris developed a process model of addiction that illuminates how many young adults get caught in the contaminative processes of what we have been describing but also illustrates a redemptive way out.[43]

Many authors in recent decades, including myself, have addressed the many transitions, new experiences, performance expectations, plurality of choices, and developmental tasks that are now pressing on emerging adults. The result is that pain and distress of some kind are inevitable in the young adult years. Pain serves as the pinnacle of the Harris model. It is an inclusive word that captures many of the phenomena increasingly prevalent at this life stage: spikes in anxiety; mental health crises of fear, depression, and loneliness; increases in suicide and suicidal ideation; and comorbidities, relational woundedness, or neglect from the family.

The process model begins by recognizing that every young adult experiences some growth or nonnormative pain by virtue of the life stage they are in. Critical is the behavioral response a young adult chooses to alleviate this pain and the consequential results that follow (see fig. 5.6 and follow the central column downward).

Moving to the left column of the model, we see that some choose a compulsive behavior to diminish or mask or escape or run from the pain or woundedness.

42. McAdams et al., "When Bad Things Turn Good."
43. Harris, Jordan, and Wilkes, "Relapse Resilience."

FIGURE 5.6
HARRIS PROCESS MODEL

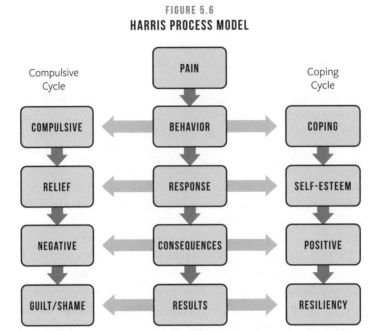

Smock, Froerer, and Blakeslee, "Systemic Interventions in Substance-Abuse Treatment."

Hence, a depressed woman turns to binge eating comfort food; a man fears he is not worthy of love and so turns to pornography; a student feels numb and engages in at-risk behavior to feel a buzz; a marginalized and floundering young adult fears they cannot succeed through conventional means and so turns to delinquent behavior to find a semblance of respect. Quite often, this compulsive behavior works. It alleviates the pain and provides the sought-after relief, at least in the short term (see the next box in the left column). Yet, accompanying the relief are often negative consequences. Binge eating increases one's appetite in the future and leads to poor health outcomes; pornography diminishes the capacity for healthy relationships; stronger and more frequent hits of alcohol or drugs are needed to alleviate the pain; running from fear becomes a pattern of avoidance, disrupting healthy functioning. Internally, self-respect begins to diminish; guilt is felt for what has been done to others or for responsibilities neglected; a pervasive sense of shame that one is deeply flawed results. Furthermore, the pain that started the whole cycle is never resolved; it is simply masked. Now there are more negative emotions to contend with. The buzz from the compulsive behavior left a trace on the neurobiology of the brain that now reminds the anxious person where to find relief . . . back in the compulsive behavior. Soon the behavior becomes a repetitive cycle, trapping the despairing person in an addictive cycle.

Moving to the right column of the chart, we see that pain and woundedness can alternatively be managed by choosing a coping behavior. A person can begin by developing emotional literacy and becoming mindful of what is causing their distress. Then they can choose behaviors that are on a trajectory to boost their self-esteem rather than diminish it through sudden but temporary relief. In common therapeutic practice, mindfulness techniques, meditation, exercise, yoga, practicing mental hygiene, learning gratitude, developing social support, prayer, turning outward toward others, and staying busy have all been found to have positive consequences. These behaviors all correlate with higher self-esteem and are ways to increase self-control and confidence so a person can avoid the undertow of compulsive behavior when and if the negative emotions return.

A number of theological concepts operate beneath this model. For example, Clement, one of the early church fathers, regarded humans in their fallen state as a conglomerate of obsessive emotions, attitudes, and desires, much in the way we talk about psychological complexes today.[44] Appetites and desires that were created to guide the person in healthy ways become distorted by the fall. We become tone-deaf to all that we should care about, and with inordinate desires or disordered loves, we misread reality and invest energy in the wrong things. The very nature of sin is toward excess. In our natural state, thought the ancients, we are a runaway train—unbridled and out of control. Our tendency in this state is to let what should be secondary and hence more marginal move to the center of our lives. As Anders Nygren describes, the human psyche can organize itself around a particular fundamental motif[45]—for example, the saint centers life on agape or sacrificial love, while the pornography addict centers life around erotic fantasy. Needed are graced ways of gaining discipline over our speech, appetites, and possessions.

Further, Augustinian theology portrays a grave reorientation that occurred as a result of the fall.[46]

In creation: Our *reason* could direct our *will*, which then had the capacity to regulate our *desire*.

$$\text{Reason} \rightarrow \text{Will} \rightarrow \text{Desire}$$

44. Hall, *Living Wisely with the Church Fathers*, 138.
45. Nygren, *Agape and Eros*, 53–60.
46. This portrayal of Augustine's theology is well summarized by Krause, "Augustine: On the Fall of Man, Part 1."

Freedom is the experience of desire being governed by the will. The will, subject to revealed truth, reasons toward rational choices in alignment with divine prerogative. As Jesus said "If you abide in my word, you are truly my disciples, and you will know the truth, and the truth will set you free" (John 8:31–32). (Note the correlation this has to the coping cycle of choosing behaviors that build self-esteem by regulating self-gratification and building resilience.)

After the fall: Our *desire* comes to direct our *will*, which rationalizes behavior via *reason*.

$$\text{Desire} \rightarrow \text{Will} \rightarrow \text{Reason}$$

Here we find ourselves in bondage to appetitive desire because our will is held captive, making even our best intentions and decision-making subject to its persuasions. Augustine wrote of the *libido dominandi*, a lust for domination whereby lower appetites become irresistible without the restraint of a social structure and the operations of grace that enable the will to be re-mastered.[47] (This condition bears strong resemblance to the compulsive cycle in which indulgent behavior is rationalized because it brings relief or release to desire.)

Finally, more contemporary ethicists and practical theologians are finding inspiration in Alasdair MacIntyre and his recovery of Aristotle's theory of virtue and character.[48] This view purports that virtue (e.g., excellence in courage or knowledge) is gained through participation in spiritual practices such as the communal telling of stories whereby internalization of the moral vision held by particular communities is inculcated. In the same way that the process model shows how to overcome pain and anxiety and break compulsivity through choosing coping behaviors with the help of a supportive community, this theological framework suggests that by corporately engaging in formative practices as means toward an ultimate shared good, one can gradually shed old dispositions and acquire a second nature.

The process model may also prove helpful in illuminating why common strategies of families, educational intuitions, and legislative bodies often become unfruitful if not counterproductive. Quite often, the focus is directed toward the aberrant behavior instead of toward the pain. Hence, a parent will attempt to manage the behavior of a young adult by increasing pressure to conform (intervention of negative consequences) rather than by asking, "Where does

47. See "Augustine."
48. MacIntyre, *After Virtue.*

it hurt?" or "What is causing you pain and anxiety?" Educational institutions will try to remedy a student's failing grades through mandatory study periods or remediation that never addresses why the student is floundering, only making the negative self-attributions driving the cycle worsen. Politicians, assuming that fear of consequences serves as a deterrent, want to be "hard on crime," but their actions rarely address the issues that give rise to the delinquent behavior.

Though not made explicit in the model, the process model, like the twelve steps of Alcoholics Anonymous, operates best within a spiritually focused, and better than average, community. Carl Anderson said to me at one point that he had never met a person whose addiction was not rooted in spiritual abuse or neglect. I asked him to elaborate further, and what I understood him to say was that often-flawed images of God created by harsh, judgmental, or vindictive spiritual authority figures can scramble or desecrate one's spiritual belief system, or one can simply be ignorant or indifferent to spiritual life. When this spiritual bypass occurs, something counterfeit often occupies the central priorities of a person's life. Critical then for recovery is spiritual enablement that comes about by reconnecting with God or, in the language of twelve-step programs, surrendering to a "power greater than ourselves."[49]

The process model shows one pathway toward transforming one's life by turning away from compulsivity to mitigate pain and anxiety and turning toward coping behaviors that lead to prosocial outcomes such as resiliency. Hence, a young adult begins to author a redemption narrative for their life.

Narrating the Broader Christian Journey

In this chapter, I focused on two grand themes that are dominant in the young adult years of the life course, but there are numerous other facets of Christian identity that can be shaped through story. Traditional means whereby God's mission to the world is told include preaching, teaching, worship, fellowship, and acts of service. But unconventional means are also being used, such as poetry slams, hip-hop, rap, comedy, museum presentations, and other artistic expressions. These platforms allow artists to tell the journey of Abraham as God covenants with him and summons him to walk before God and be blameless; to recount the tale of Esther, her providential placement in a royal court, and her plea that saves her people; to capture David's confidence that God would deliver a giant warrior into his hand; to imagine Mary as a handmaiden surrendering her womb for God's arrival in human flesh.

49. Alcoholics Anonymous, "The Twelve Steps."

Through such means we learn God's character of longsuffering, mercy, and justice. Identifying with these characters and hearing God's invitations, promises, and commands allows him to speak into our lives and shape them by the continually unfolding story of God. Christian authors have made the metanarrative and stories of Scripture accessible through *The Chosen* drama series, Sean Gladding's *The Story of God, the Story of Us*, Joshua McNall's *Long Story Short: The Bible in Six Short Movements*, Zondervan's *The Story: The Bible as One Continuing Story of God and His People*, and Eugene Peterson's *The Message: The Bible in Contemporary Language*.

The power of story is that it forms us in meaningful ways. Our centers of learning are commonly built on cognitive models that end with an accumulation of information devoid of life transformation, or on competency-based learning that teaches skills but may not form the inclination to practice what is learned. More difficult but more formational is the reformation of desire, persuading a person to act in a different manner. This may come about most profoundly when people begin to enact a different story for their lives.[50]

CONCLUSION

James K. A. Smith's work with cultural liturgies has given us avenues for discerning how sometimes hidden scripts are so embedded in the activities we engage in every day that we may not really love what we thought we loved or portend to love.[51] For example, the frequent utilization of our smartphones dozens of times a day with thousands of touches, regardless of the content we are appropriating, forms in us the expectation that we can manipulate the world to meet whatever desire or curiosity we have.[52] If we find something distasteful, we can easily discard it and swipe to a different screen that presents a reality more amenable to our current disposition. Notice how contrary this might be to a spiritual discipline, through which a person seeks to conform their life more and more to a truth that is being revealed.

Christian Smith and company, in describing the dark side of emerging adulthood, document the rampant practice of binge drinking, defined as having five or more drinks within a few hours, on college campuses. We might ask what

---

50. I learned this insight from David Setran, who draws on Nicholas Wolterstorff's distinction between cognitive learning, ability learning, and tendency learning. See Setran, "Living a Better Story in Emerging Adulthood."

51. J. K. A. Smith, *You Are What You Love*, 27–38.

52. J. K. A. Smith, "You Are What You Love: Genesis 1:1–2:4."

compels someone to relinquish their will, cause harm to their body, and make themselves susceptible to risky or deviant behavior. Smith and his team found that quite frequently young adults' rationale for binge drinking comes down to being socialized into a cultural script that in essence admits that "we do exactly what we were told to do."[53] They were following the social script that culture indicated was the norm for emerging adults. They were performing the role that was expected of them once they emerged on the young adult stage of life. Smith's broadest analysis of the religious and spiritual lives of emerging adults can be found in *Souls in Transition*. He concludes his analysis there in a way that is only fitting to close this chapter as well:

> If emerging adults want in fact to pursue lives that are genuinely free and self-directed in ways that are worthy of their commitment and devotion, they will have to come to terms with many of the larger social and cultural forces to which their lives are now subject that do not obviously serve that end. They will have to exercise understanding and agency in ways that do not simply reproduce but rather challenge some of the more problematic aspects of emerging adult culture and life. . . . If anyone in the future is ever to know what is really good, right, and true, the challenges of the crisis of knowledge and value that beset American public culture today, described earlier, must be addressed, in order to learn more justifiably surefooted ways to understand reality and the moral good. Lacking that, American culture has little to pass on to American youth with which they can navigate life beyond their experiences of their own subjective desires and feelings—on which alone it is not possible to build good lives.[54]

The Psalter is the prayer book of ancient Israel. Over and over, the Psalms tell Israel's story to new generations, reminding them that they are people of the covenant, a nation chosen to be God's own people, blessed to be a blessing. The challenge for young adults is akin to the challenge of Isaac. Isaac is not the founder of the nation—the one who witnessed a burning torch pass through the splayed carcasses of animals to establish a covenant (Gen. 15), the one who was taken to witness the destruction of Sodom and Gomorrah (18:17–33), the one visited by three men who made the most improbable of birth promises (18:1–16). Isaac comes to young adulthood with some pretty peculiar stories vying to define his existence. He has a father who is as old as the hills (21:5), a name that people literally laugh at on account of his mother (21:1–7), an older brother who is trying to figure out his own peculiar blessing story (17:19–20), the excruciating conundrum of a place in Moriah called "the LORD will provide"

---

53. C. Smith et al., *Lost in Transition*, 142.
54. C. Smith and Snell, *Souls in Transition*, 298–99.

(22:14), and a trusted servant of his father who shows up with a woman to be his wife (Gen. 24). Yet, as Isaac finds deeper and deeper identification with these stories, the Lord speaks through them to Isaac the very same life-defining covenant promises made to the founder (26:3). Isaac then begins to author his own story with God. He takes Rebekah and loves her (24:67). He sows and reaps in the land of Gerar (26:6, 12). He digs his own wells (26:17–22), and in it all he prospers (26:13, 22).

6 | Middle Adulthood
Finding Practices Sufficient to Sustain

In a seminary class titled Young and Middle Adult Development and Discipleship, I invite students to create two columns, one for young adulthood and one for middle adulthood, and then to post words or phrases that characterize for them what each of these life stages is like. Some inevitably self-identify as fitting in both categories. Some resist pejorative labels for their age cohort, and others are eager to tell it like it is. Here is a sampling from three female students enrolled in the class online.[1] You can likely detect which category they put themselves in.

Young Adulthood	Middle Adulthood
confused	grounded
short-sighted	seeing a bigger picture
judgmental	graceful
less responsible	more responsible
self-focused	focused on family/others
daring and stronger	reserved and breakable
energetic	slower moving
sharp (snappy)	brain fogged
limited opinion	freer and better able to see the importance/ beauty of things/issues/precious moments
finding purpose	living out purpose
expectancy	consistency
gaining financial independence	financial stability

1. My gratitude to Abby Salazar, Kerri Bigler, and Luann Bigler for these contributions.

Young Adulthood	Middle Adulthood
building a family	caring for family (both children and parents)
acquire more	give more physically, gain strength/beauty, physical maintenance
focus on being successful	focus on being content
ignorance	wisdom
physical beauty	intellectual beauty
searching for a place to belong	established roots (grounded)
passionate about many things	understand what matters and what does not

Many things are striking about these lists. First is the underlying confirmation that middle adulthood unmistakably differs from young adulthood. Richard Rohr, for example, in *Falling Upward*, implies that the spirituality of the second half of life is distinct from the spirituality of the first half of life.[2] Men begin with an upward ascent, needing to feel a sense of power and a sense of their goodness in the first half of life, but then they need to learn a humility for the second half of life.[3] By contrast, women in most parts of the world start in an inferior position, with descent as the dominant feature of their lives. The important turn for them is a turn toward ascent and discovering their own strength.[4] Second is the many different elements these students came up with in their lists, suggesting that adulthood may not unfold in a linear, continuous direction but may instead involve multiple crises and many turning points.[5] (One might also observe that in Erik H. Erikson's theory, middle adulthood is the longest stage in the life course, so there may be more years to allow such variety.)[6] Closely related is a third observation—that this variety of answers correlates with what some social pundits have pointed to: there is growing pluriformity in the life course and an increased freedom to act on individual propensities beyond strict adherence to social expectations.[7] With an increased freedom to author your own life and the societal mandate to become your own person, it follows that mapping the middle years is complicated. Further, if individuation expands throughout the adult stages of life, then subjective perception, interpretation of experiences, and how one responds to experiences all seem particularly germane to the integrity of the life cycle.

2. Rohr, *Falling Upward*, vii–xviii.
3. See the diagram that depicts this in Rohr and Martos, *Wild Man's Journey*, xxxiv–xxxv.
4. Rohr, *Men and Women*.
5. Schweitzer, *Postmodern Life Cycle*, 86.
6. See, e.g., McLeod, "Erik Erikson's Stages of Psychosocial Development."
7. Schweitzer, *Postmodern Life Cycle*, 16–17.

Characterizing Middle Adulthood

In comparison with other life stages, the boundaries of middle adulthood are more difficult to define: "When does middle adulthood begin, and how do I know when I am there?" In traditional developmental theories, little development was expected beyond adolescence and young adulthood (e.g., Jean Piaget's cognitive theory ends with formal operational thought emerging in young adulthood).[8] In many cultures, the stages of a woman's adult life were defined by the raising of her children. She was a wife and mother, with few role changes imagined once her children were raised. Would such a conceptualization imply that women reach old age sooner than men?

Historians credit the nineteenth and early twentieth centuries as giving rise to our contemporary conceptualizations about midlife.[9] It was then that pension funds and other institutionalized financial supports for the first time in history made the end of work possible. Hence, the outer boundary of midlife came to

6.1. *Das Stufenalter der Frau* by F. Leiber

8. See Cherry, "Piaget's 4 Stages," for a depiction of Piaget's stage theory.
9. Willis and Martin, *Middle Adulthood*, 10.

6.2. *Das Stufenalter des Mannes* by F. Leiber

be associated with retirement, and the caliber of middle age was associated largely with the quality of one's work.

Midlife quite literally points one to the midsection of one's life course. Yet, this reality has evoked various images carrying different emotional valences. If one's life is thought of as a staircase, then midlife is a sort of pinnacle or apex, the most dominant period of life but also the transition period before one begins regression and a downward decline.[10] Depictions of this view, known in German as *Lebenstreppe*, were popular for both men and women from the seventeenth through the nineteenth centuries, disappearing only through the fighting of two world wars (see figs. 6.1 and 6.2). Most often these depictions divided life into ten stages of ten years each, hence centering the fifth decade as the high point and elevating it as the age when people came closest to perfection.

Or is midlife better thought of as a bridge whereby the early lessons and developmental resolutions of life provide the confidence for moving into the later years of life with vitality and a continued ascendance? Is midlife better thought of in relation to the accomplishments of younger years or as the determination of what older life might be? When in the life course does human maturity reach its zenith? Or to pose it in light of the Christian gospel, if the aim of the Christian life is to part with childish ways (1 Cor. 13:11) and be made mature

10. Willis and Martin, *Middle Adulthood*, 14–16.

or complete or perfect in Christ (Matt. 5:48; 1 Cor. 14:20; Col. 1:28–29), then at what age or stage of life might we reasonably expect this to happen?

My college-aged son recently evoked an image from his childhood that captured for me some of what I feel while writing this text during my middle adult years. In his childhood years, Samuel was engaged in gymnastics classes. The gym was located in a two-story facility that had several ropes suspended from the ceiling. Climbing these became a regular part of strength training. My son described what he experienced descending the rope. At the halfway point, the rope above him was taut, representing stability in the history of where he had been and continuity in how he perceived the Lord had been present and shown himself faithful throughout the first decades of his life. Despite the stability of what came before, the remainder of the rope below was flailing around, creating precarious feelings as he groped for the grip that would lead him to a safe landing.

This is often the psychological experience of the midlife passage. On the one hand, a person has lived long enough to experience stability. Most crises in life have been encountered in some form and lived through, building confidence and resilience. Yet on the other hand, midlifers often shoulder responsibilities and occupy senior leadership positions of significant consequence in work and family. With some years left in their professional lives, many reevaluate the self in the hope of discovering what would allow the remainder of the rope to optimize impact and satisfaction.

Midlife Changes in the Domains of Life

Earlier stages of the life course may be easier to identify and more commonly referenced because developmental changes in the body often parallel a change of societal status—for example, children move from middle school to high school about the time of pubescence, young adulthood corresponds often with college years and movement into a career. This is less identifiable and less uniform in middle adulthood, though some common physiological, familial and societal changes may still be observed.

Biologically

Though no clear physiological marker signifies when middle adulthood begins or ends, many report that midlife brings changes to the body that no longer permit an illusion of unrestricted health. Physical changes occur with hair graying and thinning, skin wrinkling, sight and hearing decreasing, bone mass lessening, and sleep decreasing. At the same time, susceptibility to cancer and heart disease increases.[11] Other conditions may also emerge, such as diabetes and arthritis. On the whole, medical research tells us that in middle adulthood, we physiologically experience more losses than gains,[12] though psychologically we may continue on a pathway of growth, good health, and increased maturation. Some life span theorists regard successful development during middle adulthood as the "relative maximization of gains and the minimization of losses."[13]

For men, physical diminishment can create a struggle to relinquish physical dominance, and they may turn to compensatory behavior. Quite often, an incident in their own life or in the life of one of their peers awakens a mortality crisis. I recall when one of the men in our Sunday school class had a heart attack. Though he survived, we were all suddenly struck by the fact that this had happened to one in our own generation rather than to someone a generation or two ahead of us. I also recall leading a small group of men at the seminary, one of whom decided that for part of his bachelor party he would enjoy a game of flag football. Having loved athletics most of my younger life, I was ready to show a bit of my prowess to these younger bucks. On one play, Rudy took a pass in the backfield, and I thought I had him by a couple of steps. Rudy came around the corner, and I was a stubborn, stick shift pickup truck grinding away but not able to find third or fourth gear. Rudy done gone, and so was my pride!

For women, diminishment may create a struggle to relinquish physical beauty that may be resolved by activating sources of internal value. During midlife, women encounter perimenopause and the gradual reduction of reproductive ability typically over six years that ends in menopause and the cessation of the menstrual cycle (usually between age forty-two and fifty-eight). Many physiological changes accompany the lowering of estrogen, which triggers the release of other hormones, creating hot flashes, the reddening of skin, mood changes, and depression.[14] The impact of menopause varies, however, and may be determined in part by a culture's valuation of motherhood and by one's personal sense of the importance of childbirth.

Men also experience a decrease in hormone production, sometimes referred to as andropause, which is typically less dramatic than menopause for women. A decrease in testosterone may contribute to a loss of muscle mass, less energy, a decrease in the quantity and quality of sperm, and changes in sexual functioning.[15] About half of men experience erectile dysfunction, increasing anxiety about impotence and fueling a market for Viagra and male enhancement

---

11. Arnett and Jensen, *Human Development*, 478–87.
12. Broderick and Blewitt, *Life Span*, 506.
13. Broderick and Blewitt, *Life Span*, 507.
14. Arnett and Jensen, *Human Development*, 480.
15. Arnett and Jensen, *Human Development*, 482.

supplements, though most men remain fertile into old age. Correlations have been found between how sexually active a man is in older age and the strength of his sex drive in younger years.[16]

Despite these diminishments and biological changes, studies in self-concept reveal that most people grow more self-accepting in the middle years of life.[17]

Psychologically/Cognitively

Accompanying physical changes to the body are psychological changes. Many report that they awakened to the reality that they were now "counting backward," "playing the back nine," or "over the hill." Instead of counting the number of years since birth, they were now thinking "How many years do I have left?"[18] Though mandatory retirement was abolished by Congress in the United States in 1986,[19] many still see age sixty-two to seventy-two as most typical for retirement and use a number in that range to determine how many years they have left. For others, psychological change may connect with losing one or both parents to death during midlife, placing one as the matriarch or patriarch of the family and/or causing one to begin contemplating one's own mortality in greater depth for the first time. Richard Rohr makes the stunning observation that in the first half of life, we seek to "have what we love," whereas in the second half of life, we learn to "love what we have."[20]

Daniel J. Levinson reported several decades ago in his study of men in midlife that most carried from young adulthood a vocational ideal of where they hoped to be in midlife, often symbolized by a key event that signified affirmation in his occupational and social world[21]—such as becoming a senior manager, evidence that his enterprise has flourished; those in ministry might imagine pastoring at a high-steeple church. If this has not been realized, then midlife becomes a time of recalibrating what could still be or grieving what now seems elusive. In comparison to young adults, many feel their options have narrowed in midlife, as it is often perceived as more difficult to start over and/or too disruptive to primary relationships. Whereas in earlier years the tendency is toward social comparison, in midlife people tend to judge themselves based on their own expectations. Recall William James's insight that self-esteem depends on the "number of successes relative to our aspirations."[22] For many who are

---

16. Broderick and Blewitt, *Life Span*, 513.
17. Broderick and Blewitt, *Life Span*, 563–65.
18. Broderick and Blewitt, *Life Span*, 514–16.
19. Von Wachter, "End of Mandatory Retirement."
20. Rohr, *Falling Upward*, 64.
21. Levinson, *Seasons of a Man's Life*, 191.
22. Broderick and Blewitt, *Life Span*, 257.

faith-focused, a significant turn can occur as the aim of learning now becomes less about acquisition of new skills and knowledge and more about meaning and spirituality. George Vaillant in *The Wisdom of the Ego* characterizes work in late middle adulthood as possessing the quality of "keeper of the meaning," indicative of a shift away from a preoccupation with productivity or making a contribution and toward preserving what is regarded as valuable to culture.[23]

Living longer allows many to retool and start new endeavors. A quick Google search for "midlife career change" yields over five million results, giving some indication of how prevalent this pattern has become. Involuntary unemployment, however, can be especially unsettling if finding new work proves difficult. Marginalization is keenly felt, as people feel they are not needed in the community. Many choose to stay where they are and adjust expectations downward, and some women encounter glass ceilings. Sometimes this manifests in anger and frustration directed toward children and/or spouse, as the family is the only area where they feel they still have some power.

Erikson characterizes the unsuccessful resolution of the developmental tasks of this stage of life as stagnation.[24] For some, midlife confronts them with gaps between the real and the ideal. Yet, even when the internal ideal has been realized, there can yet be costs to reconcile. Success may have come at the price of a divorce, absence from the lives of children, or physical health liabilities. Hence, the midlife journey can involve forgiving people who failed you and forgiving yourself for ways you failed in order to get on with the second half of life.

The combination of physiological and psychological changes, when attuned to, can create a great deal of internal evaluation. Levinson believes that both men and women live through various seasons in their life span. A season is typically about twenty years long and has a distinct characteristic. The years from twenty to forty are typically about giving structure to the adolescent dream and showing ourselves and others that we can be competent in the work and family roles we adopted. Around age forty to forty-five, Levinson believes, we realize that we are bigger than the roles we have played, and we begin to listen to and for those aspects of ourselves that we may have stowed away while managing the responsibilities of parenting and work life.[25] Often in midlife, polarities are addressed that allow us to better embrace a character trait opposite of what has often been cultivated. Some characterize this as growing the "shadow self" or underdeveloped parts of the self.[26] Others have given credence to gender

---

23. Vaillant, *Wisdom of the Ego*, 158–60. For a helpful discussion that treats Vaillant's insights as an extension of Erikson's eight stages of life, see Broderick and Blewitt, *Life Span*, 516–17.
24. McLeod, "Erik Erikson's 8 Stages."
25. Levinson, *Seasons of a Man's Life*, 200.
26. Villines, "What Is Shadow Work?"

convergence or gender crossover whereby men mellow and women grow more assertive so that men and women become more similar in middle age[27] (though this may be less pronounced in our gender fluid society than when Levinson conducted his research). Levinson believes renewal comes when a person is willing to confront the polarities of young-old, destruction-creation, feminine-masculine, and engagement-separation.[28]

"Midlife crisis" became common parlance for more radical expressions of change in one's life as one attempted to resolve discontent between the ideal and the real. Scientists of midlife, however, have not found strong support for broad or acute crises at midlife and regard such a concept as largely overdramatized. More common are micro adjustments within an existing life structure and qualitative changes made for further development.[29] Adding another twenty years to Levinson's schema, we arrive at age sixty (plus or minus), with retirement on the horizon, setting the contours for the next season of life.

Socially/Culturally

In the early years of middle adulthood, many parents are still raising their adolescent children, creating a rather challenging dynamic. While their teenage children are confronting an adolescent identity crisis, parents may be facing a myriad of identity questions themselves. Teenage bodies are gaining new capacities and moving toward cultural ideals, while midlifers feel their bodies incrementally losing peak capacities and moving further away from cultural ideals. Research tells us relationships with children tend to improve once children move out of the house and are freer to become their own person[30] apart from parental surveillance and relational conflict. Some evidence suggests that fathers experience more distress with the structural changes to the family, perhaps associated with how the changes modify their role as decision-maker, whereas a mother experiences more relief, as she can now begin to release some duties.[31]

For many, midlife is the stage when one carries the most social roles and experiences society making the most demands on them. Some have speculated that this correlates well with what could be perceived as the life stage of greatest stability, power, and influence.[32]

27. Goldin, "Grand Gender Convergence."
28. Levinson, *Seasons of a Man's Life*, 209–44.
29. Balswick and Balswick, *Family*, 157–69.
30. Levinson describes tension between parents and teenage boys over the BOOM experience—discrepancy concerning when one is ready to "be one's own man." *Seasons of a Man's Life*, 144–49.
31. Allen, "Parents and Adult Children."
32. Willis and Martin, *Middle Adulthood*, 24–26.

In my graduate school research, we conducted what we called the Adult Role-Related Identity Interview. The interview started by identifying four primary family roles that a person occupied: at midlife one is a daughter or son, a sister or brother, often a parent and an aunt or uncle, often a husband or wife, and possibly a granddaughter or grandson; added to this are a person's professional role or roles, community roles, and organizational roles to support their children's school and extracurricular activities. Our interviews would often probe what expectations were associated with each of the roles a person occupied, what changes they had made in those roles, and whether those changes were prompted by normative life events, initiated by the person being interviewed, or brought about by nonnormative life events (divorce, unexpected unemployment, traumatic life event, a move, etc.).[33] Fascinating in these interviews was what they revealed about how social roles and spirituality interweave and create catalysts for midlife change. One man spoke, for example, of how his persistent care for his convalescing wife was understood as a religious discipline atoning for deficiencies he perceived in his role of father when his daughter was younger. One female pastor who was in a second marriage concluded that she would more readily give up her role as wife than mother as this was more central to her spiritual identity. My research attempted to distinguish what changes occurred naturally as part of the developmental journey and which were precipitated by crises in the roles people held and so initiated with the intention to change.

Mark R. Shaw, in his book *Work, Play, Love*, recognizes that at midlife a person is responding not to one calling but to multiple callings.[34] The task is often to balance these multiple callings well. This can be especially challenging, as midlifers often experience role overload, role strain, and role conflict. Finding work-life balance is a prevalent issue among midlifers. Despite women typically finding that parenting limits their career options more so than it does for men, many women find that role buffering via social support contributes to life satisfaction.

In latter middle adult years, parents can generally spend less time overseeing children and for the first time in many years explore their own interests again. Carl Jung describes midlife as an attempt to reexperience in one's inner world what one had discovered in the collective themes of one's outer worlds.[35] Decades of research suggests that generally marital satisfaction tends to follow a U-shaped curve and begins increasing as couples have more time and energy to invest in each other, though some find the pattern can be misleading.[36] However,

---

33. For more on this, see Kiesling and Sorell, "Joining Erikson and Identity Specialists."
34. M. Shaw, *Work, Play, Love*, 21–25.
35. Willis and Martin, *Middle Adulthood*, 20–21.
36. Arnett and Jensen, *Human Development*, 515.

strong links have been found between a mother's and father's feelings of well-being/generativity and their children's functioning. Cultural differences also affect how parents experience the empty nest, with parents in more interdependent cultures experiencing greater loneliness and exhibiting greater welcoming if their unmarried, adult children boomerang and want to return home to live.[37]

A life span study of how friendships are formed at different stages of life shows that a person's social convoy changes through their life based on their marital status and whether they have children.[38] For parents, friendships for years are formed around temporary communities contingent on their kids' extracurricular activities—for example, for six months out of the year, a woman is a soccer mom and friends with other soccer parents. For singles, work and leisure choices typically structure friendships. At midlife, what Erikson calls "generativity" often compels marrieds and singles, women and men, to seek greater contribution to their community in civic and community groups.

Subjective Well-Being

Greek philosophers crafted philosophical essays focused on *eudaimonia*, meaning "happiness, welfare, or human flourishing."[39] The concept captured the notion of living well, and the authors attempted to think philosophically about what constitutes the good life and procures a sense of happiness for people. Most notable in this regard was the famous dictum attributed to Socrates: "The unexamined life is not worth living."[40] In our day, social scientists continue the search for factors that contribute to living well or to providing happiness. Instead of the Greek connotation of *eudaimonia*, this is expressed in social science research as "subjective well-being" and is measured by a formula that resembles the following:

Subjective well-being (SWB) = overall life satisfaction + the frequency of positive moods + the infrequency of negative moods[41]

Patricia C. Broderick and Pamela Blewitt consider much of this research, evaluating the correlation between subjective well-being and wealth accumulation. Data reveals that the percentage of North Americans in the latter half

37. Broderick and Blewitt, *Life Span*, 537–38.
38. Broderick and Blewitt, *Life Span*, 604.
39. See Duigan, "Eudaimonia."
40. This quotation is from Plato's *Apology* 38a5–6.
41. Broderick and Blewitt, *Life Span*, 555.

of the twentieth century who self-reported as "happy" remained steady or even declined as income level per capita increased, while rates of depression and other pathologies increased.[42] Despite a culture that foments materialistic aspirations, gains in wealth cannot deliver on the promise of happiness and often carries deleterious side effects. This provides a stark contrast to levels of contentedness in countries that instead elevate the primacy of family, friends, and socially valuable work above money and possessions. To qualify this further, research now shows that people need modest though adequate income to alleviate discontent and worry, but once an adequate amount is gained, there is little difference in life satisfaction between those with modest incomes and the very wealthy. To say this another way, being delivered out of poverty and given economic and food security dramatically increases well-being, but once a basic standard of living is achieved, the law of diminishing returns sets in such that more money does not provide a lot of happiness and may even put it at risk.

Critical for well-being is a sense of connection to others and the capacity to trust—qualities that can be elusive with increased wealth. Several theories have been advanced to explain why materialistic gains don't always contribute to better life satisfaction.

- The hedonistic treadmill suggests that we habituate to a particular level of wealth and then end up wanting for the next level of wealth. Our whole marketing enterprise seems bent on creating a sense of discontent in what one has, exploiting it to keep the economy flourishing.
- Affluence reduces other forces that ordinarily help create support. For example, the more money a person has, the less need they have for others. With wealth a person can buy childcare or eldercare rather than looking to family or friends. Notice on a hot summer afternoon that parks are full where there is no air-conditioning in a neighborhood but empty where people can stay in their artificially cooled homes. Or observe how neighbors hardly know each other in gated communities where everyone has a garage and a remote control in order to exit and enter their house in relative privacy.
- Gaining control creates the expectation that a person can create the perfect life, setting them up for disillusionment—that is, if a person's life is primarily what they make of it, then anything less than a glamorous life can burden them with a sense of culpability that then turns to self-accusation and internalized blame.[43]

42. Broderick and Blewitt, *Life Span*, 557.
43. Broderick and Blewitt, *Life Span*, 559–60.

Hence, there may be real differences between those who function as "maximizers" with an eye toward always making and having a little more and "satisfiers" who have learned that having "enough" is what one needs for contentment.[44] Miroslav Volf, in his research on joy, found that a great deal of depression results from the sense that a person can never achieve enough. Unattainable goals, self-achievement, competitiveness, and the like often function to inhibit joy.[45] By contrast, suggests Volf, joy is yearning for what one already has.

What might help a person get off the hedonistic treadmill and reach for what Paul describes as "godliness with contentment" (1 Tim. 6:6) in these middle years of life? If the center of the life span is especially critical in bringing coherence to the whole life course, and if it opens people to things like evaluation of the self, recalibration of social roles, and contemplation of mortality, then what spaces and rhythms allow for this kind of reflection? If the key to life satisfaction is connection to God and to others, then what kind of practices may help people order their loves well and flourish at this stage of life?

Finding Practices to Sustain Us and Grow Virtue through the Middle Years

In the Greek philosophical system, building on the teaching of Aristotle, finding happiness largely depended on two things. First, one needed a clear vision of what the good life was (*eudaimonia*); second, one needed to know the means whereby this could be attained. Following the lead of philosopher Alasdair MacIntyre, several theologians, such as N. T. Wright, Craig R. Dykstra, and Dorothy C. Bass, have offered theological means that follow this stream of thought. Wright provides a corrective to the conventional notion that the Christian life is primarily about getting our souls saved and getting to heaven, arguing instead that there is much more intended for the Christian "after they believe."[46] The final goal is not heaven but a resurrected life that begins here on earth and that contributes to the new heaven and the new earth that Jesus intends to bring about. Believers serve the redemption of the cosmos, exercising dominion and stewarding care of all creation as in the garden of Eden. But it is critical to discern how this transformation of our being is to come about.

Mainstream thought seems to offer two options. Either there is a system of rules, moralisms, and/or a code of conduct by which to live, or we can follow our own heart. Checking off the boxes in a system of rules, we seek assurance that we are good people and have not offended God. When we do, forgiveness is

44. Broderick and Blewitt, *Life Span*, 560.
45. Banks, "Miroslav Volf."
46. N. T. Wright, *After You Believe*.

available through confession, by which we can get on track again. The problem with this strategy is that we can conform our external behavior to rules without a transformation of our inner character. Further, because of the complexities of the midlife journey, we can never compose enough rules to guide us through. We are confronted with raising teenage children, all of whom have unique personalities and different vulnerabilities, while at the same time beginning to care for aging parents. All the while, we are managing work responsibilities that require more discernment because more is at stake than ever before. The other option is the conventional, cultural directive to be yourself, follow your heart, live according to your deepest longings. According to this strategy, we rely on the inner feelings of our heart to ascertain what is right, trusting that if we do what comes most naturally, it will lead to the promised land. The problem with this strategy is that if we acknowledge the fallenness of human nature and are humble enough to recognize the possibility of self-deception, we may find that what is natural is not always bent toward what is good. Which depths of the human heart are to be trusted, and what limitations are there to our own knowledge and capacity to know what is trustworthy?[47]

As an alternative, and as a way that gleans the best from both of these options, Wright advocates for the ancient way, substantiated by philosophers and biblical theologians, of developing Christian character through practices that lead to virtue. Developing habits of the mind and heart is critical, thereby one, enabled by grace, acquires a second nature continually being renewed by God's future promises. This is largely the center of Dallas Willard's proposal for spiritual formation as well.

> Christian formation is inescapably a matter of recognizing in ourselves the idea system (or systems) of evil that governs the present age and the respective culture (or various cultures) that constitute life away from God. The needed transformation is very largely a matter of replacing in ourselves those idea systems of evil (and their corresponding cultures) with the idea system that Jesus Christ embodied and taught and with a culture of the kingdom of God.[48]

For Wright, a practice is something we do habitually in order to become a certain kind of person, like an athlete engaging in a vigorous exercise regimen to develop a natural instinct for how to react to a crucial moment in a game situation. Practices are also things people do together over time to meet a particular human need or become a particular kind of community. The rural church I served in Arkansas had a practice of welcoming every newcomer to the

47. N. T. Wright, *After You Believe*, 1–26.
48. Willard, *Renovation of the Heart*, 98.

church with a fresh-baked homemade pie. Families pray together and celebrate birthdays, practices aimed at conveying that they value persons and want to secure a prosperous and meaningful future for them. As the early church was being established, members engaged in practices of regular fellowship, worship, service, and listening to the teaching of the apostles.[49]

Virtue, defined by my retired colleague Burrell Dinkins, is "an acquired excellence of the soul," a quality of Christian character that is gained through the steadfast strengthening of the enabled will.[50] Virtue, then, is a hard-won second nature. Virtues guide the kind of practices we might engage in to become a particular kind of person, ordering our loves according to objects meant to meet the desires we bring to them.

Virtues move us beyond rule making and beyond moralistic preaching. When rules are driven by a sense of duty, they quite easily turn into legalisms that impose identity on others. Virtues, by contrast, before imposing a spiritual discipline, begin by asking, "What sort of people are we desiring to become?"[51] When vision has motivated a response, practices then become the avenue of attaining that vision. Virtues also move us beyond simply trying to discover what we are to be by doing what comes naturally or by looking within to find all the answers. Virtues turn the focal point away from the self and our own desires and toward discerning what God values and what his character is like, and love of neighbor.[52] A good place to see this reflected is in Peter's last address to the church recorded in 2 Peter 1. Peter knows his time on earth is coming to a close. Eager to keep before believers what he found most important in his momentous walk with Jesus, he admonishes that God has granted us all that is needed for life and godliness. In fact, he declares that we have the promise to become partakers of God's own divine nature. So he exhorts every believer to add to their faith virtues that guarantee that their life will bear fruit.

Let me return a final time to putting virtue and practice together by borrowing a helpful illustration from Wright.

My youngest son had been wanting to learn to play the guitar, and so he found a chord book to teach him where to place his fingers and jumped right into strumming. With natural musical ability on the piano, he assumed that he could produce melody rather easily on the guitar. But his fingers were not yet

49. My former colleague Christine Pohl did marvelous scholarship helping the church think of other communal practices, such as promise keeping, truth telling, showing gratitude, and practicing hospitality.

50. Burrell taught a class called Vocation of Ministry that worked through what he called the "matrix of vocation." A key piece of it was seeking after virtue.

51. I am indebted to my colleague Phil Meadows for this insight. He teaches it as part of the Inspire movement, which can be found at https://inspiremovement.org/.

52. N. T. Wright, *After You Believe*, 27–71.

habituated to move in particular ways, and frustration set in quickly when the noise coming from the strings didn't sound at all like the music he imagined he could produce. If he wants to play with elegance, he will have to learn, through years of practice, the fingering of notes. If he engages diligently in practice, something new is likely to emerge: a capacity to play music in a joyful way. This is what Peter and Wright and Willard have in mind. Christian character can be built by repeated and habitual choices through the enablement of grace by the power of the Holy Spirit that gradually shape us until we begin to take on the divine nature. This is what I want to point to for living the middle adult years.

Spiritual Practices for the Midlife Journey

Sabbath

Abraham Joshua Heschel poses this intriguing question: "What is the first holy object in the history of the world?" Much to our surprise, it is not a location like a holy mountain or city, nor is it an object like an altar. Rather, it is a day.[53] Time is the first thing in the history of the world that was set aside to be holy. My earliest understanding of Sabbath was having a day off to become a couch potato after a big Sunday meal and watching the Dallas Cowboys romp over their opponents. But the deeper I explore Sabbath, the richer the theological meanings become and the more central it becomes to my Christian identity. There are at least four places in the story of Scripture where we can draw out the meaning of Sabbath, supplementing them with some very practical insights from Marva J. Dawn's book Keeping the Sabbath Wholly: Ceasing, Resting, Embracing, Feasting to make this an important practice for the middle adult journey.

First, in the book of Genesis God blesses the seventh day and sanctifies it because in it he rests from all his work (Gen. 2:2–3). Lauren F. Winner contrasts the story of Genesis with other ancient creation stories.[54] In most other stories, humans are created to be a labor force for the gods; Genesis is unique in portraying a God who creates humans to be in fellowship with him and invites them into his rest as he walks with them in the cool of the day. The book of Proverbs describes wisdom as God's partner in creation (Prov. 8:22–31). Mark Shaw describes wisdom's role as summoning us to playful partnership whereby we learn to delight in (a) whatever we do each day, (b) whomever we do it with, and (c) wherever we discover God at work in the world.[55] This is Eden, described in rabbinic commentary as serenity, tranquility, repose, delight,

---

53. Heschel, Sabbath, 3–9.
54. Winner, "Sleep Therapy."
55. M. Shaw, Work, Play, Love, 29–36.

paradise—humans given dominion over all God created to experience with him the joy of his creation.[56]

Biblical scholars also find significance in the Jewish way of ordering days reflected in the phrase that occurs at the end of each day of creation: "there was evening and there was morning." The impression most people have is that if they can just get through Friday and complete household chores on Saturday, then they can finally recover on Sunday. Hence, Sabbath is the means for restoring strength at the end of exhaustion. Quite to the contrary, the biblical account seems to imply that we begin with rest in God and allow this to characterize the rest of our existence. God begins his work even while we are sleeping; we awaken to join him in the task of having dominion over the world, looking after its well-being. Sabbath is written into the creation story—a time set apart for rest.[57]

Second, Exodus conveys the importance of Sabbath, embedding it in the Ten Commandments: "Remember the Sabbath day, to keep it holy" (Exod. 20:8). The commandments are given after Israel is delivered from the tyrannical rule of Pharaoh. For four hundred years, Israel endured harsh labor as slaves, living in a culture that elevated productivity and alienated Israelites from the product of their own labor. Everything produced belonged to Pharaoh. No longer did humans have sovereignty, as in the creation story. Then God sends Israel a deliverer in the person of Moses, drowns all who oppressed them in the waters of the Red Sea, and delivers them with the hope of entering the promised land. Yet, while Israel came out of Egypt, Egypt was not as easily taken out of them. In the commandments, Israel is given a framework for freedom to keep them from self-destruction. Eugene Peterson captures it best by saying, "Nothing less than a command has the power to intervene in the vicious, accelerating, self-perpetuating cycle of faithless and graceless business."[58] To rest for a day was to remember that a time existed in Eden before the ground was cursed and before the sweat of the brow was required to bring forth fruit.

Third, centuries later Israel is taken into exile. Having failed to destroy all nations whose detestable practices became their own, Israel turns from God's laws, directing the desires of their hearts to idols. God's intent for Israel to be a distinct people—holy just as God is holy (Lev. 19:2)—is lost until Israel is driven into foreign lands and led to repent. Yet, in exile there is no temple, and seldom is permission given to worship as a gathered community. Home becomes the place where Israel can still do something religious, where they

56. See, e.g., "Deeper Hebrew Meaning."
57. Dawn, *Keeping the Sabbath Wholly*, 57–58.
58. E. Peterson, "The Pastor's Sabbath," 55–56.

can preserve their identity through storytelling. Observing Sabbath reminds them of who they are and what they are called to be as a nation. Chaim Grade illuminates the practice by recalling a story from World War II, when he was sent to flee from encroaching German forces. As he left his family, his mother said to him, "Never forget that you are a Jew. Keep the Sabbath."[59] The implication was clear: if he did this one intentional thing weekly, he would not forget who he was.

Finally, in the New Testament, a shift occurs in the practice of Sabbath from not only looking back to the mighty works of God in history but also looking present and forward because Christ has defeated death and brought eternal life. Ultimately, rest will be granted again to all creation. Entering God's rest becomes a metaphor for sanctification in the New Testament (Heb. 4:1–11). Just as the kingdom has an "already but not yet" dynamic to it, so too, by faith, we can find rest in "the conviction of things not seen" (11:1).

So how might we appropriate all this rich meaning into the midlife passage?

- Cease from anxiety, not just from work.[60] Once a week, relinquish productivity and the sin nature that is habituated to find worth only in achievement and accomplishment. Cast all earthly anxieties or faithless fears on God and remember that the aim of life is to enjoy him forever.
- Learn real rest. Sabbath was meant as much more than just being lazy. It meant replenishing. For some, that may come via a closer connection with creation. Others may find that tapping into their creativity through play or hobby helps them experience the image in which they were created. I liken this to discovering what puts the fizz back into your Dr Pepper.
- Feast with family, friends, and "foreigners." Sabbath for the Jew was sacred assembly. For Dawn, Sabbath is the day to invite special guests and familiar friends for dinner, serving them with her best silverware.[61] She greets "Queen Sabbath" with preparation, as if a bride were to visit her abode. She lights candles at the beginning of the day and extinguishes them at the end, creating a posture of waiting with longing for the next time Queen Sabbath comes around.
- Practice looking back, looking present, and looking forward. Look back over last week and ask, "For whom did I do my work?" Look present and ask, "What is giving life, and what is draining life?" Look forward, pray

59. Grade, My Mother's Sabbath Days, 247.
60. Dawn, Keeping the Sabbath Wholly, 22–27.
61. Dawn, Keeping the Sabbath Wholly, 180–89.

over upcoming appointments, and ask, "What does God wish to bring about in us and from that time together?"[62]

- Start small. If taking a full day to rest creates more anxiety than it relinquishes, then look for a four-hour block of time. If work or family does not permit a four-hour block of time, then follow a directive from Jessica LaGrone and begin with seven-minute Sabbaths during the day. Breathe deep, recenter, tune back into the natural rhythms of grace.[63]

Sabbath sanctifies time, and when time is regarded as sacred, the metric by which we gauge the rest of our lives also changes. I listed Sabbath first not only because of its significance in the Bible and in the lives of the Israelites but also because for me it serves as a beachhead from which the remaining territory of life is much more easily taken captive for Christ and his purposes.

Solitude

A second practice that relates to the inherent nature of midlife is solitude. Henri J. M. Nouwen's work alerted me to the reality that our incessant use of technology may actually betray a deep-rooted fear of being alone. We avoid encountering our inner restlessness because we harbor deep-seated suspicions about the absence of God. Nouwen believes the roots of such loneliness lie in childhood experiences that create in us a suspicion that there is no one who cares and offers love without condition, no place we can be vulnerable without being used. So we stay busy to convince ourselves that we are fine and valuable and doing something meaningful. Solitude helps us realize how unconducive modern culture is to the spiritual life—seducing us into being too busy, too ambitious, too self-indulgent.[64]

In 2021, research from Barna reported that 31 percent of adults indicated feeling lonely some of each day, and over 50 percent reported feeling lonely at least once a week. The numbers are only slightly lower for church folks. Susan Mettes, an investigator who partnered with Barna for the study, defines *loneliness* as "the distress someone feels when their social connections don't meet their needs for emotional intimacy."[65] Recall the title of David W. Smith's popular book from decades ago, *The Friendless American Male*, or remember that Erikson describes the stage of life prior to middle adulthood as intimacy versus isolation.[66]

62. MacDonald, *Ordering Your Private World*, 190–207.
63. LaGrone, "Keep the Sabbath."
64. Nouwen, *Reaching Out*, 14–24.
65. Barna Group, "31% of U.S. Adults."
66. Erikson, *Childhood and Society*, 263–66. Erikson's description of intimacy entails being able to fuse one's identity to another without fearing that one might lose something of oneself in doing so—a conception foundational to what many find in differentiation today.

We may not even be aware of our loneliness or be willing to call it by this name, but it drives us to find a new friend, community, or lover, and it is echoed in song lyrics like "I still haven't found what I'm looking for."[67] Quite often, the more convinced we are that we have found it in a rushed relationship, the harder the fall comes when disillusionment is accompanied by self-recriminations, accusations, repressed anger, jealousies, or even violence. Dante wrote, "When in my middle stage of life, I found myself entangled in a wood obscure,"[68] and Henry David Thoreau penned the penetrating words "Most men lead lives of quiet desperation."[69]

When there is an emptiness within, we become especially vulnerable to intimacy that is offered for sale in pornography. Further, our socialization into a competitive individualism undermines our longing to find a sense of unity and connection.[70] Dietrich Bonhoeffer describes the dynamic that then happens often in community. We bring an unexamined desire to find our "wish community" and impose upon it unrealistic expectations for what they will be and how they will embrace and elevate us.[71] Marriages too can easily be ruined by the illusion that the final solution to loneliness and restlessness is found in human togetherness. Communities are abandoned and judged as hypocritical because they do not measure up to our idealized image. Nouwen portends, however, that becoming aware of our loneliness rather than seeking to evade it or prevent it in others may actually offer entrance into a deeper spiritual life.[72]

Solitude is the first practice that many ancient spiritual writers taught. How one experiences community depends on what one does in solitude. When solitude is neglected, we tend to engage people as those who can be used for our own fulfillment—to meet some hidden need for self-gratification and aggrandizement.[73] Jesus often withdrew to a quiet place to be alone with the Father (Matt. 14:23; Luke 5:16; John 6:15). This is stunning to contemplate given that the whole purpose of his life was to save humanity. When we come to community empty, we seek strokes and salve to help us feel better. People often ask for support, advice, and counsel from others because they have lost contact with their inner self. Insecurities lead us toward each other for support or against each other in self-defense. In developing a capacity to listen to our inner selves

67. U2, "I Still Haven't Found What I'm Looking For."
68. Dante, The Divine Comedy, "Inferno," Canto I.
69. Thoreau, Walden, 4.
70. Nouwen, Reaching Out, 15–16.
71. Bonhoeffer, Life Together, 17–39.
72. Nouwen, Reaching Out, 22–23.
73. Nouwen, Reaching Out, 25–30.

is often the discovery that we are coming closer to inner necessity, what we must be about, a sense of unique vocation.[74]

In solitude we discern the important difference between what Gordon Mac-Donald calls living as a called person and living as a driven person.[75] The driven person is gratified only by accomplishment and is preoccupied with symbols of achievement. Self-aggrandizement seizes the soul and leads to an uncontrolled hunger for expansion that can cause a person to compromise their integrity. Busyness and competitiveness become driven by an obsessive comparison with others but often end with diminished self-esteem. Eventually, being driven leaves us feeling poorly about the work we are invested in and feeling little enjoyment in relationship with God or others.

The called person, by contrast, understands life as vocation and steward-ship. Knowing who they are before God, they can separate identity from per-formance metrics. They can step away from excessive work in the realization that the purpose of life is more than making a name for themselves (Gen. 11:4) and managing impressions others have of them.[76] Yet, they can also engage suffering and difficult challenges when convinced that God has called them to the task. They focus attention on the depth of ministry, leaving the breadth of their influence in the hands of God. Notice the "musts" in Jesus's life: preaching the kingdom of God (Luke 4:43); working the works of the one who sent him (John 9:4); being in his Father's house (Luke 2:49); passing through Samaria (John 4:4); and suffering and even being killed (Luke 9:22).

Solitude is the pathway to finding divine resources to fill our emptiness, to discerning pathways that flow from a well of living water within and that emerge not from restlessness but from assurance of God's mercy and provision. In solitude we give ourselves permission to feel and to respond to distresses within ourselves. By doing so, Nouwen believes, we gain a solidarity with the pains of the world, expanding our capacity to respond in compassion. Solitude, in this light, is not a movement toward withdrawal but a movement toward deeper engagement. When solitude is rightly practiced, we convert fearful and anxious reactions into loving and thoughtful responses. This is why the practice is so crucial at midlife, when social roles are at their peak. When we shirk solitude and evade our pain, our responses to suffering occur without our entering into it ourselves, and we become like a parent trying to save a child from a burning house without risking being hurt. Solitude offers us a compassionate solidarity from which to respond. Solitude then actually makes

74. Nouwen, *Reaching Out*, 27–28.
75. MacDonald, *Ordering Your Private World*, 57–74.
76. For a penetrating exploration of this topic, see Borgman, *Genesis*.

a new life possible—detached from false ties and more present to others and to God.[77]

Discernment

Discernment is a close companion to solitude, but unlike solitude it often has a communal component to it or may even become the practice of a community. Discernment, writes Ruth Haley Barton, is "first of all, a habit, a way of seeing that can permeate our whole life. . . . it is the movement from seeing things from a human perspective to seeing from a spiritual vantage point, continually looking for evidence of the work of God in order to join him in it."[78] Too often we assemble a group of professionals, successful in their own technical fields, and assume their decision-making aligns with this way of seeing. Overlooked are corporate and secular mindsets that may be devoid of foundational elements of discernment. Barton names these essentials:

- commitment to a communal process governed by the work of the Trinity, especially the conviction that the real and immediate presence of the Holy Spirit can be ascertained
- the relinquishment of asserting our own will
- trust in God's goodness despite previous disappointments or those that may occur in the group process
- setting the heart to love God, love self, love others, and love the world as the driving motivation of decision-making so often lost in meetings
- firm willingness to act on that which is discerned, even before it becomes apparent[79]

At midlife, the situations can be endless for which we yearn to find divine guidance—providing leadership for a team, navigating relational strife, pondering a vocational shift, guiding a recalcitrant teen, managing conflict with a coworker, figuring out whom to support when the social or political landscape changes, and so on. By this stage of life, most will recognize the very real possibilities the ego presents for self-deception but also the remarkable guidance the Holy Spirit can provide in leading us into all truth (John 16:13). The challenge is, of course, that no foolproof method ensures that God's ways are infallibly known. The Spirit eludes, and the frailties and infirmities of the

77. Nouwen, *Reaching Out*, 41–44.
78. Barton, *Pursuing God's Will Together*, 56–57.
79. Barton, *Pursuing God's Will Together*, 51–56.

human condition are persistent. Yet, ancient wisdom heightens the possibility that God's will can be known.

Here I want to supplement Barton's foundations with further insight from Frank Rogers for establishing the proper disposition of the heart to ensure integrity in discernment. First, to cultivate the right attunement of the heart, Rogers advocates for regular practice of the normative means of grace that include prayer, the study of Scripture, worship, fellowship, and works of mercy and justice.[80] Second, Scripture serves as the primary normative criteria against which any decision must be weighed. In his teaching about discerning the will of God for a person's life, John Wesley admonishes that some things are already known. God wills a person's sanctification—that they be made holy (1 Thess. 4:3)—and he wills that all people should be about doing good (Gal. 6:10). Hence, a person could begin discerning by asking questions such as, "In this decision, where will I be made most holy?" "Where can I do the most good?" "How might I avoid harm?" Beyond Scripture, Wesley looks to tradition, reason, and experience as guides to proper discernment.[81] Third, right discernment most commonly yields cardinal virtues and the fruit of the Spirit. Hence, in discernment, look for what brings about love, what requires and increases faith, what brings peace and joy, what grows self-control and patience, what is kind and gentle and not arrogant or insistent on its own way (Gal. 5:22–23). Though the Spirit sometimes operates against majority opinion, most often it seeks reconciliation, healing, and harmony. Fourth, God's Spirit hovered over creation and brought forth life (Gen. 1). John begins his Gospel declaring that in Christ is life and light (John 1). So authentic promptings of the Spirit should be generative of life, illuminating the mind, juicing creativity, and enhancing personhood and dignity both in self and others. In Ignatian prayers of examen, one asks what brings consolation and what smacks of desolation.[82] If a decision leads a person to become more anxious, entangled, unstable, or fearful, then this may be an indication that they need to remain in solitude or seek further spiritual guidance.

It is interesting to note that different faith traditions practice discernment in different ways. Quakers seek communal consensus brought about by returning often to silence and attunement to the Spirit.[83] Other communities see majority vote as an apparent protocol of discernment, and others rely on an appointed leader for discernment. Yet, most all these processes at some level involve the

80. Rogers's work is presented as one of a cluster of practices advocated for in the Valparaiso Project. It can be found in Bass, *Practicing Our Faith*, 107–10.
81. Bounds, "Wesleyan Quadrilateral."
82. V. Wright, "Consolation and Desolation."
83. "Decision-Making."

following actions: (1) all dimensions of a decision are brought before God and considered; (2) possible actions and their consequences are weighed along with who will be affected and how; (3) emotions, sensations, and thoughts are allowed to stir when staying with a particular direction, and effort is given to understand where these originate and to what they might be attributed; (4) guidance is sought from those who are deemed trustworthy and are willing to speak truth and to confront (again, the Quakers are exemplary; no one is permitted to give evaluative judgments, but instead everyone is encouraged to ask penetrating questions); and (5) a direction is taken or postponed as the consequences and reactions of others become known.[84]

Practicing discernment quite often summons individuals and communities to additional practices of forgiveness, promise keeping, truth telling, acts of mercy, and gratitude. As virtues surface, giving confirmation to a particular decision, so also do we become more aware of vices, purification of motives, the dismantling of the false self, and what the Book of Common Prayer calls the "devices and desires of our own hearts."[85] "Search me, O God, and know my heart! Try me and know my thoughts! And see if there be any grievous way in me, and lead me in the way everlasting," writes David in Psalm 139:23–24.

What's needed in the course of the midlife journeys is spaces, faces, and places.[86] Space is finding time in our schedule when we can seek discernment as to why the waters have been troubled in the interior of our lives. Faces are connection with those who, instead of draining us, inspire and motivate us to keep going. These are friends and spiritual guides and mentors who provide what the proverb alludes to when it says, "The purpose in a man's heart is like deep water, but a man of understanding will draw it out" (Prov. 20:5). Places are those "thin" locations between heaven and earth where we reclaim a sense of connection to the one who holds the universe and our lives in his hand.[87]

Much interior work begins by listening with a spiritual guide, friend, mentor, or therapist to one's own inner struggle. Rather than too quickly alleviating the aloneness, the needed spiritual guide offers us a chance to stay alone and take the risk of entering into our own experience more deeply and finding there a living well. By converting loneliness to solitude, we create a space where we can discover the voice telling us about our inner necessity—which is in effect

84. Bass, *Practicing Our Faith*, 107–17.
85. Book of Common Prayer, 12.
86. "Spaces, faces, and places" is my handy summation of what Gordon MacDonald called for in *Restoring Your Spiritual Passion* after his ministry collapse.
87. Koch, *Thin Places*.

our vocation.[88] Could it be that in the midst of our loneliness we can start to find beginnings of a quiet solitude, a way of ordering life with inner resources adequate to meet the demands of the midlife labyrinth? Such solitude, when developed, is more an inner quality than physical isolation. This human capacity, spiritual writers tell us, can exist, be developed, and be maintained in a busy city, in the context of a meeting, in the midst of productive life. This capacity is not to be pulled apart by divergent stimuli of the surrounding world but instead to perceive and experience the world from a quiet inner center.

Hospitality

Hospitality is creating the space where strangers become friends. This seems especially critical given that there were an estimated 280 million migrants in 2020, with the number increasing across each of the previous decades.[89] When Nouwen speaks of hospitality on the heels of addressing solitude, he aims at helping us turn anxious reactions into loving responses.[90] This is especially needed in the new media landscape, where it is easy to unleash our invectives in a digital conversation when we are not face-to-face with the one we are engaging.[91]

Loving, writes Tish Harrison Warren, engages us in proper names. She quotes the former archbishop of Canterbury Michael Ramsey: "Our Lord devoted himself to a small country, to small things, and to individual men and women, often giving hours of time to the very few or to the one man or woman. The glory of Christianity is its claim that small things really matter and that the small company, the very few, the one man, the one woman, the one child are of infinite worth to God."[92]

Traditionally, hospitality has often been characterized as "making room."[93] All sorts of application can be made from so simple a phrase: making room in one's schedule, making room in the pew, making room around the table, making room in one's house, making room in one's conversation. Any and all of these can convey what the ancients called "the courtesy of holiness"[94] that offers dignity and empowerment to others. Hospitality in many places is the recognition of the foreigner in our midst or the one who is often estranged in our family circles.

---

88. Nouwen, *Reaching Out*, 27.
89. International Organization for Migration, *World Migration Report 2020.*
90. Nouwen, *Reaching Out*, 46.
91. See Ed Stetzer's helpful work *Christians in the Age of Outrage.*
92. Warren, "Why We Preach for Proper Names."
93. Pohl, *Making Room.*
94. Maxie Dunnam believes this phrase characterizes the lives of the saints. Dunnam, "Dr. Maxie Dunnam."

Yet, Nouwen takes us further than simply making room. He offers that hospitality does not begin with the skill of homemaking. In fact, it requires one to detach from the need to impress or to maintain control of the exchange. Rather, it begins with learned ignorance. The highest degree of hospitality is regarding the stranger as bearing a gift. In hospitality, conditions are created where the gift of themselves that the guest brings can be revealed and an interdependency created where their story can unfold.[95] The soul, writes Parker J. Palmer, is often a wild and wounded animal that requires patient tending and quiet listening to appear.[96] Often the potential goes unrealized because fear, suspicion, or aggression sends it back into hiding. If Sabbath and solitude are what is needed on the vertical plane in our midlife journey, then hospitality that builds community may be what is needed on the horizontal plane.

For the teacher, hospitality may be attending outside classroom hours to a student who is too insecure to speak in class; for the parent, hospitality may be opening a full spectrum of options for choice rather than foreclosing on alternatives; for the friend, hospitality may be permitting vulnerable disclosures[97] or joining the midlife search to bring coherence to life and to attune to the things we care about the most. Hospitality may simply mean abiding, as this is so often what we cherish from the Trinity—the abiding presence (John 15).

Justin Whitmel Earley advocates for the practice of eating one meal a day with others. He describes how this practice in his family life made the table the "center of gravity for loving neighbor." It reordered schedules around the table rather than schedules dictating and diminishing what can happen around the table with family, friends, and guests.[98]

Space does not permit a full discussion of other practices or virtues salient for the midlife journey. I highlight these hopefully without undermining Scripture study, prayer, acts of mercy, Christian fellowship, worship, fasting, partaking of the sacraments, and giving tithes as critical to all seasons of a Christian's life. Further, the practices I highlight here are organically connected to other practices. Hospitality often leads naturally to deeper practices of intercessory prayer and the pursuit of social justice with vulnerable populations. Spiritual friendship compels generosity and allows confession. Discernment may lead one to seek a spiritual director, to journal, to read spiritual biographies, or to take a risk. I recommend further exploration of the twelve practices identified in the Valparaiso Project for the midlife journey.[99]

95. Nouwen, *Reaching Out*, 46–52.
96. Palmer, *Hidden Wholeness*, 58–59.
97. Nouwen, *Reaching Out*, 56–68.
98. Earley, *Common Rule*, 51–53.
99. See under the heading "The Valparaiso Project" at https://practicingourfaith.org/about/.

CONCLUSION

Having begun this chapter with the observation that the middle adult years are the longest and least understood stage of the life span, I am struck by the fact that it has become one of the longest chapters of this book. Perhaps it is reminiscent of the axiom that we have not yet distilled the wisdom that is on the far side of complexity and are still immersed in the plurality of forms that characterize our lives at their midpoint. On a more personal note, I often come to the end of a day with a heavy sigh when I just don't seem to be enough for all this season seems to require of me in the complexities that emerge amid the myriad roles I occupy. One consolation that guides my prayer when I am at my best is Psalm 78. The psalm captures aspects of the generativity Erikson uses to characterize this stage of life when it summons us to not hide testimony from our children, but "tell to the coming generation the glorious deeds of the LORD, and his might, and the wonders that he has done" (v. 4). Yet, all of this recounting is set in the context of chronicling a history of how Israel's propensity is to forget, to fail in their covenantal obligations, to question God's provision, to rebel, and to find that their only hope is the recurring beneficence of God to deliver them again and again. The psalm ends rather abruptly with the choosing of David, who is heralded as a paradigmatic shepherd to whom is entrusted Israel as an inheritance. The Book of Common Prayer translates the last verse as "he fed them with a faithful and true heart."[100] When I consider all that is entrusted to me at midlife in the shepherding of future generations, despite my susceptibility to falter, slowness of heart to trust, and shortness of wisdom to guide, I still want my striving for a "faithful and true heart" to be the legacy on which my shadow falls.

---

100. Book of Common Prayer, 373.

7 | Late Adulthood
Retirement, Relinquishment, and the Spirituality of Losing Life

How do we think theologically about aging? That is, what might God's purposes be for aging or how might his purposes for our sanctification be fulfilled through the process of aging? Is aging a result of the fall, or would we have aged/matured even if Adam and Eve had never eaten from the tree? Presumably, since Adam and Eve were given the command to "be fruitful and multiply" (Gen. 1:28), God's intent included children who would age, but what would they age into if death emerged only as a result of sin? What does it mean to age gracefully? My wife recently commented to me, "I am not aging gracefully like new wine. I am fermenting like cheap beer!" How might our expectations of and perspective on aging shape how we enter the later years of life?

Demographics

In 2020, the US Census Bureau reported that in the previous decade the number of people in America who were over age sixty-five grew by over a third. During the same time period, the number of those who were eighteen years of age or younger decreased due to lower fertility rates. This trend has been called the "graying of America," though similar trends are true for many parts of the world, creating concern for how we care for an increasingly aged population.[1]

Because of the extended period of time that people are now living, late adulthood is often divided into three distinct stages, each characterized by differences in physical, cognitive, and social functioning.[2]

1. "65 and Older Population Grows Rapidly."
2. The age ranges listed here are gleaned from a categorization of those who visit an emergency department. See Lee et al., "Differences in Youngest-Old, Middle-Old, and Oldest-Old," 249.

young-old = 60–69 or 65–74
middle-old = 70–79 or 75–84
old-old = 80+ or 85+

However, because functional age is regarded as a more salient indicator of how old one feels than chronology, the age for each division differs significantly among the various categorizations. Some schemas reflect the *Lebenstreppe* imaged in the previous chapter and distinguish stages based on decades of life. Others have offered a more generous appraisal based on greater longevity and suggest the following ranges:

young-old = 65–84
middle-old = 85–99
centenarians[3]

Perceptions of aging and late adulthood vary significantly by culture, with Asian, African, and Latin American cultures bestowing authority and respect on those who are aged. By contrast, in developed countries, where even toy tank engines are evaluated on the basis of their usefulness,[4] older adults who no longer work often feel devalued and put out to pasture. The older one gets, the more stereotypes may stigmatize one's life stage.[5]

More than 75 percent of the time, families care for their elderly, with women disproportionately carrying the burden.[6] The old adage holds true: "A son is a son until he takes a wife; a daughter is a daughter all of her life."[7] Although the pandemic may have altered some trends, some middle-aged adults could spend more years caring for aging parents than they did raising their own children.[8] This can put strain on a mother who was hoping for greater freedom after launching the kids. Many financial planners advise that very few families are adequately prepared financially to pay the medical bills that can accompany the aged and are not adequately covered by Medicare and Medicaid.[9]

3. Lally and Valentine-French, *Lifespan Development*, 377.
4. This is a reference to the popular English kids' show *Thomas the Tank Engine*, in which Sir Topham Hatt often comments on the "very useful engines" in the rail yard.
5. Broderick and Blewitt, *Life Span*, 602.
6. Broderick and Blewitt, *Life Span*, 599–600.
7. *Farlex Dictionary of Idioms*, s.v. "a son is a son."
8. Broderick and Blewitt, *Life Span*, 599–600.
9. According to 2020 census data, Medicaid and Medicare each provided on average about 18 percent of the needed coverage. Keisler-Starkey and Bunch, "Health Insurance Coverage."

Retirement

When the life course was shorter, it was not uncommon for people to remain working until they were no longer able to function. As people began living longer, they often became dependent on their children, putting a substantial strain on the family physically and emotionally and sometimes contributing to poverty. Only in the last century were things like national pension programs, health care, and personal savings implemented that allowed developing Western nations to create retirement the way we experience it today.[10] A person in the United States, for example, can begin to draw Social Security benefits at age sixty-two, prompting many to consider retiring in their early to mid-sixties. Counterintuitively, however, as the life span has gotten longer, the average age of retirement has been slowly decreasing.[11]

Many factors may influence why and when a person decides to retire or is forced into retirement: financial considerations, physical health issues, and current or projected levels of job satisfaction. Satisfaction in retirement increases for those with financial resources, good health, and educational achievements and who have held a relatively high-status job. Some also find that a graduated approach whereby they systematically reduce the number of hours they work or the amount of responsibility they carry eases the transition into retirement. Some companies, fearing the increasing cost of health care and wanting to invest in younger employees who have more years of service to give, make it difficult for people to continue working past a certain age. In the United States, however, government assistance and home ownership have meant that older persons now have the lowest poverty rate among all age groups.[12] Nancy Schlossberg identifies multiple pathways into retirement:

- *Continuers* use the same skills from their earlier careers either part time or in different contexts.
- *Involved spectators* remain connected to their previous work but take on different roles.
- *Adventurers* develop new skills and/or new work roles.
- *Easy gliders* relinquish work roles to keep their schedules flexible.
- *Searchers* continue searching for suitable work roles.

10. "Retirement in the U.S.: A History to Today."
11. Sato, "What Is the Average Retirement Age?"
12. This situation may be challenged by an increasing number of couples divorcing later in life and hence splitting their nest egg and living alone. Shoichet and Leipzig, "More Baby Boomers Are Living Alone."

- *Retreaters* despair that no work roles can be found that provide satisfaction.[13]

Robert Atchley developed a theory about the typical progression a person might experience in retirement. Though almost fifty years old, the theory still has value today.[14] Atchley observes that many retirees experience a *honeymoon* phase (stage 1) in their first six months of retirement. (The exception may be the quarter of those who are forced into retirement.) Work demands, dress clothes, and the pressure of schedules are relinquished, and a person feels an initial sense of relief. But once the relief wears off, a second stage of *disenchantment* (stage 2) may follow. The retiree misses the colleagues they saw regularly at work, life feels less meaningful, and feelings of control and contribution are relinquished. Furthermore, the retiree's spouse may be adjusting to them being at home all the time and sense their restless boredom. Usually with some experimentation and false starts, the retiree begins to find some *resolution or reorientation* (stage 3) to the challenges retirement presents. Life *stabilizes* (stage 4), and new investments of time are given to things that again bring meaning, satisfaction, and well-being. These may take the form of leisure activities, travel or educational programs, community or civic engagements, or volunteering with religious or medical institutions. A couple eventually finds new rhythms and begins to function better together again. Finally, toward the end of life, health declines may force dependency on others for care, creating what Atchley calls the final stage of *termination* (stage 5).[15]

Robert Peck believes that when a person retires, what is critical is that the person begins to find identity, meaning, and purpose beyond their work role. In particular, he urges four shifts to occur: a person learns to value wisdom above physical prowess, a person learns to value socializing above sexualizing, a person learns emotional flexibility to overcome relational impoverishments, and a person develops mental flexibility.[16]

Grandparenting

Grandparents—whether older adults or those still in middle adulthood—have sometimes been referred to as the "silent saviors" of a whole generation of chil-

---

13. Schlossberg's work is summarized along with other helpful explorations regarding the transition to retirement in Broderick and Blewitt, *Life Span*, 606.

14. Atchley's work, *The Sociology of Retirement*, is summarized along with other helpful explorations regarding the transition to retirement in Broderick and Blewitt, *Life Span*, 606–7.

15. Balswick, King, and Reimer, *Reciprocating Self*, 226–27.

16. R. Peck, "Psychological Developments in the Second Half of Life."

dren and youth. Some estimates suggest that 2.9 million children are being raised in their grandparents' home.[17] Grandparents are also instrumental in helping to raise children when both parents work or when time and resources run thin in single-parent families. This is especially true in multigenerational families that are more commonly Asian, African, or Latino.[18] Grandmothers and grandfathers generally find their role beneficial, allowing them to share family history, maximize fun without having to be disciplinarians, offer wisdom based on long experience, and gaining the sense that something of who they have been will live beyond their death.[19]

Declines during the Retirement Years

Most physical declines that accompany the retirement years are relatively mild. If it has not already occurred, hair tends to gray and thin. Age spots develop, hastened by exposure to the sun in earlier years. Height and weight may begin to decline. The decline in the senses that may have begun in middle life may become more noticeable, as sight, hearing, smell, and taste can become impaired. Cataracts involve the shrinking of the lens of the eye, causing one's vision to become cloudy, opaque, and distorted. Some eye conditions, such as macular degeneration (loss of acuity in the center of the visual field) and glaucoma (hardening of the eyeball due to fluid buildup), can create greater impairments to vision and present more formidable challenges to the activities of daily living. Hearing acuity, especially for high-pitched sounds, often diminishes, with about 40 percent of those over age sixty-five reporting some difficulty in hearing normal conversations. Tinnitus, a constant buzzing or ringing in the ear, can develop. The challenge with hearing loss is that it often moves an older person toward further social withdrawal and isolation, contributing to depression or loneliness. Fortunately, hearing aid technology is significantly improving, and there is less stigma connected to wearing aids. The number of taste and smell receptors also begins to decline, making dangerous smells less easy to detect and food less enjoyable and occasionally even leading to malnutrition.[20]

Typically, the amount of sleep a person needs tends to increase with age, but the quality of sleep often declines as a person grows older. A person sleeps less deeply, so the time spent in light sleep increases. Sleep can be affected by many medical conditions but also compounded by psychological issues such

17. D. Thompson, "U.S. Grandparents."
18. Arnett and Jensen, *Human Development,* 512.
19. Arnett and Jensen, *Human Development,* 514.
20. Arnett and Jensen, *Human Development,* 535.

as depression and anxiety. Common sleep problems, such as sleep apnea, grow more common with age but are also more treatable with things like a CPAP device.

The most talked about declines typically occur in the cognitive domain, referenced in common parlance as "having a senior moment." However, neurobiology is now helping us understand that the effects of aging on memory vary based on the type of memory or intelligence that is being considered. Fluid intelligence might be thought of as the processing efficiency or mechanics of the brain, the parts of thinking used in working memory and problem-solving; crystallized intelligence might be thought of as the product of that processing or the pragmatics of the brain. Crystallized intelligence may include verbal ability or factual knowledge. Whereas fluid intelligence may begin incrementally decreasing around the seventh decade of life, crystallized intelligence may continue to increase until age ninety. Some brain scans show that older adults use both sides of their brain, while younger populations favor one hemisphere over the other, perhaps because the brain is compensating for loss in one hemisphere and drawing on reserve power.[21]

The brain shrinks and total brain mass declines by about 5 to 10 percent by age eighty, leaving space between the brain and the skull and spaces within the brain as well. The production of neurotransmitters is greatly reduced in old age, the volume of neural fluid diminishes, and cerebral blood flow weakens, all contributing to the slowing of neural communication and pace of brain activation. The hippocampus, cerebellum, and frontal lobes lose efficiency, and the loss of neurons that are not replaced is notable.

Older Adulthood

Currently, 80 percent of the American population lives beyond age sixty-five. Of this group, more than 75 percent will struggle with heart disease, cancer, stroke, lung disease, or dementia during the last twelve months of life. Common health issues that intensify during this period of the life course are arthritis, osteoporosis, and hypertension.[22]

The most common chronic health problem of late adulthood is arthritis, a disease of the joints reported by about half of the adults over age sixty-five in developed countries, especially women. The cartilage that cushions the joints during movement begins to wear out. No cure has been found for arthritis, but it is generally treated with anti-inflammatory medications. Exercise can

21. Broderick and Blewitt, *Life Span*, 593–96.
22. Arnett and Jensen, *Human Development*, 536–38.

sometimes help relieve the symptoms of arthritis, and occasionally surgery is prescribed for the pain.

Osteoporosis is a loss of bone mineral density, causing a decrease in bone mass. Height slowly declines, about one and a half inches for men and two inches for women after age sixty. The decrease in bone strength also increases the risk of fractures. In about 15 percent of cases, a bone fracture leads to subsequent mortality. About 66 percent of women age sixty and older in developed countries are affected by osteoporosis. Strength-training exercises and calcium-rich foods can help delay or reverse the damage of osteoporosis.[23]

Hypertension, also known as high blood pressure, plagues about 70 percent of people in developed countries in late adulthood. Hearts become less efficient with age, worsened by bad diets, excess fat, and chronic stress. Symptoms of hypertension are often silent, but they strain the circulatory system as arteries weaken and inflammation increases. Although death resulting from cardiovascular disease is more prevalent in middle adulthood, an increasing number of effective medications can help control it.[24]

Three processes are key to coping with increasing losses and maintaining well-being. They no doubt have implication at any stage of the life course but are especially poignant in old age. Together, the processes are often referred to as selective optimization with compensation.[25] Selection simply refers to making choices about what is valued and can still be enjoyed while eliminating things that are too straining. Sometimes this happens naturally, as when a person retires and so surrenders work time to invest more deeply in family. Older adults are more selective about the friendships they maintain, choosing relationships that are low in conflict and high in mutual enjoyment, thus maximizing their emotional well-being.[26]

Optimization is characterized by channeling the energy one has into attaining remaining goals or finding places that are conducive to one's wants.[27] This might be akin to the retiree who builds a wood shop to support a latent hobby or completes a writing project as a legacy for future generations.

Compensation signifies the use of technology or other means to overcome loss in some area.[28] For example, when one older man's eyesight left him almost blind, he outfitted his home with special lighting so he could continue living independently, and he purchased a digital magnifier so he could continue to read his Bible and communicate easily with his daughter.

23. Arnett and Jensen, *Human Development*, 537.
24. Arnett and Jensen, *Human Development*, 537–38.
25. Arnett and Jensen, *Human Development*, 554.
26. Broderick and Blewitt, *Life Span*, 605.
27. Broderick and Blewitt, *Life Span*, 605.
28. Arnett and Jensen, *Human Development*, 554.

A great deal of ministry with the elderly likely hovers around facilitating selective optimization with compensation. The aim is often to allow the aging person as much control as possible to contribute to their ongoing need for autonomy, competence, and relatedness while also giving care when needed.

Participation in a faith community is especially beneficial during this stage of life. Maintaining social connection serves a protective function and enhances cognitive functioning. Across cultures and different world religions, senior followers are encouraged to relinquish worldly desires and interests to focus on spiritual enlightenment. Church attendance may decline after age eighty due to physical and health issues, but this in no way indicates a loss of faith. Religiosity is especially prominent among African Americans, where it serves many purposes, including supporting faith, socializing, and social services. Women are generally more religious in beliefs and practices than men, yet older men are the ones who mainly hold positions of power in religious organizations.[29]

Studies of social media have tended to focus on younger populations and mental health issues. However, the use of technology has significant implications for older Americans as well. Research suggests that older adults spend more than half of their leisure time, over four hours a day, using media.[30] Television is likely the most common type of media used by older generations, with women and African Americans viewing more than men and whites. While older adults are less likely to surf the internet, many are learning to use the Web to enhance their health and quality of life, including socializing with family and friends online. Families and caregivers of the elderly can benefit from the ever-expanding capabilities of assistive technology. Chat features on mobile devices, timed reminders to take medications, GPS tracking devices for those who wander, digital sharing of photographs, and motion detection systems to determine whether an elder has become immobile are all technologies enhancing quality of care.[31]

Myths of the Aged

Those in late adulthood face stereotyped attitudes and responses that can sometimes lead to patronizing talk or demeaning practices.[32] These misconceptions seem to be true across a wide variety of cultures. Elderspeak is a way of speaking to the elderly that resembles baby talk.[33] Simple, short sentences

29. For a good presentation on the correlation of religiosity to well-being, see Broderick and Blewitt, Life Span, 564–67.
30. Livingston, "Americans 60 and Older."
31. "Assistive Technology for the Elderly."
32. Broderick and Blewitt, Life Span, 602–4.
33. C. Shaw, Gordon, and Williams, "Understanding Elderspeak."

are used with repetition and exaggerated emphasis. Sometimes this can be helpful, but far too often people talk past the elderly without realizing the capacities they retain.[34]

James M. Houston and Michael Parker provide humorous epithets that help us become aware of the stereotypes we may have about the aged.[35] I have revised and added to these myths as a way of helping us think about common images and fears about the elderly that can be misleading. The myth is stated first, followed by research that provides a more accurate understanding.

Myth: To be old is to be incapacitated, severely impaired, or in poor health. The elderly spend most of their time in bed, in homes for the aged, or under "house arrest" as prisoners of fear.

- Some studies suggest that as high as 89 percent of those age sixty-five to seventy-four report no disabilities, and 75 percent of those age seventy-five to eighty-four report no disabilities.[36]
- Currently, less than 5 percent of the elderly live in nursing homes.[37]
- Medical experts are interested in "compression of morbidity"—promoting lifestyles that can prolong quality of life and minimize the time people spend being unhealthy at the end of their lives.[38]

Myth: You can't teach an old dog new tricks. The elderly lose mental capacities and are incompetent or senile.

- Older adults may be less able to screen out distractions or prevent irrelevant thoughts, thus inhibiting some communication, but many also have a greater capacity to select from extensive experience when making judgments about a particular situation.[39]
- Neurobiology confirms that we lose some capacity for quick retrieval as we reach the later years of life. However, some forms of intelligence, like looking across decades of life experience, do not decline until the seventies, and vocabulary knowledge may continue to increase until the nineties.[40]

34. Broderick and Blewitt, *Life Span*, 603.
35. Houston and Parker, *Vision for the Aging Church*, 111–20.
36. Houston and Parker, *Vision for the Aging Church*, 114.
37. Houston and Parker, *Vision for the Aging Church*, 114.
38. Stibich, "Compression of Morbidity and Reducing Suffering."
39. Houston and Parker, *Vision for the Aging Church*, 115.
40. Broderick and Blewitt, *Life Span*, 514–15, 594.

Myth: The horse is out of the barn—lost function cannot be recovered.

- Losing weight, ceasing to smoke, and beginning to exercise have been shown to reduce disease and disability and sometimes to allow a reclaiming of bone strength, muscle, and brain development. Across several domains of human functioning, the principle often seems to be "You lose what you don't use."[41]
- There are no doubt limitations to what can be restored, but there does seem to be some possibility that "neurons that fire together, wire together."[42]

Myth: The key to growing old successfully is choosing one's parents wisely— that is, one needs to have good genes.

- The later one is in the life span, the more it appears lifestyle trumps biology. Some genetic conditions persist and cannot be fully overcome, but in many cases habits are more determinative of outcome than one's inherited DNA.[43]
- Sherry Willis and K. Warner Schaie found that cognitive interventions for memory, reasoning, and processing speed were effective, substantial, and durable. Hence, mental exercises can be used to slow cognitive decline. These skills also improved confidence for everyday tasks.[44]

Myth: Old people are curmudgeons.[45] They complain all the time and are ill-tempered and bitter.

- Older adults actually tend to have fewer conflicts and resolve them more quickly when compared with younger adults. Whereas depressive symptoms may increase in old age, older adults describe themselves as having greater regulatory control over their emotions when compared to young adults.[46] They generally dwell less on sorrow and are more accepting of things they cannot change.
- Dixon Chibanda trained elderly grandmothers in Zimbabwe in basic listening and counseling skills so they could occupy friendship benches

---

41. Houston and Parker, *Vision for the Aging Church*, 117–18.
42. This principle is known as the Hebbian learning rule. Hebb, *Organization of Behavior*, 62. Cf. Krupic, "Wire Together, Fire Apart."
43. Houston and Parker, *Vision for the Aging Church*, 118.
44. Willis and Schaie, "Intellectual Functioning in Midlife," 238–39.
45. Broderick and Blewitt, *Life Span*, 602.
46. Broderick and Blewitt, *Life Span*, 613–14.

where young people could come to talk about any problems they were having.[47]

- Some studies reveal that older people are seen as lower in competence but higher in warmth than those who are younger.[48]

Myth: The lights are on, but the voltage is low—older men and women are sexless and uninterested in sex.

- John Rowe and Robert Kahn report that about 70 percent of men reported remaining sexually active at sixty-eight, though this number decreases significantly in the next decade. Even with "low voltage," the desire for affectionate contact may remain high.[49]

Myth: The elderly don't pull their weight.

- This myth flows from a diminished view of personhood. Seniors may actually play an increasingly important role in the workplace, in churches as volunteers, and in public service sectors.[50] Greatly needed is a reconceptualization of ministry that is not simply *to* seniors but *with, by,* and *from* seniors.
- One of the eightysomething-year-olds in my former parish started an after-school tutoring program for kids in an underprivileged neighborhood near the church. I was skeptical of it catching on, but in a few months she was regularly coordinating about a dozen retired schoolteachers to tutor two or three times a week.
- When my mother turned eighty-five, having recently retired from brokering a real estate company, she took a pretty bad fall that badly bruised her wrist. We feared it might signal a rapid decline, but she rallied in part because she was determined to become certified with my father (now deceased) as a Stephen Minister in their Lutheran congregation.

Autobiographical Memory and the Virtue of Mortality

Autobiographical memory is a term used to refer to the preferred "remembered self"—how we like to remember who we have been at various points in our lives, providing us in narrative form a pleasant story about ourselves that we present

47. Singh, "Friendship Bench."
48. Broderick and Blewitt, *Life Span*, 603.
49. Rowe and Kahn, *Successful Aging*, 28–30.
50. Houston and Parker, *Vision for the Aging Church*, 119.

to ourselves but that can also be shared with others.[51] In general, a memory is strongest when the event is most recent, and it declines in saliency as time passes. However, some report that there is a reminiscence bump whereby more vivid and personally relevant memories are produced from age ten to thirty than from age thirty to fifty, perhaps being encoded as highly important or first-time events.[52] My own experience with student assignments bears this out. Adapting aspects of the Human Library project,[53] I have assigned my students to interview seventy- and eighty-year-olds. From these interviews, students report that often the stage of life most remembered and talked about is the period from ten to thirty.

My graduate schoolwork was in identity formation. Once, after attending an identity conference, I was privileged to be in the airport with one of the premier researchers on identity at that time, Jane Kroger. She shared with me that one of her latest studies involved interviewing seniors who were transitioning into nursing homes and considering what objects they were choosing to take with them and what meaning they had for them.[54] The objects we choose to keep tend to contain memories, making such an inquiry a fascinating window into what life experiences are most treasured at the end of our journey.

Autobiographical memory brings our past into the present and makes it available for further contemplation. There may be something God-like in the process of hovering over all that has created one's life and bestowing upon it goodness and value. When objects and events and people of seemingly little importance are given value, virtue is fostered. Our own innate search for significance draws us in curiosity to what people value at the end of life.[55]

Houston and Parker articulate virtues they see as potentially emerging during this stage of life:

- Adoration. Born from the long experience of God's mercy, adoration inclines the heart toward God.
- Individuation. In spite of our continuity in temperament traits, God encourages uniqueness to grow so that extraordinary variety manifests in the temperament of the aged.
- Strength from suffering. As bodies retain the scars of natural aging and illness, a closeness to Christ can develop in journeying with a suffering Savior.

51. Arnett and Jensen, *Human Development*, 546.
52. Arnett and Jensen, *Human Development*, 546.
53. The Human Library promotes learning by "borrowing" people from the human library (especially those who have been stigmatized or marginalized), rather than borrowing books from a traditional library. https://humanlibrary.org/.
54. Kroger, "Identity Processes and Contents," 81–89.
55. Some of my thoughts on memory and virtue were helped by Ward, "Reading and the Virtue of Memory."

- Steadfastness and sacrifice. Through long journeys, late adults have often learned to sacrifice things of lesser value for those of greater and eternal worth. Persevering through times of trial frequently yields serenity where anxiety once reigned.[56]

A friend in high school, Kevin Evans, shared with me the perspective that the book of Job might serve as a metaphor for aging. Job moves into adulthood with all that is often cherished in life: he is married with kids, has significant possessions, owns property and livestock, has "friends" who surround him, etc. As life progresses, however, he loses more and more of what he had been gathering and clinging to (family, health, possessions, friends) until finally he is left with nothing except his relationship with God. It may be that loss throughout the life course presents us with this sanctifying dilemma: When all is stripped away and we relinquish more and more of the roles and possessions that have given our life meaning, what will we anchor in?

Seniors cultivate an atmosphere of peace because of their gentle steadiness of purpose. This is often accompanied by humor, perspective, and altruism. The aging process presents us with the "breaking of self-preoccupation" that lends itself to the cultivation of "more space for others." It may well be that a lifetime of making small sacrifices for others allows for big sacrifices also to be made.[57]

Wisdom

In Erik H. Erikson's rendering of the eight stages of life, wisdom is the culminating virtue. It is the endowment for those who can engage in life review and find in it a sense of ego integration, a confirmation that they have lived their life well. By contrast are those who find despair at choices made, opportunities squandered, or the disabling of successful resolutions to the developmental tasks of life.[58]

The Scriptures affirm wisdom in old age. The presumed oldest book in the Bible, Job, declares that "wisdom is with the aged, and understanding in length of days" (Job 12:12). Yet, other passages assume that wisdom is not solely the reward of the aged but can be acquired by any who are humble of heart, open minded, and willing to pursue it. James writes that "if any of you lacks wisdom, let him ask God, who gives generously to all without reproach, and it will be given to him" (James 1:5). Much of the Old Testament Wisdom literature is

56. Houston and Parker, *Vision for the Aging Church*, 72–78.
57. Houston and Parker, *Vision for the Aging Church*, 72–78.
58. Erikson, *Identity and the Life Cycle*, 104–5.

instruction to the young to seek after wisdom. Proverbs 2, for example, addresses "my son," imploring that "if you receive my words . . . , making your ear attentive to wisdom and inclining your heart to understanding; . . . then you will understand the fear of the LORD" (vv. 1–2, 5) that preserves, delivers, and delights. After Jesus is found in the temple reasoning with the religious leaders, the Bible states that he "increased in wisdom and in stature and in favor with God and man" (Luke 2:52).

Wisdom itself, though so recognizable in those who possess it, is hard to define. Paul Baltes and Ursula Staudinger define *wisdom* as "expertise in the conduct and meaning of life,"[59] associating it with several related concepts: "*insight* into human nature and the human condition; *knowledge* of human social relations and emotions; *strategies* for applying this insight and knowledge to everyday problems and life decisions; a concern with promoting the highest human *values*; and an *awareness* that human problems often involve multiple considerations and no easy answers."[60]

Western cultures tend to emphasize more cognitive aspects of wisdom—that is, breadth of knowledge and the ability to analyze—whereas Eastern cultures use more expansive notions of wisdom, incorporating both cognition and affect.[61] Children who become adept at reading social cues manifest earlier development of wise reasoning skills in resolving conflict.[62]

According to Staudinger, a wise person is one who becomes "expert in the psychological art of life," including such factors as motivation, emotion regulation, other-directed perspective versus remaining self-involved, tolerance of ambiguity, and insight.[63] Recognizing contradictions in life, the wise person draws insight from them, creating the capacity for integration that serves the common good. Not surprisingly, correlations have been found between high scores on wisdom and cooperative conflict management (in contrast to dominance strategies).[64] Wisdom possessors score high on involvement with people and aim at enhancing the growth and potential of people. Igor Grossman suggests that wisdom consists of intellectual humility, appreciating perspectives beyond the present issue, recognizing the possibility of change in relationships, and integrating different opinions.[65] Ann Morisy writes about nine aptitudes that wise people cultivate:

59. Baltes and Staudinger, "Wisdom," 124.
60. This summation of Baltes and Staudinger's work is in Arnett and Jensen, *Human Development*, 551–52.
61. Broderick and Blewitt, *Life Span*, 610.
62. Broderick and Blewitt, *Life Span*, 611.
63. Staudinger, "Social Cognition and a Psychological Approach to an Art of Life," 343.
64. Broderick and Blewitt, *Life Span*, 610.
65. Grossman, "Wisdom in Context."

- becoming a nonanxious presence in stressful times
- practicing systemic thinking to resist blaming others when things go wrong
- practicing gratitude—even in difficult circumstances
- engaging in small acts that serve those outside one's group, countering the inclination toward neo-tribalism rather than social cohesion (e.g., Jesus with the Samaritan woman at the well)
- imagining ways of breaking out of the constraints of circumstances
- gaining confidence in the viability of abundance rather than being beholden to scarcity
- practicing sitting lightly on the globe in recognition of our abuse of creation
- practicing compassion, conviviality, and harnessing the imagination to ward off Gnosticism
- affirming the human capacity to correct one's own errors—"to repent" or "turn about"[66]

Psalm 90:12 admonishes, "Teach us to number our days that we may get a heart of wisdom." Implicit in this admonition is that wisdom may be gained via the contemplation of one's mortality. Christopher A. Hall captures Augustine's counsel on prayer as he writes to a widow by the name of Proba who was apparently a woman of some means but yearned to dedicate more and more of her life to God.[67] Augustine examines whether Proba's reliance on her family and her wealth may present impediments to prayer because they provide false sources of security and comfort. As an antidote to these taking root and robbing her of a deeper reliance on God, Augustine prescribes that she remember and meditate on life's brevity and death's inevitable embrace, reorienting her desire toward what could provide a more lasting and genuine source of happiness. Mortality provides the wisdom that can teach one how to live life well.

I was once invited on a men's retreat designed by Lyman Coleman, one of the gurus of the small group movement, to attend my own funeral and to present my own eulogy.[68] Facing one's mortality as an avenue for enhancing living is pervasive in leadership literature. Steven Covey's second habit, "Begin with the end in mind,"[69] and writing one's mission statement based on the legacy one wants to leave come to mind. However, the principle is also found in the parables and teachings of Jesus (Matt. 25:1–13; Mark 13:35) and in Pauline

---

66. These attributes are woven throughout Morisy, *Bothered and Bewildered*.

67. Hall, *Living Wisely with the Church Fathers*, 144.

68. Coleman's creative work on men's ministry is now embedded in a retreat curriculum Lutheran Men in Mission is conducting called *One Year to Live*.

69. Covey, *7 Habits of Highly Effective People*, 95–144.

theology (2 Cor. 5:10; 1 Thess. 5:6).[70] Moral instruction, amendment of life, and true repentance are fashioned in moments of contemplating one's own mortality.

Dementia

With increased longevity to the life course comes the risk of dementia. By 2050, an estimated 13 million Americans will suffer from this disease.[71] Dementia is characterized by an irreversible loss of intellectual functioning caused by the accumulation of plaque in the cerebral cortex of the brain or by neurofibrillary tangles of protein threads. Dementia can be difficult to diagnose, as it is also associated with more than seventy other diseases. Most often it is diagnosed by excluding all other possible diseases, but it can be confirmed only by an autopsy once the patient is deceased. Alzheimer's is the most common form of dementia, accounting for about 60 percent of all cases. Other forms of dementia are frontotemporal (deterioration in the frontal lobes of the brain), vascular (related to the flow of blood to the brain), and Lewy Body (or the buildup of proteins).[72] Some common symptoms of Alzheimer's include:

- Memory loss. Beyond wondering where I left my keys, this is more akin to "How do I drive?"
- Difficulty with familiar tasks. One is no longer able to check the oil, bake a cake, address a card.
- Language problems. Frequently, one forgets how to complete a sentence or repeats a phrase over and over.
- Inability to calculate. One cannot balance a checkbook or figure out the amount of ingredients needed for a recipe.
- Confusion about time. One loses a sense of how much time has passed and confuses day and night.
- Confusion about location. One talks frequently about going home and does not feel at home wherever they are.
- Confusion about people. One thinks that their daughter is their mother who has been deceased for thirty years.
- Poor judgment. One loses common sense, can't weigh risks, and can't anticipate consequences.

70. See also Hays, *Moral Vision of the New Testament*, for a deeper rendering of virtue in light of eschatological themes.
71. Broderick and Blewitt, *Life Span*, 596.
72. Broderick and Blewitt, *Life Span*, 596–98.

- Mood and personality changes. One becomes agitated or mellow, quick to anger and to forget.
- Loss of initiative. One requires more prompting from loved ones to do simple things.
- Hiding and hoarding. One stashes money, food, clothing, paper, and other things.[73]

Women are at greater risk than men to develop dementia, and European Americans seem more susceptible than Asian Americans. However, age seems to be the primary factor, with one in one hundred showing signs at age sixty-five, but one in five has a confirmed diagnosis by age eighty-five. Early onset Alzheimer's (about 5 percent of overall cases) has a strong genetic basis, detected by the presence of the ApoE gene. Yet, even this gene is affected by environmental factors, such as a diet high in fat and sugar. The Mediterranean diet has been shown to diminish the chances of dementia, as has regular exercise and being cognitively active and educated.[74]

Dementia typically progresses in stages, depicted as anywhere from three to seven stages, with common characteristics appearing at each stage. Typically it takes three to eleven years to move through these stages, but it can take up to twenty years.[75]

Stage 1
  general forgetfulness
  failure to remember common words
  heavy reliance on others to carry on conversations
Stage 2
  more general confusion
  deficits in concentration and short-term memory
  aimless or repetitive speech
  mixed-up vocabulary
Stage 3
  dangerous memory loss (a person may get lost)
  inability to take care of basic needs
  inability to recognize people
Stage 4
  need for full-time care

73. Adapted from "10 Early Signs and Symptoms of Alzheimer's and Dementia."
74. "Basics of Alzheimer's Disease."
75. "Alzheimer's Stages."

irrational anger or paranoia

inability to recognize other people, even those they have known well

Stage 5

muteness

inability to respond with action or emotion

death[76]

Kenneth L. Carder, a professor at Duke Divinity School and a United Methodist bishop, spent over a decade caring for a beloved wife who developed the worst kind of dementia. In his deeply probing reflection on his wife's degeneration, he poses challenging theological questions.[77] Most commonly in evangelical circles, we define what it means to be a Christian assuming cognitive and relational capacities—that is, a Christian is one who believes the creeds, accepts Jesus as Lord and Savior, loves God and neighbor, and participates in the life of the church. But Ken found that none of these applied to his wife in the throes of her cognitive impairment. She often could not recognize Ken, much less affirm the creeds. She could not remember who God was, and she was disabled from participating in the life of the church. By common definitions, she could no longer qualify as a disciple of Jesus.

Ken pushes us to consider how Christian identity is embedded not simply in *our* memory but in *God's* memory. A Christian community can hold on to the identity of a person when they have lost the capacity to do so themselves. So here we have come full circle in our explorations. When a newborn is presented for baptism or dedication, we entrust their spiritual inheritance to godparents and/or a congregation. In most traditions, members of the congregation make a pledge to support and love the child and the parents so that the child will be caught up in a life of faith. In the last stage of life, many find their bodies and minds returning them to a state of vulnerability much like infancy where they must once again rely on the care, including the spiritual care, of others.

Death

My colleague Chris Johnson wrote a dissertation on John Wesley's theology of death. Though some might shun the contemplation of their own death, Johnson found evidence that in other eras of the church, the art of dying well (*ars moriendi*) actually held a prominent place in the life of believers.[78] Guidance

76. "Alzheimer's Stages."
77. Carder, *Ministry with the Forgotten.*
78. Chris Johnson, "Dying Well."

was given on how to prepare for death in a way that turned one from fear and hence witnessed to the rest of the world. Fear of death is our ultimate anxiety and the foundation of most depression and alienation. Wesley took his cues from Jeremy Taylor's *The Rule and Exercise of Holy Dying*. By normalizing death, Wesley sought to learn from those who were dying and hence to diminish the way we tend to isolate ourselves from the sick and dying.[79]

Johnson writes that for Wesley the key to dying well is living well. Contemplating the end of our lives reminds us that life is a precious gift from God and should not be squandered on penultimate pursuits. As we contemplate the short time that remains, impediments to the single intention of glorifying God are removed and new earnestness is revived. When a life is fully lived for the glory of God, death is simply one more opportunity to manifest the grace of God.[80]

Wesley regards sanctification as a movement from the fear of God to a middle stage where there is a mixture of fear and love to a final stage where love casts out fear.[81] Is this movement accelerated by those who practice sacrifice and daily dying to self? I have encountered a few folks who passed almost naturally from this life into the next as if there was a continuity between the two worlds. One was Thomas Carruth, the dean of Asbury Seminary's chapel and the first professor hired in the area of spiritual formation. Late in his life, Carruth would shuffle down the hallway to retrieve his mail from the seminary post office. Under his breath, he repeatedly whispered the name Jesus. Carruth was already living in the heavenly realm; his earthly body had just not yet let go. I recently read a commentary on Enoch, who we are told "walked with God, and he was not, for God took him" (Gen. 5:24). This may be an early foreshadowing, long before any promise of eternal life was given, that those who walk with Yahweh overcome the curse of sin in the garden.

The hospice movement and the death with dignity movement are perhaps modern equivalents of *ars moriendi*, both bringing attention to the question "What is a good death?" One study identifies from thirty-six studies the most critical features of a good death according to the reports of patients and their families. The findings focus on the following as some of the important factors to consider:

Where will dying occur? (most do not express a desire to die at home)

Who will be present?

Will it be a pain-free experience?

79. Christine Johnson, "Holiness and Death."
80. Christine Johnson, "Holiness and Death."
81. I am indebted to Donald Joy for this insight, which he developed from Wesley's sermon "On the Spirit of Bondage and Adoption" and Wesley's notes on 1 John 4:81. Joy wrote about this in "Human Development and Christian Holiness."

What emotional support optimizes the person's well-being?

Is there an opportunity to discuss the meaning of death?[82]

Many organizations now have written statements that detail the core principles they seek to follow in giving care. One of the more extensive is the statement of the International Association for Hospice and Palliative Care. Following is an abbreviated version of their two-page statement:

- Holistic concern for "all aspects of a patient's suffering," not just the medical (e.g., personality, ethnicity, religious belief, etc.)
- High regard for the "unique psychosocial needs" of the patient as opposed to care categorized on the basis of their disease
- Support for the emotional needs of the caregiver in recognition that mitigating their distress contributes to successful care for the dying
- Cultural sensitivity particularly regarding how much information is disclosed to the patient and the extent to which the family wishes to preserve the life of the patient
- Honor of patient consent, as most patients express an interest in shared information and control over decision-making
- Choice of location where care is given (though most in the West die in hospitals)
- Good communication between health-care professionals and families
- Treatment that aims to balance medical interventions to prolong life with a humanistic understanding of dying patients (may require a coordination and continuity of care when a patient is moved from one place to another)
- Forewarning of risks and contingency plans that seek to minimize the emotional toll of a crisis should it occur
- Continual reassessment as a disease progresses
- Planning in advance that addresses end-of-life options and a person to help with such decision-making[83]

Grief Work

For decades, grief work was dominated by Elisabeth Kübler-Ross's stages of grief, with each stage in the cycle representing a type of coping or defense mechanism for dealing with death.[84]

82. Meier et al., "Defining a Good Death."
83. Doyle, "Principles of Palliative Care."
84. Kübler-Ross, *On Death and Dying.*

Denial→Anger→Bargaining→Depression→Acceptance

The theory served me well in most of my pastoral work, as it (1) yielded insight into the various responses a person might experience when confronting significant loss, (2) suggested that grief may be a protracted process that can last anywhere from six months to two years or longer and should not be rushed, and (3) helped me become accepting of the aggressive skepticism of God's goodness that often accompanies good grief work.

Yet, despite the popularity of Kübler-Ross's theory, aspects of it are problematic. For example, the five stages may not be the only appropriate responses to grief, and so the theory may not be comprehensive of all grief reactions. Furthermore, by ordering these in a fixed sequence, the theory can lead a pastor or therapist to falsely evaluate what is functional adjustment. In other words, if a person has not experienced a particular stage, they may be seen as maladjusted in their grief work. Perhaps most importantly, the absence of overt, intense grief is not necessarily problematic, as the theory would seem to suggest. Encouraging a demonstration of intense grief is no more helpful than advising someone to maintain a stiff upper lip. The reality is that most people don't grieve in a linear, predictable fashion, and for some, there may not be a requisite expression of mourning. In fact, rumination as a way of coping correlates highly with depression, and a certain amount of detachment may actually predict a healthy outcome. What further research has shown is that using a theory like Kübler-Ross's prescriptively rather than descriptively likely ignores the variety of grief reactions that can prove healthy.[85]

Similarly, a central aspect of Sigmund Freud's theory posits that the key aspect of good grief is emotionally detaching from the person who was lost and reinvesting the psychic energy in other ways. He calls this decathecting.[86] John Bowlby's theory of attachment challenges Freud's assumptions, offering instead that healthy grief work actually involves holding on to the memory of the loved one and that a person heals by sensing the person's presence still abiding with them. Rather than decathecting, a person integrates the attachment into their current life.[87] Bowlby's theory mimics much of Kübler-Ross's theory but utilizes terminology that gives more flexibility to the grief process.

Shock—numbness, blunted emotion, disbelief, a sense that one has been unaffected by the loss

85. Arnett and Jensen, *Human Development*, 594.

86. For a discussion of Freud and cathexis, see Cherry, "Cathexis and Anticathexis According to Freudian Theory."

87. For a comparison between Freud and Bowlby, see Broderick and Blewitt, *Life Span*, 620–21.

Protest—irritability or restlessness; obsessive yearning or even searching for the one lost

Despair—sadness often accompanied by social withdrawal or somatic disturbances; flashbacks

Reorganization—the work of holding on to memories and reintegrating them into current life[88]

The challenge for pastors and therapists is determining when grief has become chronic, complicated, or abnormal, interfering with a person's capacity to reorient. Several findings are challenging the assumption that good grief is a cathartic experience of confronting loss and feeling distress. For example, several studies have found that some amount of detachment in the grieving process—the ability to deactivate and emotionally regulate feelings of loss—leads to better outcomes. Other studies have shown that for some the task of confronting grief head-on activates excessive preoccupation and prolonged rumination that perpetuate distress rather than heal it. One dimension of profound and protracted grief occurs when a person searches endlessly to make meaning of a loss without being able to find it. Those who adjust best to grief find something positive in the loss or reappraise it in a way that permits them to extract some

FIGURE 7.1
DUAL PROCESS MODEL OF GRIEF

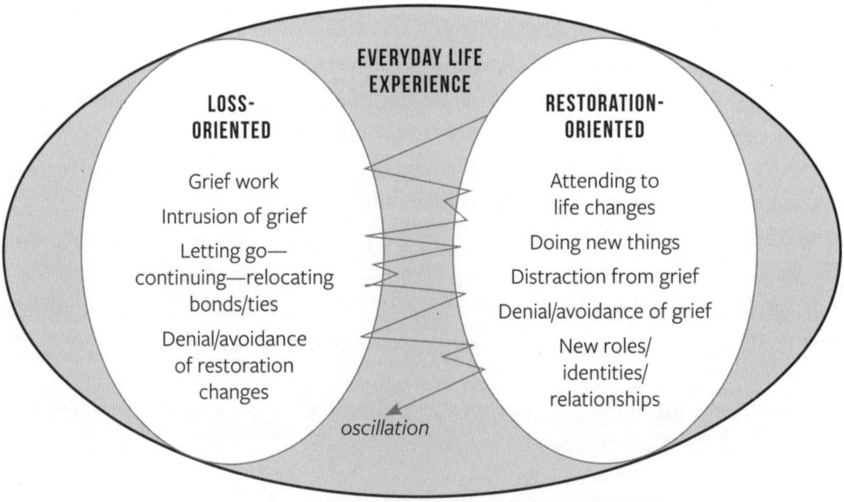

Based on Stroebe and Schut, "Dual Process Model of Coping with Bereavement."

88. Bowlby wrote about grief in a three-volume series titled Attachment and Loss.

meaning. This is, of course, quite difficult when the loss is sudden, involves a malicious or negligent act, or involves a child. Some evidence suggests that restitution made by perpetrators can help with resolving or reducing grief in the families of the bereaved.[89]

One model that takes these new findings into consideration is the dual process model from Margaret Stroebe and Henk Schut (see fig. 7.1).[90] In this model, healthy grief work moves between complementary poles of approach and avoidance. Approach tendencies confront the reality of death, give expression to sorrow, and engage the grief but are restricted and balanced with coping strategies aimed at returning to the practical tasks that sustain daily life. Hence, the coping strategy allows intense periods of grief and recounting of memories but then returns to the task of problem-solving and gaining distance for the sake of restoration.

CONCLUSION

Erikson characterizes the last stage of life as ego integrity versus despair.[91] Ego integrity indicates the capacity to look across the chapters of one's life, with all its successes and disappointments, and to conclude that on the whole one has lived life well and it was worthwhile. Conversely, despair ends in the bitterness of regret that life has not gone well and now cannot be repaired. Important pastoral work entails helping a person relate this present understanding to beliefs about the afterlife.

Workbooks, recordings, and conversations focused on life review help seniors connect their lives with the future as they tell their stories to younger generations and remember their pasts in self-affirming ways. Remembering renews links with former generations, especially when the remembering of ancestors is more of a social process than a solitary one. Life review may be crucial to helping a senior find self-worth as others recognize the significance of a life well lived.[92]

I remember watching the final scene of the movie *Saving Private Ryan* and feeling initially disappointed in what I perceived was an anticlimactic end for such an epic drama. The last scene portrays Private Ryan visiting the cemetery.

89. Broderick and Blewitt, *Life Span*, 621–23.

90. Broderick and Blewitt, *Life Span*, 624.

91. Erikson, *Childhood and Society*, 268.

92. See this helpful article on the importance of life review: Damon, "Purpose and the Life Review."

At the tombstone of Captain Miller, who risked so much to retrieve Ryan from the war, Ryan pleads with his wife to "tell me I have led a good life. Tell me I'm a good man."[93] Reading Erikson, however, I realize that this is the culminating task of the life course—taking a view from the bridge and determining whether it coheres into a narrative that we and others can regard as a well-lived life. In a small way, I suspect it is a version of that greater narrative that we as Christians live for—to one day hear the Master say, "Well done" (Matt. 25:23).

93. "Saving Private Ryan Ending Scene."

Conclusion

I conclude this book with an autobiographical story told by the famed missionary doctor Paul Brandt when he was in his ninth decade of life. Dr. Brandt shared the reflection at the dedication of a retirement center that he was living in late in his life in Seattle. My friend and mentor across my adult life, Steve Moore, shared the story with several of us who have been in a covenant group with Steve now for over thirty years.

Dr. Brandt remembered the experience of reaching what he regarded as his physical peak at age twenty-eight while he was mountain climbing in India. He came to this realization when he crossed over into his thirties and had the distinct sense that for some people, hitting that peak constituted a point where the best life had to offer was passing; life would now plateau. Then he recounted the unexpected experience of feeling that he had reached his mental peak. He was fifty-eight and performing a hand surgery that had not been done before, and he discovered that he was remarkably good at performing the surgery. He realized that, for many, crossing that mental peak meant their life was effectually over and now on a declining plane. But now in his eighties, Dr. Brandt believed he was rapidly approaching another peak, a spiritual one where goodness, joy, wisdom, mercy, and all he hoped to become had a chance to come together. And then he opined that none of those earlier peaks were a culmination at all. In fact, realizing what he did now, he could surmise that even when he crossed over from this world, "Life will not be over; it will have just begun."

For all that the social sciences can offer us about human flourishing, they can only lay hold of such a grand affirmation if they find themselves in the service of a yet greater and more transcendent story. "Come, let us go up to the mountain of the LORD . . ." (Mic. 4:2).

Bibliography

"Abstraction and Hypothetical Propositions." PowerPoint video presented in Lifespan Development class, Asbury Theological Seminary.

Alcoholics Anonymous, "The Twelve Steps." Accessed October 6, 2023. https://www.aa.org/the-twelve-steps.

Alexander, Brian. "Ideal to Real: What the 'Perfect' Body Really Looks Like for Men and Women." *Today*, March 31, 2016. https://www.today.com/health/ideal-real-what-perfect-body-really-looks-men-women-t83731.

Allen, Laura. "Parents and Adult Children: Mutually Irritating." *Popular Science*, May 8, 2009. https://www.popsci.com/scitech/article/2009-05/parents-and-adult-children-mutually-irritating/.

"Alzheimer's Stages: How the Disease Progresses." Mayo Clinic. April 29, 2021. https://www.mayoclinic.org/diseases-conditions/alzheimers-disease/in-depth/alzheimers-stages/art-20048448.

Archer, Sarah. "'Hands to Work, Hearts to God': A Post-Election Craft Manifesto." *Hyperallergic*, November 11, 2016. https://hyperallergic.com/337680/hands-to-work-hearts-to-god-a-post-election-craft-manifesto/.

Armstrong, Kim. "Carol Dwerk on How Growth Mindsets Can Bear Fruit in the Classroom." Association for Psychological Science. October 29, 2019. https://www.psychologicalscience.org/observer/dweck-growth-mindsets.

Arnett, Jeffrey J. *Adolescence and Emerging Adulthood: A Cultural Approach.* 5th ed. Boston: Pearson, 2012.

———. *Emerging Adulthood: The Winding Road from the Late Teens through the Twenties.* Oxford: Oxford University Press, 2004.

Arnett, Jeffrey J., and Lene A. Jensen. *Human Development: A Cultural Approach.* 3rd ed. New York: Pearson, 2019.

"Assistive Technology for the Elderly: A Guide to Getting Started." Age Space. Accessed October 5, 2023. https://www.agespace.org/tech/assistive-technology.

Atchley, Robert C. *The Sociology of Retirement.* New York: Wiley & Sons, 1976.

Augustine. *Confessions.* Translated by Henry Chadwick. Oxford: Oxford University Press, 1991.

"Augustine." The School of Life. Accessed March 9, 2023. https://www.theschooloflife .com/article/the-great-philosophers-augustine/#:~:text=Our%20sinful%20nature %20gives%20rise,our%20egoism%20and%.

Balswick, J. K., and J. O. Balswick. *Authentic Human Sexuality: An Integrated Christian Approach.* 2nd ed. Downers Grove, 1L: IVP Academic, 2008.

———. *The Family.* 3rd ed. Grand Rapids: Baker Academic, 2007.

Balswick, J. O., Pamela Ebstyne King, and Kevin S. Reimer. *The Reciprocating Self: Human Development in Theological Perspective.* Downers Grove, IL: IVP Academic, 2005.

Baltes, Paul B., and Jacqui Smith. "The Fascination of Wisdom: Its Nature, Ontogeny, and Function." *Perspectives on Psychological Science* 3, no. 1 (January 1, 2008): 56–64. https://doi.org/10.1111/j.1745-6916.2008.00062.x.

Baltes, Paul B., and Ursula M. Staudinger. "Wisdom: A Metaheuristic (Pragmatic) to Orchestrate Mind and Virtue toward Excellence." *American Psychologist* 55, no. 1 (2000): 122–36. https://doi.org/10.1037/0003-066X.55.1.122.

Banks, Adelle M. "Miroslav Volf Delves into the Theology of Joy: A Q&A." *Religion News Service,* May 21, 2018. https://religionnews.com/2018/05/21/miroslav-volf-delves -into-the-theology-of-joy-a-qa/.

Barfield, Robin. "Children and the Imago Dei: A Reformed Proposal Regarding the Spiritual Openness of the Child." *Christian Education Journal* 17, no. 1 (2020): 7–17.

Barna Group. "31% of U.S. Adults Report Feeling Lonely at Least Some of Each Day." December 8, 2021. https://www.barna.com/research/mettes-lonely-americans/?u tm_source=Newsletter&utm_medium=email&utm_content=Barna+Update%3A +Understanding+the+Loneliness+Epidemic+in+America&utm_campaign=2021 -12-08_Loneliness+Epidemic+Launch_BU.

Barton, Ruth Haley. *Pursuing God's Will Together: A Discernment Practice for Leadership Groups.* Downers Grove, IL: InterVarsity, 2012.

"Basics of Alzheimer's Disease." Alzheimer's Association. https://www.alz.org/national /documents/brochure_basicsofalz_low.pdf.

Bass, Dorothy C., ed. *Practicing Our Faith: A Way of Life for a Searching People.* 2nd ed. San Francisco: Jossey-Bass, 2010.

Baumrind, Diana. "The Discipline Encounter: Contemporary Issues." *Aggression and Violent Behavior* 2, no. 4 (August 1997): 321–35. https://doi.org/10.1016/S1359 -1789(97)00018-9.

Berk, Laura E. *Development through the Lifespan.* Annotated instructors ed. Needham Heights, MA: Allyn and Bacon, 1998.

Berzonsky, Michael. "Identity Style." *Journal of Adolescent Research* 4 (July 1, 1989): 268–82. https://doi.org/10.1177/074355488943002.

Bitterly, T. Bradford, Robert Mislavsky, Hengchen Dai, and Katherine L. Milkman. "Want–Should Conflict: A Synthesis of Past Research." In *The Psychology of Desire*, edited by Wilhelm Hofmann and Loran F. Nordgren, 244–64. New York: Guilford, 2015.

Blythe, Teresa A. *50 Ways to Pray: Practices from Many Traditions and Times*. Nashville: Abingdon, 2006.

Bogot, Howard I. "Making God Accessible: A Parenting Program." *Religious Education* 83, no. 4 (1988): 510–17. https://www.proquest.com/openview/f24ef03c2e17150d4 2459079b9d88e42/1?pq-origsite=gscholar&cbl=1816639.

Bonhoeffer, Dietrich. *Life Together: The Classic Exploration of Christian Community*. New York: HarperOne, 1978.

Book of Common Prayer. Huntington Beach, CA: Anglican Liturgy Press, 2019. bcp2019 .anglicanchurch.net/wp-content/uploads/2022/10/BCP-2019-MASTER-5th -PRINTING-05022022-3.pdf.

Borgman, Paul. *Genesis: The Story We Haven't Heard*. Downers Grove, IL: IVP Academic, 2001.

Bounds, Chris. "The Wesleyan Quadrilateral." The Wesleyan Church. January 24, 2022. https://www.wesleyan.org/the-wesleyan-quadrilateral.

Bowlby, John. *Attachment and Loss*. 3 vols. New York: Basic Books, 1969–1980.

Bradshaw, Matt, Blake Victor Kent, W. Matthew Henderson, and Anna Catherine Setar. "Attachment to God and Social Trust." *Sociological Perspectives* 62, no. 6 (December 1, 2019): 1001–21. https://doi.org/10.1177/0731121419870775.

Broderick, Patricia C., and Pamela Blewitt. *The Life Span: Human Development for Helping Professionals*. 5th ed. New York: Pearson, 2020.

Brown, Teresa L. Fry. *Can a Sistah Get a Little Help? Encouragement for Black Women in Ministry*. Cleveland: Pilgrim, 2008.

Brown, Warren S., and Brad D. Strawn. *The Physical Nature of Christian Life: Neuroscience, Psychology, and the Church*. New York: Cambridge University Press, 2012.

Brueggemann, Walter. *The Prophetic Imagination*. Minneapolis: Fortress, 2001.

Budd, Clair Allen, and Martha S. Bergen. "Adult Ministry in the Church: A Forty-Year Perspective." *Christian Education Journal* 17, no. 3 (December 1, 2020): 468–87. https://doi.org/10.1177/0739891320951201.

Bybee, Jane Allin, and Yvonne V. Wells. "The Development of Possible Selves during Adulthood." In *Handbook of Adult Development*, edited by Jack Demick and Carrie Andreoletti, 257–70. The Springer Series in Adult Development and Aging. Boston: Springer US, 2003. https://doi.org/10.1007/978-1-4615-0617-1_14.

Cahalan, Kathleen A., and Bonnie J. Miller-McLemore. *Calling All Years Good: Christian Vocation throughout Life's Seasons*. Grand Rapids: Eerdmans, 2017.

Carder, Kenneth L. *Ministry with the Forgotten: Dementia through a Spiritual Lens*. Nashville: Abingdon, 2019.

Cassian, John. *John Cassian: Conferences*. Translated by Colm Luibheid. New York: Paulist Press, 1985.

Cavalletti, Sofia. *The Religious Potential of the Child: Experiencing Scripture and Liturgy with Young Children*. Translated by Patricia M. Coulter and Julie M. Coulter. 2nd ed. New York: Liturgy Training Publications, 1992.

Centers for Disease Control and Prevention. "Sexual Risk Behaviors." Adolescent and School Health. Last reviewed March 16, 2023. https://www.cdc.gov/healthyyouth /sexualbehaviors/index.htm.

Chatterjee, Rhitu. "What Is Postpartum Depression? How to Recognize the Signs and Get Help." NPR, January 28, 2020. https://www.npr.org/2020/01/27/800139124 /what-is-postpartum-depression-recognizing-the-signs-and-getting-help.

Cherry, Kendra. "Cathexis and Anticathexis according to Freudian Theory." Very Well Mind. Updated July 25, 2023. https://www.verywellmind.com/cathexis-and-anti cathexis-2795843.

———. "Piaget's 4 Stages of Cognitive Development Explained." Very Well Mind. December 16, 2022. https://www.verywellmind.com/piagets-stages-of-cognitive-develop ment-2795457.

Chesterton, G. K. *Orthodoxy*. New York: Lane, 1909.

Cloud, Henry, and John Townsend. *Raising Great Kids: A Comprehensive Guide to Parenting with Grace and Truth*. Grand Rapids: Zondervan, 1999.

"Cognitive Development during Adolescence." Lifespan Development, Module 7: Adolescence. Lumen Learning. Accessed October 29, 2023. https://courses.lumenlearning .com/wm-lifespandevelopment/chapter/cognitive-development-during-adolescence /#:~:text=According%20to%20Elkind%2C%20adolescent%20egocentrism,with %20self%2Dconsciousness%20in%20general).

Cole, Michael, and James V. Wertsch. "Beyond the Individual-Social Antinomy in Discussions of Piaget and Vygotsky." *Human Development* 39, no. 5 (1996): 250–56.

Commission on Children at Risk. *Hardwired to Connect: The New Scientific Case for Authoritative Communities*. New York: Broadway, 2003.

"Comprehensive Sexuality Education." American College of Obstetricians and Gynecologists. Committee opinion 678, posted November 2016. https://www.acog.org /en/clinical/clinical-guidance/committee-opinion/articles/2016/11/comprehensive -sexuality-education.

Covey, Stephen R. *The 7 Habits of Highly Effective People: Powerful Lessons in Personal Change*. Rev. ed. New York: Free Press, 2004.

Crouch, Andy. *The Tech-Wise Family: Everyday Steps for Putting Technology in Its Proper Place*. Grand Rapids: Baker Books, 2017.

Damon, William. "Purpose and the Life Review." *Psychology Today*, July 28, 2021. https:// www.psychologytoday.com/us/blog/the-puzzles-your-past/202107/purpose-and -the-life-review.

Dante. *The Inferno of Dante*. Translated by Charles Rogers. London: J. Nichols, 1832.

Dawn, Marva J. *Keeping the Sabbath Wholly: Ceasing, Resting, Embracing, Feasting*. Grand Rapids: Eerdmans, 1989.

Dean, Kenda Creasy, and Ron Foster. *The Godbearing Life: The Art of Soul Tending for Youth Ministry*. Nashville: Upper Room, 2005.

DeCasper, Anthony J., and Melanie J. Spence. "Prenatal Maternal Speech Influences Newborns' Perception of Speech Sounds." *Infant Behavior and Development* 9, no. 2 (April 1, 1986): 133–50. https://doi.org/10.1016/0163-6383(86)90025-1.

"Decision-Making." Quaker.org. Accessed October 9, 2023. https://quaker.org/decision -making.

"The Deeper Hebrew Meaning of the 'Garden of Eden.'" Hebrewversity. Accessed March 9, 2023. https://www.hebrewversity.com/deeper-hebrew-meaning-garden-eden/.

"The Developmental Assets Framework." Search Institute. Accessed March 9, 2023. https://www.search-institute.org/our-research/development-assets/developmental -assets-framework/.

Doyle, Derek. "Principles of Palliative Care." International Association for Hospice and Palliative Care. Accessed March 13, 2023. https://hospicecare.com/what-we -do/publications/getting-started/principles-of-palliative-care/.

Duckworth, Angela. *Grit: The Power of Passion and Perseverance*. New York: Scribner, 2016.

Duigan, Brian. "Eudaimonia." *Britannica*. Last modified Jan. 27, 2023. https://www.bri tannica.com/topic/eudaimonia.

Dunnam, Maxie. "Dr. Maxie Dunham." March 5, 2021. In *The Art of Holiness*, produced by Carolyn Moore, podcast, 1:01:47. https://artofholiness.com/maxie-dunnam/.

Dweck, Carol S. *Mindset: The New Psychology of Success*. New York: Ballantine Books, 2007.

Dykstra, Craig R. *Growing in the Life of Faith: Education and Christian Practices*. 2nd ed. Louisville: Westminster John Knox, 2005.

Earley, Justin Whitmel. *The Common Rule: Habits of Purpose for an Age of Distraction*. Downers Grove, IL: InterVarsity, 2019.

"Edwards, Jonathan (1703–1758)." Biographies. Boston University School of Theology. Accessed August 12, 2023. https://www.bu.edu/missiology/missionary-biography /e-f/edwards-jonathan-1703-1758/.

Eisenhandler, Susan. *Keeping the Faith in Late Life*. New York: Springer, 2003.

Elkind, David. "Instructive Discipline Is Built on Understanding: Choosing Time In." *Child Care Information Exchange*, no. 141 (September–October 2001): 7–8.

Erikson, Erik H. *Childhood and Society*. 2nd ed. New York: Norton, 1993.

———. *Identity and the Life Cycle*. New York: Norton, 1980.

———. *Identity: Youth and Crisis*. New York: Norton, 1994.

Farlex Dictionary of Idioms. S.v. "a son is a son until he takes a wife." Accessed March 13, 2023. https://idioms.thefreedictionary.com/a+son+is+a+son+until+he+takes+a+wife.

Fay, Charles. "Are You a Helicopter, Drill Sergeant, or Consultant Parent?" Love and Logic. April 29, 2022. https://www.loveandlogic.com/blogs/our-blog/are-you-a -helicopter-drill-sergeant-or-consultant-parent.

Fowler, James W. *Stages of Faith: The Psychology of Human Development and the Quest for Meaning*. New York: HarperOne, 2010.

Fowler, Larry. *Raising a Modern-Day Joseph: A Timeless Strategy for Growing Great Kids*. New ed. Colorado Springs: David C. Cook, 2009.

Garber, Steven. *The Seamless Life: A Tapestry of Love and Learning, Worship and Work*. Downers Grove, IL: InterVarsity, 2020.

Garland, Diana R. *Sacred Stories of Ordinary Families: Living the Faith in Daily Life*. San Francisco: Jossey-Bass, 2003.

Gillette. "This Father's Day, Go Ask Dad." YouTube video, 2:36. Posted October 18, 2016. https://www.youtube.com/watch?v=0m9WLRMkYRA.

Gilligan, Carol. *In a Different Voice: Psychological Theory and Women's Development*. Cambridge, MA: Harvard University Press, 2016.

Gladding, Sean. *The Story of God, the Story of Us: Getting Lost and Found in the Bible*. Downers Grove, IL: IVP Books, 2010.

Goldin, Claudia. "A Grand Gender Convergence: Its Last Chapter." *American Economic Review* 104, no. 4 (April 2014): 1091–119. https://www.aeaweb.org/articles?id=10.1257/aer.104.4.1091.

Gorrell, Angela Williams. *Always On: Practicing Faith in a New Media Landscape*. Grand Rapids: Baker Academic, 2019.

Grade, Chaim. *My Mother's Sabbath Days: A Memoir*. Translated by Channa Kleinerman Goldstein and Inna Hecker Grade. Northvale, NJ: Aronson, 1997.

Granqvist, Pehr, and Lee A. Kirkpatrick. "Attachment and Religious Representations and Behavior." In *Handbook of Attachment: Theory, Research, and Clinical Applications*, edited by Jude Cassidy and Phillip R. Shaver, 906–33. 2nd ed. New York: Guilford, 2008.

Grossman, Igor. "Wisdom in Context." *Perspectives on Psychological Science* 12, no. 2 (March 2017): 233–57. https://doi.org/10.1177/1745691616672066.

Guinness, Os. *In Two Minds: The Dilemma of Doubt and How to Resolve It*. 2nd ed. Downers Grove, IL: InterVarsity, 1976.

Haidt, Jonathan. "Why the Past 10 Years of American Life Have Been Uniquely Stupid." *The Atlantic*, April 11, 2022. https://www.theatlantic.com/magazine/archive/2022/05/social-media-democracy-trust-babel/629369/.

Hall, Christopher A. *Living Wisely with the Church Fathers*. Downers Grove, IL: IVP Academic, 2017.

———. *Worshiping with the Church Fathers*. Downers Grove, IL: IVP Academic, 2009.

Hample, Stuart, and Eric Marshall, *Children's Letters to God: The New Collection*. New York: Workman, 1991.

Harris, Kitty, Sara Smock Jordan, and McKenzie Wilkes. "Relapse Resilience: A Process Model of Addiction and Recovery." *Journal of Family Psychotherapy* 22 (July 1, 2011): 265–74. https://doi.org/10.1080/08975353.2011.602622.

Hart, Betty, and Todd R. Risley. "The Early Catastrophe: The 30 Million Word Gap by Age 3." *American Educator* 27, no. 1 (Spring 2003): 4–9.

Hays, Richard B. *The Moral Vision of the New Testament: A Contemporary Introduction to New Testament Ethics.* New York: HarperSanFrancisco, 1996.

Hebb, D. O. *The Organization of Behavior: A Neuropsychological Theory.* New York: Psychology Press, 2012.

Helms, Harold E. *God's Final Answer.* Maitland, FL: Xulon, 2004.

Hersch, Patricia. *A Tribe Apart: A Journey into the Heart of American Adolescence.* New York: Random House, 2013.

Heschel, Abraham Joshua. *The Sabbath.* New York: Farrar, Straus & Giroux, 2005.

Hillman, Os. *The 9 to 5 Window: How Faith Can Transform the Workplace.* Ventura, CA: Gospel Light, 2005.

"History Cloth—42 Chronological Bible Stories." International Orality Network. September 23, 2016. https://orality.net/content/history-cloth-42-chronological-bible-stories/.

Hoffman, Martin L. *Empathy and Moral Development: Implications for Caring and Justice.* Cambridge: Cambridge University Press, 2001.

Holcomb, Gay L., and Arthur J. Nonneman. "Faithful Change: Exploring and Assessing Faith Development in Christian Liberal Arts Undergraduates." *New Directions for Institutional Research* 2004, no. 122 (2004): 93–103. https://doi.org/10.1002/ir.112.

Holland, John L. *Making Vocational Choices: A Theory of Careers.* Englewood Cliffs, NJ: Prentice Hall, 1973.

Hosack, Lisa. *Development on Purpose: Faith and Human Behavior in the Social Environment.* Botsford, CT: North American Association of Christians in Social Work, 2019.

Houston, James M., and Michael Parker. *A Vision for the Aging Church: Renewing Ministry for and by Seniors.* Downers Grove, IL: IVP Academic, 2011.

Igniter Media. "The Marshmallow Test." YouTube video, 3:27. Posted September 9, 2009. https://www.youtube.com/watch?v=QX_oy9614HQ.

"Impact of Media Use on Children and Youth." *Paediatrics & Child Health* 8, no. 5 (2003): 301–6.

International Organization for Migration. *World Migration Report 2020.* https://publications.iom.int/system/files/pdf/wmr_2020.pdf.

Izard, Carroll E. *The Psychology of Emotions.* New York: Springer, 1991.

Johnson, Adam J. Review of *The Gravity of Sin*, by Matt Jenson. *Themelios* 34, no. 2 (July, 2009). https://www.thegospelcoalition.org/themelios/review/the-gravity-of-sin-augustine-luther-and-barth-on-homo-incurvatus-in-se/.

Johnson, Chris. "Dying Well according to John Wesley." Seedbed. April 17, 2012. https://seedbed.com/dying-well-according-to-john-wesley/.

Johnson, Christine. "Holiness and Death in the Theology of John Wesley." YouTube video, 50:10. Posted March 15, 2021. https://www.youtube.com/watch?v=6B8tTH7QWl4.

Johnson, Kirk, Lauren Noyes, and Robert Rector. "Sexually Active Teenagers Are More Likely to Be Depressed and to Attempt Suicide." The Heritage Foundation. June 3,

2003. https://www.heritage.org/education/report/sexually-active-teenagers-are
-more-likely-be-depressed-and-attempt-suicide.

Jones, E. Stanley. *The Christ of the Mount.* Nashville: Abingdon, 1931.

Jones, Jeffrey M. "LGBT Identification in U.S. Ticks Up to 7.1%." Gallup. February 17,
2022. https://news.gallup.com/poll/389792/lgbt-identification-ticks-up.aspx.

"Journey to Adulthood." Church Publishing. Accessed October 10, 2023. https://www
.churchpublishing.org/journeytoadulthood#.

Joy, Donald M. *Empower Your Kids to Be Adults: A Guide for Parents, Ministers, and Other
Mentors.* Nappanee, IN: Evangel, 2000.

———. "Human Development and Christian Holiness." *Asbury Seminarian* 31, no. 2
(1976): 5–27. https://place.asburyseminary.edu/asburyjournal/vol31/iss2/3/.

———. *Unfinished Business: How a Man Can Make Peace with His Past.* Wheaton: Victor
Books, 1989.

"The Joyful Mysteries." Rosary Center & Confraternity. Accessed September 3, 2023.
https://rosarycenter.org/the-joyful-mysteries-without-distractions.

Kagan, Jerome, and Nathan A. Fox. "Biology, Culture, and Temperamental Biases." In
Social, Emotional, and Personality Development, edited by Nancy Eisenberg, 167–225.
Vol. 3 of *Handbook of Child Psychology,* edited by William Damon and Richard M.
Lerner. New York: Wiley & Sons, 2006.

Kang, Shimi K. *The Dolphin Parent: A Guide to Raising Healthy, Happy and Self-Motivated
Kids.* Toronto: Penguin Random House, 2015.

Keisler-Starkey, Katherine, and Lisa N. Bunch. "Health Insurance Coverage in the
United States: 2020." United States Census Bureau. September 14, 2021. https://www
.census.gov/library/publications/2021/demo/p60-274.html#:~:text=Of%20the%20
subtypes%20of%20health,2.8%20percent)%2C%20and%20Department%20of.

Keller, Helen. *My Religion.* San Francisco: Book Tree, 2007.

Kett, Joseph F. "Reflections on the History of Adolescence in America." *The History of
the Family* 8, no. 3 (January 1, 2003): 355–73. https://doi.org/10.1016/S1081-602X
(03)00042-3.

Kiesling, Chris. "My Sense of Spiritual Self." PhD diss., Texas Tech University, 2002.

Kiesling, Chris, Tapiwa N. Mucherera, and Anne Kiome Gatobu, eds. *Tri-Level Identity
Crisis: Children of First-Generation Immigrants.* Eugene, OR: Pickwick, 2020.

Kiesling, Chris, and Gwen Sorell. "Joining Erikson and Identity Specialists in the Quest
to Characterize Adult Spiritual Identity." *Identity* 9, no. 3 (November 27, 2009):
252–71. https://doi.org/10.1080/15283480903344554.

Kinlaw, Dennis. "The Family: Sacred Pedagogy." In *Confessing the Faith: Reclaiming
Historic Faith and Teaching for the 21st Century,* edited by Craig M. Kibler, 77–88.
Lenoir, NC: Reformation Press, 2003.

Kinnaman, David, with Aly Hawkins. *You Lost Me: Why Young Christians Are Leaving
Church . . . and Rethinking Faith.* Grand Rapids: Baker Books, 2011.

Kinsler, Jim. "Grandparenting the Next Generation: Fanning the Flames of Faith." PhD diss., Asbury Theological Seminary, 2013.

Kirkpatrick, Lee A. "An Attachment-Theory Approach to the Psychology of Religion." *International Journal for the Psychology of Religion* 2, no. 1 (1992): 3–28. https://doi.org/10.1207/s15327582ijpr0201_2.

Koch, Kevin. *The Thin Places: A Celtic Landscape from Ireland to the Driftless.* Eugene, OR: Wipf & Stock, 2018.

Koteskey, Ronald L. *Understanding Adolescence.* Wheaton: Victor Books, 1987.

Krause, Paul. "Augustine: On the Fall of Man, Part I." Hesiod's Corner. November 1, 2017. https://hesiodscorner.wordpress.com/2017/11/01/augustine-on-the-fall-of-man/.

Kroger, Jane. "The Epigenesis of Identity—What Does It Mean?" *Identity* 18, no. 4 (October 2, 2018): 334–42. https://doi.org/10.1080/15283488.2018.1523730.

———. *Identity Development: Adolescence through Adulthood.* 2nd ed. Thousand Oaks, CA: Sage, 2006.

———. "Identity Processes and Contents through the Years of Late Adulthood." *Identity* 2, no. 1 (January 2, 2002): 81–99. https://doi.org/10.1207/S1532706XID0201_05.

Krupic, Julija. "Wire Together, Fire Apart." *Science* 357, no. 6355 (2017): 974–75. https://www.science.org/doi/10.1126/science.aao4159.

Kübler-Ross, Elisabeth. *On Death and Dying: What the Dying Have to Teach Doctors, Nurses, Clergy and Their Own Families.* New York: Scribner, 2014.

LaGrone, Jessica. "Keep the Sabbath." Asbury Theological Seminary chapel service. February 11, 2015. Video, 24:33. https://place.asburyseminary.edu/ecommonsats chapelservices/5539.

Lally, Martha, and Suzanne Valentine-French. *Lifespan Development: A Psychological Perspective.* 2nd ed. Grayslake, IL: College of Lake County, 2017.

Larson, Mimi L. "The Child in Our Midst: The Shifting Trends in Ministry with Children and Families over the Past Forty Years." *Christian Education Journal* 17, no. 3 (December 1, 2020): 434–48. https://doi.org/10.1177/0739891320943902.

"Learn How the CliftonStrengths Assessment Works." CliftonStrengths. Gallup. Accessed January 26, 2024. https://www.gallup.com/cliftonstrengths/en/253676/how -cliftonstrengths-works.aspx.

Lee, Sang Bum, Jae Hun Oh, Jeong Ho Park, Seung Pill Choi, and Jung Hee Wee. "Differences in Youngest-Old, Middle-Old, and Oldest-Old Patients Who Visit the Emergency Department." *Clinical and Experimental Emergency Medicine* 5, no. 4 (December 31, 2018): 249–55. https://doi.org/10.15441/ceem.17.261.

Levinson, Daniel J. *The Seasons of a Man's Life: The Groundbreaking 10-Year Study That Was the Basis for "Passages!"* New York: Ballantine Books, 1986.

Lewis, C. S. *The Four Loves.* New York: Harcourt, Brace, 1991.

———. *A Grief Observed.* New York: HarperCollins, 1961.

———. *Mere Christianity.* San Francisco: HarperOne, 2015.

Lim, Annabelle G. Y. "Big Five Personality Traits: The 5-Factor Model of Personality." Simply Psychology. Updated September 7, 2023. https://www.simplypsychology.org /big-five-personality.html.

Livingston, Gretchen. "Americans 60 and Older Are Spending More Time in Front of Their Screens than a Decade Ago." *Pew Research Center* (blog). Accessed August 19, 2022. https://www.pewresearch.org/fact-tank/2019/06/18/americans-60-and-older -are-spending-more-time-in-front-of-their-screens-than-a-decade-ago/.

Loder, James E. *The Logic of the Spirit: Human Development in Theological Perspective.* San Francisco: Jossey-Bass, 1998.

"Love Stories Influence Your Partner Choice, Relationship Satisfaction, and Behavior." The Love Multiverse. Accessed March 9, 2023. https://lovemultiverse.com/under standing-love/different-kinds-of-love-stories/.

Lykken, David T., T. J. Bouchard Jr., Matt McGue, and Auke Tellegen. "Heritability of Interests: A Twin Study." *Journal of Applied Psychology* 78, no. 4 (1993): 649–61. https://doi.org/10.1037/0021-9010.78.4.649.

Lyness, D'Arcy. "Normal Childhood Fears." Kids Health. October 2018. https://kids health.org/en/parents/anxiety.html.

MacBeth, Sybil. *Praying in Color: Drawing a New Path to God.* Brewster, MA: Paraclete, 2013.

Maccoby, Eleanor E. *The Two Sexes: Growing Up Apart, Coming Together.* Cambridge, MA: Belknap, 1999.

Maccoby, Eleanor E., and Carol Nagy Jacklin. "Gender Segregation in Childhood." In *Advances in Child Development and Behavior,* vol. 20, edited by Hayne W. Reese, 239–87. San Diego: Academic Press, 1987.

MacDonald, Gordon. *Ordering Your Private World.* Nashville: Nelson, 2007.

———. *Restoring Your Spiritual Passion.* Nashville: Nelson, 1986.

MacIntyre, Alasdair. *After Virtue: A Study in Moral Theory.* 3rd ed. Notre Dame, IN: University of Notre Dame Press, 2007.

Maddix, Mark A., and Dean G. Blevins, eds. *Neuroscience and Christian Formation.* Charlotte, NC: Information Age, 2016.

Mahan, Brian J., Michael Warren, and David F. White. *Awakening Youth Discipleship: Christian Resistance in a Consumer Culture.* Eugene, OR: Cascade Books, 2008.

Manduley, Aida. "The Real Origin of the African Birth Song: Surprise, It's Racist." March 10, 2015. https://aidamanduley.com/the-real-origin-of-the-african-birth-song/.

Marcia, James E. "Development and Validation of Ego-Identity Status." *Journal of Personality and Social Psychology* 3, no. 5 (1966): 551–58. https://doi.org/10.1037/h0023281.

Markus, Hazel, and Paula Nurius. "Possible Selves." *American Psychologist* 41, no. 9 (1986): 954–69. https://doi.org/10.1037/0003-066X.41.9.954.

Marquardt, Elizabeth. *Between Two Worlds: The Inner Lives of Children of Divorce.* New York: Three Rivers, 2006.

Mason, Mike. *The Mystery of Marriage: Meditations on the Miracle.* New York: Crown, 2005.

McAdams, Dan P., and Bradley D. Olson. "Personality Development: Continuity and Change over the Life Course." *Annual Review of Psychology* 61 (2010): 517–42. https://doi.org/10.1146/annurev.psych.093008.100507.

McAdams, Dan P., Jeffrey Reynolds, Martha Lewis, Allison H. Patten, and Phillip J. Bowman. "When Bad Things Turn Good and Good Things Turn Bad: Sequences of Redemption and Contamination in Life Narrative and Their Relation to Psychosocial Adaptation in Midlife Adults and in Students." *Personality and Social Psychology Bulletin* 27, no. 4 (2001): 474–85. https://doi.org/10.1177/0146167201274008.

McLeod, Saul. "Erik Erikson's 8 Stages of Psychosocial Development." Simply Psychology. February 24, 2023. https://simplypsychology.org/Erik-Erikson.html.

McNall, Joshua. *Long Story Short: The Bible in Six Short Movements*. Franklin, TN: Seedbed, 2018.

Meier, Emily A., Jarred V. Gallegos, Lori P. Montross Thomas, Colin A. Depp, Scott A. Irwin, and Dilip V. Jeste. "Defining a Good Death (Successful Dying): Literature Review and a Call for Research and Public Dialogue." *American Journal of Geriatric Psychology* 24 (April 2016): 261–71. https://doi.org/10.1016/j.jagp.2016.01.135.

Mindell, Jodi A., Avi Sadeh, Benjamin Wiegand, Ti Hwei How, and Daniel Y. T. Goh. "Cross-Cultural Differences in Infant and Toddler Sleep." *Sleep Medicine* 11, no. 3 (March 2010): 274–80. https://doi.org/10.1016/j.sleep.2009.04.012.

Montessori, Maria. *The Absorbent Mind*. Translated by Claude A. Claremont. 10th ed. Madras: Kalakshetra, 1992.

Moon, W. Jay, and Fredrick J. Long. *Entrepreneurial Church Planting: Engaging Business and Mission for Marketplace Transformation*. Wilmore, KY: GlossaHouse, 2018.

Morgan, G. Campbell. *Life Applications from Every Chapter of the Bible*. Grand Rapids: Revell, 1994.

Morisy, Ann. *Bothered and Bewildered: Enacting Hope in Troubled Times*. New York: Continuum, 2009.

Neal, Cynthia Jones. "The Power of Vygotsky." In *Nurture That Is Christian: Developmental Perspectives on Christian Education*, edited by James C. Wilhoit and John M. Dettoni, 123–38. Grand Rapids: Baker, 1995.

Nouwen, Henri J. M. "Being the Beloved." YouTube video, 17:58. Posted November 22, 2012. https://www.youtube.com/watch?v=v8U4V4aaNWk.

———. *Reaching Out: The Three Movements of the Spiritual Life*. Garden City, NY: Image, 1975.

Nygren, Anders. *Agape and Eros*. Chicago: University of Chicago Press, 1982.

Online Etymology Dictionary. S.v. "infancy." Last modified November 18, 2015. https://www.etymonline.com/word/infancy#:~:text=infancy%20(n.),speak%22%20(see%20infant).

Outler, Albert C. *John Wesley's Sermons: An Anthology*. Nashville: Abingdon, 1991.

———. "A New Future for Wesley Studies: An Agenda for 'Phase III.'" In *The Future of the Methodist Theological Traditions*, edited by M. Douglas Meeks, 34–52. Nashville: Abingdon, 1985.

Palmer, Parker J. *A Hidden Wholeness: The Journey toward an Undivided Life.* San Francisco: Jossey-Bass, 2009.

Paulsell, Stephanie. *Honoring the Body: Meditations on a Christian Practice.* Minneapolis: Fortress, 2019.

Pearce, Lisa, and Melinda Lundquist Denton. *A Faith of Their Own: Stability and Change in the Religiosity of America's Adolescents.* New York: Oxford University Press, 2011.

Peck, M. Scott. *The Road Less Traveled: A New Psychology of Love, Traditional Values, and Spiritual Growth.* New York: Simon & Schuster, 1979.

Peck, Robert. "Psychological Developments in the Second Half of Life." In *Psychological Aspects of Aging,* edited by John Edward Anderson, 42–53. Washington, DC: American Psychological Association, 1956.

Peniel, Binu. "Salvation and Wholeness—the Theological Understanding of the *Summum Bonum* of the Human." *Binu Peniel* (blog). June 16, 2011. http://www.binupeniel.com /2011/06/salvation-and-wholeness-theological.html.

Peterson, Eugene. "The Pastor's Sabbath." *Leadership* (Spring 1985): 52–58.

Peterson, Sarah. *Let Us Pray: Prayer Journal for Kids.* N.p. 2022.

Piaget, Jean. *The Moral Judgment of the Child.* New York: Free Press, 1997.

Pierpoint, Folliott Sandford. "For the Beauty of the Earth." Hymnary.org. https://hymnary.org/text/for_the_beauty_of_the_earth.

Pipher, Mary, and Ruth Ross. *Reviving Ophelia: Saving the Selves of Adolescent Girls.* New York: Riverhead Trade, 2005.

Plato. *Plato in Twelve Volumes.* Vol. 1. Translated by Harold North Fowler. Introduction by W. R. M. Lamb. Cambridge, MA: Harvard University Press, 1966.

Pohl, Christine D. *Making Room: Recovering Hospitality as a Christian Tradition.* Grand Rapids: Eerdmans, 1999.

Popenoe, David. "American Family Decline, 1960–1990: A Review and Appraisal." *Journal of Marriage and Family* 55, no. 3 (1993): 527–42. https://doi.org/10.2307/353333.

Poulin-Dubois, Diane, and Lisa Serbin. "La connaissance des catégories de genre et des stéréotypes sexués chez le jeune enfant." *Enfance* 58, no. 3 (2006): 283–92. https://doi.org/10.3917/enf.583.0283.

Powell, Kara. "Can Social Distancing Reinvent Youth Ministry?" *Christianity Today,* April 15, 2020. https://www.christianitytoday.com/pastors/2020/april-web-exclusives /coronavirus-social-distancing-reinvent-youth-ministry.html.

———. "How to De-Stress Your Family's Pandemic Holidays." *Fuller Youth Institute* (blog). November 25, 2020. https://fulleryouthinstitute.org/blog/how-to-de-stress.

Powell, Kara, and Brad M. Griffin. *3 Big Questions That Change Every Teenager: Making the Most of Your Conversations and Connections.* Grand Rapids: Baker Books, 2021.

Pritchard, Gretchen Wolff. *Offering the Gospel to Children.* Boston: Cowley, 1992.

Ramshaw, Elaine. *The Godparent Book: Ideas and Activities for Godparents and Their Godchildren.* Chicago: Liturgy Training, 2020.

Regnerus, Mark D. "Linked Lives, Faith, and Behavior: Intergenerational Religious Influence on Adolescent Delinquency." *Journal for the Scientific Study of Religion* 42, no. 2 (2003): 189–203. https://doi.org/10.1111/1468-5906.00172.

"Retirement in the U.S.: A History to Today." Fisher Investments. June 13, 2023. https://www.fisherinvestments.com/en-us/insights/business-401k/retiring-in-the-us-brief-history.

Richter, Sandra L. *The Epic of Eden: A Christian Entry into the Old Testament.* Downers Grove, IL: IVP Academic, 2008.

Roehlkepartain, Eugene C., Pamela Ebstyne King, Linda M. Wagener, and Peter L. Benson. *The Handbook of Spiritual Development in Childhood and Adolescence.* Thousand Oaks, CA: Sage, 2005.

Rohr, Richard. *Falling Upward: A Spirituality for the Two Halves of Life.* San Francisco: Jossey-Bass, 2011.

———. "Growing Up Men." Interview by Krista Tippett. *On Being with Krista Tippett*, April 13, 2017. https://onbeing.org/programs/richard-rohr-growing-up-men/.

———. *Men and Women: The Journey of Spiritual Transformation.* Read by the author. Cincinnati: St. Anthony Messenger Press, 1999.

Rohr, Richard, and Joseph Martos. *Wild Man's Journey: Reflections on Male Spirituality.* Cincinnati: St. Anthony Messenger Press, 1992.

"Rosary for Life: The Joyful Liturgies." US Conference of Catholic Bishops. Accessed September 3, 2023. https://www.usccb.org/prayers/rosary-life-joyful-mysteries.

Rowe, John W., and Robert L. Kahn. *Successful Aging.* New York: Pantheon, 1998.

Sato, Gayle. "What Is the Average Retirement Age?" Experian. October 30, 2021. https://www.experian.com/blogs/ask-experian/average-retirement-age/.

"Saving Private Ryan Ending Scene." YouTube video, 3:39. Posted by David Benson. https://www.youtube.com/watch?v=IZgoufN99n8.

Schafer, Thomas A. "Jonathan Edwards." Britannica. Accessed August 12, 2023. https://www.britannica.com/biography/Jonathan-Edwards/Dismissal-from-Northampton.

Schweitzer, Friedrich. *The Postmodern Life Cycle: Challenges for Church and Theology.* Des Peres, MO: Chalice, 2012.

Searle, Mark. Preface to *The Religious Potential of the Child: Experiencing Scripture and Liturgy with Young Children* by Sofia Cavalletti, xvii–xxvi. Translated by Patricia M. Coulter and Julie M. Coulter. 2nd ed. New York: Liturgy Training Publications, 1992.

Seltzer, Vivian C. *The Psychosocial Worlds of the Adolescent: Public and Private.* Hoboken, NJ: John Wiley and Sons, 1989.

A Service of Christian Marriage I. Discipleship Ministries, the United Methodist Church. November 9, 2014. https://www.umcdiscipleship.org/resources/a-service-of-christian-marriage-i.

Setran, David. "Living a Better Story in Emerging Adulthood." In *Formation for Mission: Discipleship and Identity for Emerging Adults,* edited by Mary T. Federline, Andrew MacDonald, and Rick Richardson, 67–83. Bellingham, WA: Lexham, 2022.

Setran, David P., and Chris A. Kiesling. *Spiritual Formation in Emerging Adulthood: A Practical Theology for College and Young Adult Ministry.* Grand Rapids: Baker Academic, 2013.

Shaw, Clarissa, Jean Gordon, and Kristine Williams. "Understanding Elderspeak: An Evolutionary Concept Analysis." *Innovation in Aging* 4, supplement 1 (December 16, 2020): 451. https://doi.org/10.1093/geroni/igaa057.1459.

Shaw, Mark R. *Work, Play, Love: A Visual Guide to Calling, Career and the Mission of God.* Downers Grove, IL: IVP Books, 2014.

Shoichet, Catherine E., and Parker Leipzig. "More Baby Boomers Are Living Alone. One Reason Why: 'Gray Divorce.'" CNN Health. August 5, 2023. https://www.cnn.com/2023/08/05/health/boomers-divorce-living-alone-wellness-cec/index.html.

Singh, Maanvi. "The Friendship Bench Can Help Chase the Blues Away." NPR, January 10, 2017. https://www.npr.org/sections/goatsandsoda/2017/01/10/508588401/the-friendship-bench-can-help-chase-the-blues-away.

"65 and Older Population Grows Rapidly as Baby Boomers Age." United States Census Bureau. June 25, 2020. https://www.census.gov/newsroom/press-releases/2020/65-older-population-grows.html.

Smith, Christian, Kari Christoffersen, Hilary Davidson, and Patricia Snell Herzog. *Lost in Transition: The Dark Side of Emerging Adulthood.* New York: Oxford University Press, 2011.

Smith, Christian, and Patricia Snell. *Souls in Transition: The Religious and Spiritual Lives of Emerging Adults.* Oxford: Oxford University Press, 2009.

Smith, David W. *Friendless American Male.* Ventura, CA: Gospel Light, 1983.

Smith, James K. A. "You Are What You Love: Genesis 1:1–2:4." Sermon delivered at Wheaton College, Wheaton, IL, August 31, 2016. https://www.youtube.com/watch?v=-xVV4lrOBXIat.

———. *You Are What You Love: The Spiritual Power of Habit.* Grand Rapids: Brazos, 2016.

Smock, Sara A., Adam S. Froerer, and Sara E. Blakeslee. "Systemic Interventions in Substance-Abuse Treatment: Past, Present, and Future." *Journal of Family Psychotherapy* 22, no. 3 (2011): 177–92.

Sroufe, L. Alan. *Emotional Development: The Organization of Emotional Life in the Early Years.* Cambridge: Cambridge University Press, 1997.

Stanley, Scott M., Galena Kline, Rhoades Howard, and J. Markman. "Sliding versus Deciding: Inertia and the Premarital Cohabitation Effect." *Family Relations* (2006): 499–509.

Staudinger, Ursula M. "Social Cognition and a Psychological Approach to an Art of Life." In *Social Cognition and Aging,* edited by Thomas M. Hess and Fredda Blanchard-Fields, 343–75. New York: Academic Press, 1999.

Steinberg, Laurence, and Kathryn C. Monahan. "Age Differences in Resistance to Peer Influence." *Developmental Psychology* 43, no. 6 (2007): 1531–43. https://doi.org/10.1037/0012-1649.43.6.1531.

Sternberg, Robert J. *Love Is a Story: A New Theory of Relationships.* New York: Oxford University Press, 1998.

———. *The Triangle of Love: Intimacy, Passion, Commitment.* New York: Basic Books, 1988.

Stetzer, Ed. *Christians in the Age of Outrage: How to Bring Our Best When the World Is at Its Worst.* Carol Stream, IL: Tyndale Momentum, 2018.

Stibich, Mark. "Compression of Morbidity and Reducing Suffering: Reducing Age-Related Suffering." Very Well Health. September 7, 2021. https://www.verywellhealth.com/compression-of-morbidity-2223626#.

Stonehouse, Catherine. *Joining Children on the Spiritual Journey: Nurturing a Life of Faith.* Grand Rapids: Baker, 1998.

Stonehouse, Catherine, and Scottie May. *Listening to Children on the Spiritual Journey: Guidance for Those Who Teach and Nurture.* Grand Rapids: Baker Academic, 2010.

The Story: The Bible as One Continuing Story of God and His People. 3rd ed. Grand Rapids: Zondervan, 2011.

Strahan, Bradley J. *Parents, Adolescence, and Religion.* Cooranborg, Australia: Avondale Academic, 1994.

Stroebe, Margaret, and Henk Schut. "Dual Process Model of Coping with Bereavement: Rationale and Description." *Death Studies* 23, no. 3 (1999): 197–224.

Stumpf, Samuel Enoch. *Philosophy: History and Problems.* New York: McGraw-Hill, 1983.

Super, Donald E. "A Life-Span, Life-Space Approach to Career Development." *Journal of Vocational Behavior* 16, no. 3 (June 1, 1980): 282–98.

"10 Early Signs and Symptoms of Alzheimer's and Dementia." Alzheimer's Association. Accessed October 10, 2023. https://www.alz.org/alzheimers-dementia/10_signs.

"The Thomas Theorem of Sociology Explained with Examples." PsycholoGenie. Accessed March 9, 2023. https://psychologenie.com/the-thomas-theorem-of-sociology-explained-with-examples.

Thompson, Dennis. "U.S. Grandparents Are Raising Millions of Kids, and It's Tough." Medical Xpress. August 4, 2020. https://medicalxpress.com/news/2020-08-grandparents-millions-kids-tough.html.

Thompson, Marjorie J. *Family: The Forming Center; A Vision of the Role of Family in Spiritual Formation.* Nashville: Upper Room, 1998.

Thoreau, Henry David. *Walden.* Las Vegas: Empire Books, 2012.

The Trinity Forum. "After Babel: Reclaiming Relationship in a Technological World." Online webinar aired live May 6, 2022. https://www.ttf.org/portfolios/online-conversation-with-andy-crouch/.

Trentham, John David. "Reading the Social Sciences Theologically (Part 1): Approaching and Qualifying Models of Human Development." *Christian Education Journal* 16, no. 3 (December 2019): 458–75.

———. "Reading the Social Sciences Theologically (Part 2): Engaging and Appropriating Models of Human Development." *Christian Education Journal* 16, no. 3 (December 2019): 476–94.

Turner, Victor, Roger D. Abrahams, and Alfred Harris. *The Ritual Process: Structure and Anti-Structure*. New York: Routledge, 2017.

"The 26 Love Stories That Shape Our Views of Relationships." Poly.Land. February 23, 2019. https://poly.land/2019/02/23/the-26-love-stories-that-shape-our-views-of-relationships/.

U2. "I Still Haven't Found What I'm Looking For." *The Joshua Tree*. Island Records, 1987.

Vaillant, George E. *The Wisdom of the Ego*. Cambridge, MA: Harvard University Press, 1993.

Vanauken, Sheldon. *A Severe Mercy: C.S. Lewis's Influence on a Moving and Tragic Love Story*. London: Hodder & Stoughton, 2011.

Villines, Zawn. "What Is Shadow Work?" Medical News Today. Updated February 16, 2023. https://www.medicalnewstoday.com/articles/what-is-shadow-work.

Vincent, Kristen E. *A Bead and a Prayer: A Beginner's Guide to Protestant Prayer Beads*. Illustrated ed. Nashville: Upper Room, 2013.

Volf, Miroslav. *Exclusion and Embrace: A Theological Exploration of Identity, Otherness, and Reconciliation*. Rev. ed. Nashville: Abingdon, 2019.

von Rad, Gerhard. *Old Testament Theology*. New York: Harper & Row, 1962.

von Wachter, Till. "The End of Mandatory Retirement in the US: Effects on Retirement and Implicit Contracts." http://www.econ.ucla.edu/tvwachter/papers/vonwa_mr_2009.pdf.

Wangerin, Walter, Jr. *As for Me and My House: Crafting Your Marriage to Last*. Nashville: Nelson, 1990.

———. *The Orphean Passages*. Grand Rapids: Zondervan, 1996.

Ward, Thomas M. "Guest Post: Reading and the Virtue of Memory." Christian Scholar's Review. May 17, 2022. https://christianscholars.com/guest-post-reading-the-virtue-of-memory/.

Warren, Tish Harrison. "Why We Preach for Proper Names." *Christianity Today*, June 21, 2022. https://www.christianitytoday.com/ct/2022/july-august/tish-harrison-warren-preaching-small-local-church.html.

Wenegrat, Brant. *The Divine Archetype: The Sociobiology and Psychology of Religion*. Lanham, MD: Lexington Books, 1989.

Wesley, John. "The Use of Money." Sermon 50. Wesley Center Online. Accessed October 6, 2023. http://wesley.nnu.edu/john-wesley/the-sermons-of-john-wesley-1872-edition/sermon-50-the-use-of-money.

Westerhoff, John H. *Will Our Children Have Faith?* Harrisburg, PA: Morehouse, 2000.

White, David F. *Practicing Discernment with Youth*. Eugene, OR: Wipf & Stock, 2018.

Wiesel, T. N., and D. H. Hubel. "Comparison of the Effects of Unilateral and Bilateral Eye Closure on Cortical Unit Responses in Kittens." *Journal of Neurophysiology* 28, no. 6 (November 1965): 1029–40. https://doi.org/10.1152/jn.1965.28.6.1029.

Willard, Dallas. *Renovation of the Heart: Putting On the Character of Christ.* Colorado Springs: NavPress, 2002.

Willis, Sherry L., and Mike Martin. *Middle Adulthood: A Lifespan Perspective.* Thousand Oaks, CA: Sage, 2005.

Willis, Sherry L., and K. Warner Schaie. "Intellectual Functioning in Midlife." In *Life in the Middle: Psychological and Social Development in Middle Age,* edited by Sherry L. Willis and James D. Reid, 233–47. San Diego: Academic Press, 1999.

Winner, Lauren F. "Sleep Therapy." *Books and Culture,* January/February 2006. https://www.booksandculture.com/articles/2006/janfeb/2.07.html.

Wolpe, David J. *Teaching Your Children about God: A Modern Jewish Approach.* New York: HarperCollins, 1994.

Wood, Alex M., Alex Linley, and Stephen Joseph. "Gratitude—Parent of All Virtues." British Psychological Society. January 20, 2007. https://www.bps.org.uk/psychologist/gratitude-parent-all-virtues.

Woolf, Steven, Ryan K. Masters, and Laudan Y. Aron. "Changes in Life Expectancy between 2019 and 2020 in the US and 21 Peer Countries." *JAMA Network Open* 5, no. 4 (April 13, 2022). https://jamanetwork.com/journals/jamanetworkopen/fullarticle/2791004#:~:text=The%20high%20prevailing%20mortality%20rates,by%201.8%20years%20in%202020.

Wright, N. T. *After You Believe: Why Christian Character Matters.* New York: HarperOne, 2012.

Wright, Vinita Hampton. "Consolation and Desolation." Ignatian Spirituality. Accessed March 10, 2023. https://www.ignatianspirituality.com/consolation-and-desolation-2/.

Yust, Karen-Marie. *Real Kids, Real Faith: Practices for Nurturing Children's Spiritual Lives.* The Families and Faith Series. San Francisco: Jossey-Bass, 2004.

Zhitnik, Alexander P. "Eden and Erikson: Psychosocial Theory and the Garden of Eden." *Journal of Pedagogy, Pluralism, and Practice* 6, no. 1 (Fall 2014): 142–52. https://digitalcommons.lesley.edu/jppp/vol6/iss1/10/.

Index